THE SPACE BETWEEN

THE SPACE BETWEEN
Experience, Context, and Process in the Therapeutic Relationship

Edited by

Carmel Flaskas, Barry Mason, and Amaryll Perlesz

Foreword by

John Byng-Hall

Systemic Thinking and Practice Series

Series Editors
David Campbell & Ros Draper

Routledge
Taylor & Francis Group
LONDON AND NEW YORK

First published 2005 by
Karnac Books Ltd.

2 Park Square, Milton Park, Abingdon, Oxfordshire OX14 4RN
52 anderbilt Avenue, New York, NY 10017

Routledge is an imprint of the Taylor & Francis Group, an informa business

First issued in hardback 2019

British Library Cataloguing in Publication Data

A C.I.P. for this book is available from the British Library

ISBN 978-1-85575-365-5 (pbk)
ISBN 978-0-367-32886-3 (hbk)

Edited, designed, and produced by The Studio Publishing Services Ltd, Exeter EX4 8JN

CONTENTS

SERIES EDITORS' FOREWORD

This is the first time the Systemic Thinking and Practice Series has published a second collection of papers based on a previously published theme. You could say this is "Therapeutic Relationship II", but this would do a great injustice to not only the authors, but the field of systemic therapy. Instead we see this book as a marker in time.

We can now look back and say: "Why was the therapeutic relationship so important ten years ago?"; and ask, "What does it mean to us and to the field that we can now take the importance of this topic for granted and begin to look closer at its contexts and its inner workings?"

So this book, edited by Flaskas, Mason, and Perlesz, is not about releasing therapists from the grip of theory and technique, because it has already happened . . . and it happened for many of the reasons discussed in Carmel Flaskas' introduction. Rather the taken-for-grantedness of this second volume allows the reader to look at the topic with a cool eye, somewhat removed from the ground-breaking agenda of the first volume, and, we think, enables the reader to build 'thicker', more complex ideas on the topic.

Part of the richness springs from the diversity of the chapters, nevertheless bound by the common exploration of one theme. The contexts are diverse, the theoretical models of therapy are diverse, the client groups are diverse, cultures are diverse, and, interestingly, the diversity of writing styles also adds to the development of new thoughts. Our maturing field is even able to produce a body of research evidence which gathers diverse studies to justify our attention to the therapeutic relationship. It is as though, ten years on, we are now secure enough to appreciate the diversity and enjoy it for its potential rather than its threat.

We hope the reader will be stimulated by this thoughtful, contemporary, and honest collection on the topic which lies at the very heart of therapy, and if you are captivated by the historical development of this topic, as we were, may even decide to revisit volume number one: *The Therapeutic Relationship in Systemic Therapy* edited by Carmel Flaskas and Amaryll Perlesz, Karnac, 1996.

David Campbell
Ros Draper
London, 2005

ABOUT THE AUTHORS

The Editors

Carmel Flaskas is a Senior Lecturer in the School of Social Work, University of New South Wales, Sydney, where she convenes the Masters programme in couple and family therapy. Her contributions in family therapy include her work on the therapeutic relationship, on the translation of psychoanalytic ideas in the systemic context of work, and on knowledge and postmodernist ideas in therapy. With Amaryll Perlesz, she edited *The Therapeutic Relationship in Systemic Therapy* (1996, Karnac).

Barry Mason is the Director of The Institute of Family Therapy in London. He has been involved in the training of family therapists and systemic practitioners since the early 1980s. He chairs the advanced training in supervision at the Institute, and co-chairs the doctoral programme. He is also involved in developing clinical, training, and research aspects of a relational approach to the management of chronic pain.

Amaryll Perlesz is a Senior Lecturer in Family Therapy and manages the academic programme at The Bouverie Centre, La Trobe

University, Melbourne. Her current research interests include engaging rural schools around issues of homophobia and discrimination, exploring the interface between the private and public worlds of lesbian families, and using Theatre of the Oppressed techniques in training and supervision of family therapists. With Carmel Flaskas, she edited *The Therapeutic Relationship in Systemic Therapy* (1996, Karnac).

The Contributors

Rhonda Brown is a researcher and family therapist with The Bouverie Centre, La Trobe University Melbourne. Her current research interest is in lesbian families and she is completing a PhD on lesbian co-parents.

John Burnham is a Consultant Family Therapist and Director of Systemic Training Parkview Clinic, Birmingham Children's Hospital NHS Trust, and formerly Director of Training in Systemic Teaching, Training and Supervision, KCC Foundation, London.

Alan Carr is the Director of the Doctor of Psychological Science Programme in Clinical Psychology at University College Dublin and Marital and Family Therapist at the Clanwilliam Institute, Dublin.

Jo Howard is a social worker and family therapist. She manages the Child, Youth and Family Health Programme at the Inner South Community Health Service in Melbourne and has written *Mothers and Sons*, a book for sole mothers who raise boys.

Alfred Hurst is a qualified social worker and family therapist. He works as a systemic organizational consultant within the health and voluntary sectors and runs therapeutic groups within the gay and HIV communities in London.

Ellie Kavner is a systemic psychotherapist currently working at the Tavistock Clinic as Senior Organizing Tutor and in private practice in central London. She also works as a clinical supervisor on the Masters course at the Institute of Family Therapy.

Sebastian Kraemer has been working in the UK National Health Service for thirty-four years. He is a consultant child and adolescent psychiatrist at the Whittington Hospital, London, and until 2003, at the Tavistock Clinic, London.

Inga-Britt Krause is a social anthropologist and a family therapist. She is a Training and Development Consultant at the Tavistock and Portman NHS Trust, London.

Sue McNab is a systemic psychotherapist. She is currently employed by Oxford Mental Healthcare Trust and also works as a clinical supervisor on the Masters course at the Institute of Family Therapy.

Rabia Malik is a part time Family Therapist and Minority Ethnic Services Development Officer at the Marlborough Family Service. She is also a part time Senior Lecturer in psychosocial studies at University of East London.

Maeve Malley is a Northern Irish systemic therapist and supervisor working in the statutory and voluntary sectors. She trained at the Institute of Family Therapy and Birkbeck College, University of London. She lives and works in London.

Michael Maltby is a clinical psychologist and a group analyst. He is Clinical Director of the Doctoral Programme in Clinical Psychology at Salomons: Canterbury Christ Church University College, Kent, UK, and a Consultant Clinical Psychologist in the NHS.

David Pocock is a family therapist and psychoanalytic psychotherapist working in an NHS Child and Adolescent Mental Health service and in private practice in Swindon, UK.

Hitesh Raval is a clinical psychologist and systemic family therapist, and a trainer in these disciplines. He is Clinical Research Director of the Doctoral Programme in Clinical Psychology at Salomons: Canterbury Christ Church University College, Kent, UK.

Justin Schlicht has been working with families for many years in both adult and child and family mental health settings. He now works as a child and adolescent psychiatrist in Nottinghamshire, UK.

Lennox K. Thomas is a family and individual psychotherapist in private practice, London, UK.

FOREWORD

John Byng-Hall

Former Consultant Child Psychiatrist, The Tavistock Clinic, London, UK and Founder Member and Past Chair, The Institute of Family Therapy, London.

This book, which comprises contributions from many well-known authors, takes an important step in the field of family therapy towards linking many fruitful approaches. Sheila McNamee (2004) recently suggested that we have reached the point when we should be promiscuous rather than remaining faithful to one pure approach. This allows us to enrich our skills rather than confining them. Nevertheless, we still need a shared focus. What better place to start than by exploring the space between the therapist and client. So much of our thinking has centred on both what therapists do, or what families are. Since the emergence of second order perspectives, however, there has been an increasing interest in how family and therapists mutually influence each other in the therapeutic relationship.

The history of family therapy started with the development of models of change: ideas about what has gone wrong in families that inform us about what to do to put it right. These led to schools of family therapy exploring, with much enthusiasm, particular ways of working. This was helpful in that each approach was thought about, tried out and "perfected". Each needed a label or flag around which their followers could gather. These labels, however, marked a boundary smaller than the whole; either by focusing on a particular function of the family system such as narrative, or a technique such as the Milan approach. What is needed is a versatile capability to deal with all aspects of family functioning and adapt them to the various contexts in which we work. How can features of these pure schools be linked together to increase the versatility of family therapy while remaining coherent? What is common to all approaches is the therapeutic relationship. It is also the most important.

Postmodernism has focused our attention on the hierarchy of expertise, and asked questions about the certainty with which the schools portrayed their ideas as truth. To counter this certainty the concept of "not knowing" (Anderson & Goolishian, 1992a) emerged. This idea was helpful in that it made us listen to our clients much more and find out what their views were. In addition, important issues of prejudice, including racism and sexism, have increasingly been addressed in our practice. The role of expertise, which was scrutinized under the magnifying glass of Foucault's philosophy, highlighted the potential for the abuse of power within the expert role of the therapist. Yet, at the same time, I was always surprised by this because it seemed to me that the problem could be more about how to have enough influence on the family system, rather than having too much power. We can damage by pathologizing families, but we have been trying to avoid this since the origins of family therapy.

This preoccupation with the dangers of the experts and their knowledge has made it unfashionable to own, or sometimes even to be seen to seek, knowledge and expertise. In the healthy struggle to be the best therapist that we can be, we might be drawn into the invidious position of being proud of "not knowing", reminiscent of the man who gave himself 99% for humility. There are many dimensions to ethics, however. It seems to me that the most significant ethic in the therapeutic contract is that of being able to be effective in helping the family find its own solutions. Anxiety should then be more about not having enough expertise rather than too much. Of course, ethically we need both: to have adequate expertise but not misuse it. Perhaps the term capability should replace expertise. Our aim could then be versatile capability.

Barry Mason uses the concept of authoritative doubt to put alongside the "not knowing" position. This allows us to own our expertise as well as knowing that we do not know. This gives us space for curiosity and exploration, which of course involves taking some risks. The more you know about a particular issue the more you appreciate what is missing, and can see where to explore for new answers. As the saying goes, a little knowledge is a dangerous thing. This is because you do not know its limitations, I have now been working for thirty-five years with families and feel more comfortable with what seems to work, while wishing I had time to explore those intriguing areas of which I am ignorant. I am so impressed by how fascinating and complex families are, and feel so lucky to have been in this profession.

Collaboration within the therapeutic relationship is very well discussed in this book and innovative ways of establishing it are described. Collaboration is much more effective in empowering the family to find its own solutions, than by informing. This more equal relationship thus meets the requirements of the ethics of both power and of effectiveness. Amaryll Perlesz and Rhonda Brown describe how family therapy can be conducted in the form of a shared piece of "research". The family has expertise in what happens in their family and the therapist has experience across many families, both contributing to the investigation. The research is the therapy. John Burnham describes how the therapist's self reflectivity, asking one's self questions about what is going on, can be extended to include the family in this reflecting process; making it a joint project. Maeve Malley and Alfred Hurst describe how supervision within the room with open discussion between supervisor and therapist creates transparency and sense of equality and collaboration in their work with gay and lesbian couples.

The book includes some marvellous work on making cross-cultural work more collaborative and adaptive. Hitesh Raval and Michael Maltby describe how the interpreter, in work with intercultural therapy, can be made a co-worker who can be valuable in translating not only words but also cultural values and significant information about the family's situation. In cross-cultural work Lennox Thomas describes how ideas from both psychoanalytic and systems thinking can lead to seeing which ideas work best in which situation within intercultural work. Rabia Malik and Britt Krause use an anthropological perspective to see how our bodies are the source of our shared humanity, embodying our capacity to communicate between cultures highlighting our similarities, but also our differences. Two chapters bring further fresh ideas about how we experience the therapeutic relationship. Ellie Kavner and Sue McNab tell us about the role of shame and embarrassment in the relationship. This is instantly recognizable. It is embarrassing that such an important experience has had such little discussion. Thank you for showing how useful and important being aware of this emotion is to our work. David Pocock writes about the sharing of emotions in relationship creating what he calls a shared ethos. He also gives a valuable affirmation to the notion that ideas from both modernism and postmodernism can be valued rather than polarized. This is important in our attempts to bring together ideas to enrich our work rather than be pure.

Carmel Flaskas addresses the issues therapists can learn most from; when it all gets in a mess. There should be far more of these publications. She explores the experience of the therapist in these uncomfortable situations and discusses ways in which these impasses can be understood from within the contexts of narrative, systemic, and psychoanalytic understandings. This chapter is an affirmation that varied ideas can be linked to tell an empathic story about how the therapist and the family are both feeling stuck, and how to use this experience therapeutically. Just in case the reader thinks it has all been explained, Justin Schlicht and Sebastian Kraemer have a fascinating dialogue about what they call informed spontaneity; things that happen beyond the theory. As they discuss each other's clinical work a vista opens up beyond what we think we know. We can glimpse new angles. Jo Howard shows how there are times when work needs to be done outside the family for the family, in this case working with men who use violence.

One of the most satisfying developments in the field of family therapy, for me, in the last ten years has been the increasing respect that has been given to the place of research. No longer does it seem to reside in the marginalized position that it once occupied. Alan Carr reminds us that research can inform us in a most interesting way and it highlights for me how description of the research on the therapeutic relationship indicates what could be done in establishing a therapeutic alliance that can be empirically linked to good outcome. As I read it I could recognize experiences in my own work and learned something. It is astonishing that some people coming from a postmodern orientation, dismissed non-postmodernist research from a view that there was no such thing as truth. I can sympathize with concerns about how research findings can be misused. Nevertheless, we can learn so much from a wide range of research perspectives. I have, for example, seen attachment theory being validated by research during my career. It has elaborated the theory as well as validating it. Research tells us what is the most likely story in those arenas that have been adequately researched so far. This then defines the boundary between knowledge currently held at that level and where we need to rely on theories. This is part of the authority held within authoritative doubt.

Lastly I asked myself how some of my own thinking could fit with the message of the book. Attachment theory, which I use as a way of thinking about therapeutic relationships, seems to fit well. I see the therapist as providing a secure base from which the family can feel safe enough to improvise in their relationships and find new ways of relating. Secure attachments encourage curiosity and exploration. As a way of making my therapeutic relationships more collaborative I have been sharing my models of what happens in families or couples with them. When I have a hunch about what is going on I may say, "In my experience in this situation many families . . . I don't know about you. There will be things that are not so for you, there may be some which are." As my uncertainty is real, it becomes a shared way of exploring how family members relate to each other. In this way, it is possible to develop a shared model which can be revised or discarded through dialogue between us. This is how I learned most about family scripts; the gains can be mutual. In the same way, when I have relevant research information, say about their attachments, I tell them about the research and that it has been done with many different kinds of families. The relief that they are not abnormal or uniquely awful, or the same as others, can be palpable. We can also use our shared models in the work. I would think most other ways of thinking about therapeutic relationships could also be linked to ideas in this book and enriched by it.

INTRODUCTION

Orientating to therapeutic relationships and the space between

Then and now

It is nine years since the first edited collection on the therapeutic relationship was published in Karnac's *Systemic Thinking and Practice Series* (Flaskas & Perlesz, 1996a). At the time, this book placed the therapeutic relationship squarely on the agenda in the family therapy literature after a long period of neglect. The introduction we wrote then (Flaskas & Perlesz, 1996b) located the neglect as part of the historical development of family therapy and its earlier opposition to the individual (and especially intrapsychic) therapies, and we also plotted the changes that had brought pressure to bear on our thinking about this important aspect of theory and practice. Three important factors in the 1980s were drawn out— the shift to second-order theory, the feminist critique of the mechanical and rather de-humanizing language of the earlier biological systems metaphors, and the implications of postmodernist ideas that were beginning to filter into our field. These three influences together allowed (and even demanded) that we start seriously attending to developing our understandings of the therapeutic relationship in family therapy.

Now, writing the introduction to this second collection, I am struck by how the themes that needed to be so carefully mapped in 1996 can simply be taken for granted. We have moved well and truly beyond the need to justify attention to the therapeutic relationship. The last decade has seen creative developments in theory and practices in family therapy with the continuing elaboration of postmodernist, social constructionist, narrative, and "post-Milan" ideas. Systemic and narrative therapies have been embedded more firmly in a politics that at least acknowledges power and abuse, intimacy and emotionality, and contexts of race, culture, class, gender, and sexuality. Understandings that were effectively pitched within the frame of a normalizing sameness have been challenged by political and ethical demands that we relate to, and across, difference. The developments in our ideas about the therapeutic relationship throughout this time have been part of this broader milieu that continues, albeit in quite a different way, to address the enduring systemic concerns of context and relationship.

In a recent review of the development of ideas about the therapeutic relationship over the past decade, I drew out the following sets of themes as being important: the adoption of collaborative and therapist-present descriptions of the therapeutic relationship; the continuing elaboration of therapist practices of curiosity and not-knowing; the re-emphasis on therapist listening and witnessing; the attention to practices of transparency; the more specific considerations of the therapist's use of self, particularly in contexts of difference; and the engagement with psychoanalytic ideas and beginning discussions of therapeutic failure and impasse (Flaskas, 2004). These sets of themes may not be all of one piece, but none the less they each resonate with the broader currents in contemporary family therapy knowledge.

Thus, the context now of this collection of papers on the therapeutic relationship is very different to the context of the last collection. The contributors are in a position to show the results of a sustained period of attention to the therapeutic relationship, and are writing from a position informed by the more recent developments of family therapy knowledge. It will come as no surprise to find that this collection is able to be more specific and more contextually grounded in its explorations of the many forms of therapeutic relationships that emerge in the different practice and social contexts, and the umbrella themes just named are woven in and out of the chapters' discussions. We have titled the book *The Space Between: Experience, Context and Process in the Therapeutic Relationship*, and this choice of title flags very clearly the more specific kind of attention that we are now able to give when we orientate ourselves to the therapeutic relationship in systemic family therapy.

The parameters of this collection

But more should be said about the parameters of this collection. We talk about "the space between" as recognition of the recursive nature of relationships in general, and the therapeutic relationship in particular. It is an idea which is very much in harmony with the systemic project across time, for of course a foundational premise of systems thinking is that the whole of a system is greater than the sum of its parts, and that being in-relationship-with allows possibilities beyond the capacities of constitutive parts. Postmodernism has brought a very different set of metaphors to our theory, yet just as powerfully places relationships at the core of its knowledge. "The space between", then, is the space within the therapeutic relationship between therapist and family, where mutual influence and change is possible.

To single out experience, context, and process in the title also speaks of a particular set of commitments that inform the book and its discussion. The lived experience that families bring with them is the territory of therapeutic endeavour. However, in the process of the therapy, there is also the experience of the therapy itself, for both therapist and family. Trying to think about and make sense of that experience, and staying curious about both the therapist's and family's experience, is one of the main parameters of the enquiry of this book and its chapters.

To hold a focus on the specificity of context is another, and this enables us to begin to move beyond general descriptions of "the" therapeutic relationship, to a more layered set of understandings that begin to meet more fully the diversity of contexts in the practice of family therapy, and the influence of these contexts in shaping the possibilities and limits of particular kinds of therapeutic relationships. And process, an idea so central to psychotherapy, becomes a third parameter that marks the explorations in this book, moving the discussion beyond abstract and static understandings of "the" therapeutic relationship to the richness of the constructions of therapeutic relationships in different contexts and with different families.

As editors, we are aware that we are in some ways simply stating explicitly core concerns of systemic and narrative ideas in our choice of title, though in fact the title came mid-way through the project rather than at the beginning. Moreover, in the process of planning the collection, we were not programmatic in soliciting specific content, or indeed prescriptive about the way in which contributors might approach the topics of their chapters. Instead, we asked contributors to write on topics that were of interest to them, and to develop their ideas in whatever way best showed the directions of their current understandings.

The chapters cover a wide range of topics. Through different mixes of reflections on practice experience and theory ideas, they all orientate very clearly to experience, context, and process in the therapeutic relationship.

The chapters

However, it is time now to give a more detailed picture of the chapters and their content. The first two chapters give contrasting and detailed explorations of process in the therapeutic relationship. John Burnham simultaneously investigates and develops the idea of relational reflexivity as a way of more deliberately nurturing the therapeutic function of the therapeutic relationship and socially constructing a sensitivity to relationship and process. He writes of the use of therapeutic immediacy in questions the therapist may use to open conversations, and of different ways of "warming" the context of therapeutic invitations, coordinating resources, and attending to emotionality, language, and time within therapy.

In Chapter Two, Justin Schlicht and Sebastian Kraemer enter into a free-flowing dialogue about their experiences as therapists and their own use of self with different families. They describe, question, and reflect on the specifics of their use of self in the different pieces of work, drawing out the dynamics of thinking and feeling, the intersections of theory, the shifts in practice from theory to intuitive leaps, and the back-and-forth "from system to psyche"' in the therapeutic process.

Chapters Three and Four give more particular case studies of the way in which the context of practice, and the choice of particular practices, shape the kind of therapeutic relationships that then emerge, and they also explore the challenges within the form of these therapeutic relationships. The contexts are different, the expressions of collaborative and respectful practice vary markedly, and the therapeutic relationships show a finely-tuned fit to agency practice and philosophy as well as the practitioners' own politics. Maeve Malley and Alfred Hurst, as supervisor and therapist, reflect on their experience of in-the-room supervision in work with clients in a voluntary counselling service for lesbians and gay men. They explore the shaping of the supervisory relationship and the shaping of the therapeutic relationships, and also the effects of their choice for supervisory transparency, as well as more personal transparency, with their clients.

Jo Howard writes of the kind of therapeutic relationship shaped in a very different context—a group programme for men who use violence and control, which is guided by a feminist politics that deliberately and transparently prioritizes the safety of women and children, and which is provided by narrative and systemic practitioners in a community health service. The challenges of engagement and bearing witness to the men's experience while privileging the stories of their partners and children, the parallel processes of building a therapeutic relationship while inviting other-centeredness in the men's relationship with others, and the question of the different experiences of therapists as women and men in this context, are all topics of the chapter's exploration.

Chapters Five, Six and Seven continue to investigate the effects and possibilities of context, examining cross-cultural contexts of work. Hitesh Raval and Michael Maltby take the focus beyond the space between (just-the-) therapist and family, to a wider focus on the multi-levelled therapeutic system that is formed when therapists join with bilingual co-workers and interpreters in their work with families. The challenge here is for the therapeutic part of the therapeutic relationship not to get "lost in translation". Within a frame that situates bilingual workers and interpreters collegially and inclusively within the therapeutic system, this chapter offers a step-by-step guide to the construction and negotiation of relationships within the therapeutic system in order to maximize the therapeutic space with families.

In Chapter Six, Lennox K. Thomas uses a broad lens to give a commentary on the influences of psychoanalytic and systemic ideas in shaping the practices of intercultural therapy. Tracing his exposure to different therapeutic traditions in his own career, he argues strongly for the need to embrace a diversity of ideas to meet the challenge of intercultural relationships in therapy. He also argues for the need for therapists to tackle their own experience of race and culture, and racism and social dominance and marginalization—and for creating space for clients' stories about their experience of race and culture.

Rabia Malik and Britt Krause then take the attention back to a more specific focus on the process between therapist and families in cross-cultural relationships in a chapter that finely interweaves the development of theory understandings and experience. Chapter Seven critiques and extends social constructionist ideas, arguing that any sole privileging of language can miss the complexities of cross-cultural communication in general, and within the therapeutic relationship in particular. They argue for an understanding of embodiment, its symbolization and relationship to language and the therapeutic process, and they make this theory argument through their reflection on pieces of their own practice experience.

The methodologies of Chapters Eight, Nine and Ten use a similar movement between theory and practice in the development of core theory themes and, although contrasting in topics, they each orientate to emotionality in the therapeutic process. In Chapter Eight, Carmel Flaskas examines impasse in the therapeutic process, highlighting the experience of the therapist, and the shared emotional territory for families and therapists, when the therapy becomes stuck and messy. This chapter argues that in the interactional constellation of impasse, it becomes very easy for the therapist to enter into "anti-therapeutic sequences" in the therapeutic relationship, and that narrative and systemic and psychoanalytic understandings may all be used to guide a reflective practice that actively uses the therapist's experience of impasse, and orientates the therapist back to the "therapeutic" function of the therapeutic relationship.

David Pocock in Chapter Nine pares the exploration of process down to the moment-by-moment use of the "feeling self" of each person involved in the therapeutic system. His chapter is strongly orientated to understandings of the self-in-relationship, and the recursiveness of the "feeling self" that simultaneously shapes and is shaped by the relational context. It uses understandings from relational psychoanalysis and object relations, which Pocock puts alongside systems thinking, social constructionism, and ideas from attachment and infant research. The therapist's attention to the construction and use of her or his own feeling self in the course of meeting the feeling selves of the family members provides a rich source of understanding and allows something more of the family's experience to be known.

Chapter Ten reflects on the powerful emotion of shame for families and therapists that is so often an unnamed aspect of the therapeutic process, and the challenges and complexities of the negotiation of shame in the therapeutic relationship. Ellie Kavner and Sue McNab echo the interest in contributions from psychoanalysis (particularly the relational ideas of the Stone Centre) and add to these ideas the more systemic concerns of personal, social and cultural contexts. The chapter maps some of the effects of clients' stories of shame on the therapeutic relationship, the challenge for the therapist in respectfully witnessing clients' stories of shame, and the way in which clients' stories of shame may interact with, and sometimes trigger, therapists' stories of shame.

Chapters Eleven and Twelve continue the examination of process in the therapeutic relationship, and they are each angled toward particular explorations of collaboration. In Chapter Eleven, Barry Mason spotlights risk and risk-taking, and he does this from a position that is appreciative and yet critical of the thinking about collaboration and the not-knowing position. The chapter's position is effectively "both/and", recognizing the benefits of collaborative practices, yet being concerned about the self-marginalization of therapist expertise and restraints in the therapist's readiness to take risks. The activities of establishing trust and therapist risk-taking are seen as recursive rather than sequential, with risk-taking aiding the establishment of trust and vice versa, as well as inviting a different kind of exploration in the therapeutic work. Conceptualizing a therapeutic position of safe uncertainty and authoritative doubt allows more space for the process of risk-taking in the therapeutic relationship.

Chapter Twelve remains firmly allied with the collaborative ideal, and explores the fit between this ideal and different research and theory frameworks. Here Amaryll Perlesz and Rhonda Brown wind their discussion around three "case" examples, the first a qualitative family research interview on lesbian-parented families' experience, the second being the historical ethnographic research done by Margaret Mead in Samoa, the third a family therapy interview with lesbian parents. The discussion juxtaposes the collaborative practices of participatory cooperative research with the ideas more common to family therapy via social constructionist understandings, as well as David Epston's narrative ideas of the "co-research" of local knowledges. A combination of "co-research" and a lens drawn from the collaborative research paradigm is used to reflect back on the process of the research/therapeutic relationship in the original three case examples.

Chapter Thirteen maps the empirical research on the therapeutic alliance in family therapy and the findings so far in this research programme. Alan Carr considers the way in which empirical research can guide us in thinking about the usefulness of particular types and aspects of therapeutic relationships. The chapter makes very accessible the therapeutic alliance assessment scales that may routinely be used in clinical practice, and summarizes the research that shows a strong relationship between therapeutic alliance and outcome in couple and family therapy. It also gives a selective review of process research which points to specific practices that therapists may incorporate into their own styles in the therapeutic relationship. The helpfulness of the offerings so far of empirical research is a good ending to a collection which emphasizes more the generation of clinical and theory knowledge in family therapy.

Finally, something like a postscript

Having given an overview of the project and parameters of the book, and the content of its chapters, I cannot resist some comments which really stand more like a postscript to this introduction.

As editors, we always had in mind a collection that would represent the different threads of current thinking about the therapeutic relationship in systemic family therapy—we wanted, if you like, to show a sample of the developments. We also thought that the collection would look quite different to the collection produced nearly a decade ago, and across the chapters, the clinical and theory reflections do indeed show the influences of broader discussions within our field as well as the building on earlier discussions of the therapeutic relationship. This much I suppose was expected.

Yet we were surprised, first by the specificity of topics chosen by our contributors and then, once the chapters started rolling in, by the very different kinds of angles taken and the themes developed in their particular explorations. Now it may well be that our surprise says more about the limitations of our expectations. When we talked about it, though, we were struck by the way in which contributors seemed to be choosing explorations that were finely tuned to the particularities of their practice and practice contexts. It seems to us that we have moved beyond the level of generality that comes with the first layer of exploration in the generation of knowledge. We were left with the perhaps rather belated, but none the less very welcome, recognition that in systemic family therapy we now seem more able to resist unified descriptions and analyses of what "the" therapeutic relationship should look like or be like and how we should think about it.

An effect of this, of course, is that we are left with multiple descriptions, multiple practices, and multiple theory understandings. But yet, to use this collection as a kind of case example itself in the production of knowledge, there is no sense of the "anything goes" relativism so often feared in a postmodernist epistemology. Instead, one sees a purposeful crafting bounded by common parameters. So, having fallen into the rather irritating postmodernist habit of giving first an oppositional description (the idea of the need to resist unified descriptions), let me claim more wholeheartedly and more positively what we do seem to be doing. As editors, we think that across the collection as a whole, there is a greater readiness and ability to grapple with the specificity of experience, context and process—and that it is an important step to begin to do this, rather than simply to keep saying as a field that this is what we want to do.

Who knows in another decade what another collection about "the" therapeutic relationship might look like? No doubt quite different. But we feel confident that family therapy will continue to orientate to this topic, and look forward to the diversity of ways in which the space between therapist and family will be explored.

Carmel Flaskas

CHAPTER ONE

Relational reflexivity: a tool for socially constructing therapeutic relationships

John Burnham

Introduction

When clients come for therapy, the relationship that develops between therapist and clients is seen as a significant factor in whether there is a therapeutic outcome (Hubble, Duncan, & Miller, 1999). Naming one person in the relationship as "therapist" doesn't automatically make it a "therapeutic relationship". It takes hard work as well as imagination to coordinate the resources of client and therapist to create and maintain a relationship that is experienced as therapeutic for the client. One of the questions I regularly ask myself (in the spirit of self-reflexivity) is "How can I practise so as to increase the chances of this relationship becoming therapeutic for the people I work with?" This chapter is an account of some of the ways in which I have enjoined the people I work with in working with me (in the spirit of relational-reflexivity) towards answering that question. I will begin with a practice example, relating to theory, and offer definitions as I go, since this more accurately reflects how the praxis of relational reflexivity developed in my work. The initial development was mainly in my work as a therapist but I have since easily transferred these questions and practices to my work as a supervisor and trainer.

A beginning: socially constructing sensitivity

A particularly significant episode in developing relational reflexivity happened a number of years ago (1991), when I was guest supervisor at a Kensington Consultation Centre venue in Hertfordshire, in the UK. Julia Wigglesworth was then a therapist in training with Susan Lang as supervisor and (all female) team members. Julia requested that I do a "demonstration interview" with a couple with whom she had been working with for five sessions. She was uncertain about how the work was going, and she was very concerned to be particularly sensitive in relation to: *race*—the couple were mixed race Indian and African-Caribbean and Julia was English-white; and *sexuality*—the husband had hinted at some sexual difficulties. I eagerly accepted this invitation and, with their agreement, began to interview the couple in the presence of Julia and the team.

After about fifteen minutes of interviewing I was beginning to feel that the interview was not going so well and asked the couple, "How is today's interview going compared to the ones that you usually have with Julia?" Both agreed that it was similar to what usually happened, and the couple agreed to my request to talk with them about the interviews with Julia. As this progressed I had in mind the concerns that Julia had expressed before the session. The following is an example of an episode in the session in which I asked some "questions about questions":

"Does Julia tend to ask you more questions that are easy to answer or difficult to answer?"
"Easy to answer."

"Which questions are most useful to you, the easy ones or the difficult ones?"
"The difficult ones, we know the answers to the easy ones because we've thought about them already. The difficult ones make us think about things differently."

"If Julia asked you questions that were really too difficult for you to answer, for whatever reason, would you be able to tell her?"
"Yes, yes, that would be no problem" (both nodding in agreement).

These "questions about questions" caught my imagination during the rest of the session. They seemed to have the effect of directly involving the couple in decisions about the process and content of interviewing. Sensitivity, as well as being a self-reflexive posture of the therapist, became socially constructed between this therapist and these particular clients, through the practice of relational reflexivity. It became a "made to measure" sensitivity related to, but not restricted by, the therapist's intentions or training.

My interest in "questions about questions" grew and became a regular part of my interviewing style in therapy, consultation, and supervision. Previously, I, like many others in the field (for example, Hoffman, 1992) had been more concerned with developing self-reflexivity. I think of self-reflexivity as a process in which a therapist makes, takes, or grasps an opportunity to observe, listen to, and question the effects of their practice, then use their responses to their observation/listening to decide "how to go on" in the particular episode or the work in general. Their responses might include: continuing with what they are doing, recalibrating slightly, or repositioning radically in how they act in relation to self and others. The practice of self-reflexivity tends to emphasize the "internal" activity of the therapist, as they search their own resources (similar to Tomm's (1988) notion of "strategizing"). Self-reflexive activity can be prompted by a therapist's reading of their own responses (where is this interview going? . . . I need to introduce more structure . . . I must pay more attention to gender and culture . . . what kind of questions can I ask?) and/or their empathic sensing of clients' experience. With regard to the latter I might be thinking in the followinng ways: "The family seem to be liking these kind of questions . . . I'll keep going"; "The children seem disconnected from the conversation . . . perhaps I will introduce more play". In the interview with Julia and her clients, using self-reflexive activity ("this interview isn't going well . . . what shall I do differently?") as a prompt ("let me see what the couple think about how it is going") to initiate questions about the questions, seemed to open a relationally reflexive space for the clients to experience empowerment in co-constructing with the therapist a relationship with therapeutic potential.

The responses of clients, supervisees, and therapists in training to this kind of collaborative conversation encouraged me to include other aspects of a session and components of systemic practice within this frame. In a development of the initial definition (Burnham, 1993) I would now describe relational reflexivity as:

> the intention, desire, processes, and practices through which therapists and clients explicitly engage one another in coordinating their resources so as to create a relationship with therapeutic potential. This would involve initiating, responding to, and developing opportunities to consider, explore, experiment with, and elaborate the ways in which they relate.

The rest of this chapter explores a range of ways to transform this ethical aspiration into practical activity. I imagine that many practitioners will recognize aspects of their own practices. Perhaps they may already call it "checking out", or "talking about talk". It is my hopeful intention that by giving a name to this process (relational reflexivity), and exploring its usefulness in a range of ways, it will help to make this a more reliably creative tool for making the relationships we form with clients therapeutic. The generation of different forms of questions that follows is situated in, and owes much to, the traditions created by the great "question makers" such as de Shazer, 1994; O'Hanlon and Weiner-Davis, 1989, Madigan, 1993; Selvini Palazolli, Boscolo, Cecchin, and Prata, 1980; Tomm, 1987a,b, 1988; White, 1988; White & Epston 1991. I hope that what I offer is both within this tradition and extending it, by the explicit inclusion of clients in the creation of the therapy they receive. In my attempts to theorize this development of praxis, I feel I am working alongside and variously inspired by such concepts as *coherence, coordination, and mystery* (Pearce, 1989), *knowledge of the third kind* (Shotter, 1993), *language and action* (Cronen & Lang, 1994), and *relational responsibiity* (McNamee & Gergen, 1999).

Warming the context

Bateson (1972) talks of "warm ideas" as having a greater chance of survival than "cold ideas". In the same way, if the context for conversation is "warmed", and made less scary/more inviting, then generally participants may feel more willing/able to join the conversation/relationship more productively, openly, and wholeheartedly.

Warming the context would be all the ways that the therapist can, self-reflexively, help to create a "readiness" in the person(s) they are talking to or an audience that is listening to the conversation. When the therapist explicitly engages the client(s) in this process it becomes relationally reflexive.

Preparing a question to fit (I'm not sure whether to begin with . . .)

There is a preference in certain parts of the field to begin a question about change with the word "When . . . [a desired change] happens", rather than "If . . . [a desired change] happens" on the grounds that "when" creates a greater emphasis on the inevitability of change. I think this is "unfair" on those people who are at the stage of "If" and could impose the idea that "When" is the best place to be. So I now ask routinely, "I would like to ask a question, and I am not sure whether to begin it with "when" or "if". The question is "When, or if, the changes that you want to happen do happen . . . what will life be like?" Shall I begin the question with "When" or "if"? My intent is to coordinate my resources (different kinds of questions) with the client's coherence in relation to being certain (when) or tentative (if). In doing so I am being irreverent (Cecchin, Lane, & Ray, 1991) to the injunction to "follow the field" and insist on "when". Some people respond immediately with their preferred choice, while others think a while and the question about the question seems to have a reflexive effect. When people respond with "if" then we can talk about how close they are to "when", and what steps they might take to get to "when". The broad aim is to create a context which is "warm" or receptive to considering the direction of the question rather than imposing "when" as better than "if". I find that this time is well spent for a variety of reasons.

1. The eventual question chosen/asked fits more closely with the coherence (personal preferences, family style, cultural values) of the client(s).

2. The client(s) have a sense of being able to make active choices in the session in creating "bespoke" questions as well as having "off the peg" questions.
3. They have the sense that the therapist is receptive (warm) to their answers and therefore they can be more willing to answer.

A fascinating episode happened when I asked a young woman of seventeen, who had a very quiet voice (literally and metaphorically) this question, that is "How should I begin this question . . . with 'when' or 'if.' " She thought for a while and then said "When". I began to continue the conversation and the father interrupted and said that he thought she had answered "when" to please me as she was by now very familiar with what professionals wanted. (I was indeed pleased when she made this choice.) I asked the young woman what she thought about her father's idea. She said yes, she had thought I might be more pleased if she said "when" because professionals want you to move on. I said what if she knew that I would be pleased if she chose the answer *she* wanted to give, what would she choose, when or if? She thought and said, "It's somewhere in between when and if". I spontaneously suggested the invention of "Whif" (amidst general amusement) as something in-between "when" and "if" and which was accepted. "Whif" became a catchword during the therapy.

When the therapy was ending we discussed "Whif" as an important part of the therapeutic process. It was a catchword that seemed to have meaning at different levels. It was a word we had made together and became part of our local grammar (Cronen & Lang, 1994) or ways of talking. When a word didn't fit it could be made to fit or a new one could be invented. The episode in which the word was created and the future episodes in which it was used (in humour, for reflection, to tease) helped to shape the relationship. The relationship became reflexive, and one in which co-creation was a regular and practical event.

As the family members realized and experienced the context as "warm", that is, receptive to their suggestions, they began to exercise choice and imagination. They also became receptive to ideas from the therapist and so "warming the context" (at different points in the process) contributed towards creating a therapeutic relationship in which all voices were heard, including family members, therapist, and team. The family members came to realize that they could ask for things to be different and that the choices offered could be accepted, rejected, or modified. The girl "played" with her self story of, "I am someone who does things to please other people" and experimented with "I am someone who is saying and doing things for myself". All relationships have a "local grammar" that creates the shared meanings created within that relationship. The shared meanings are created within and partly define the relationship. Such episodes of creating new language can help to create a relationship as therapeutic.

Warming/preparing an audience to respond ("While we are talking . . .")

When parents or a member of a couple say something like "Will you talk to him/her?" in a session, I would, previously, decline this invitation for a number of reasons. Now I am inclined to say something like: "I am willing to do that and I wonder if, as I am talking to your son/daughter/partner you would listen to the conversation that I have with him/her and take note of things that we talk about that you have not thought about or would like to know more about. Perhaps you could note which questions I ask that helps your son/daughter/partner to talk about their experiences?" In this way the young person hears (I hope) the intentions I have in accepting the parents' request to talk with them and thus it is more likely that a warmer context has emerged when I turn to talk with him/her. Similarly, as I am talking with him/her I will be asking things like "Of all the things you have talked about so far, what do you hope your parents/partner have understood . . . and what difference would that make to you if they understood that? (Here I am aware of the parents or partner) as the context of audience to our conversation?" If I talked and then turned to ask them without "warming" the listening audience context, I might just put them on the spot whereas by framing my questions in the way I have the son/daughter/partner has been able to give them clues or coach them about how to respond.

I realize, as I write, that this could sound strategic, but it is not my intention to cause the parents to have a particular response, only to increase the chances of coordinating with their son's/daughter's wishes to be heard and understood in a particular way.

Warming the context for praise (How much praise can you take . . .?)

Not all clients can respond easily to glowing compliments and the "Wow" utterances by enthusiastic therapists and/or reflecting teams. One father said "I don't know who they are talking about, but it certainly isn't me!" after a reflecting team had been complimenting him during their reflections. Asking clients about their relationship with praise and compliments, for example, "How much praise can you take" or "If I or the team wanted to say something positive or appreciative about what we have heard, how might we say it in ways that you could accept?", can create a context in which the therapist and team members can offer their appreciation without embarrassing the client into accepting something that doesn't fit or giving him a feeling of not being heard.

Warning about warming

The term "warming" is not used to imply "cuddly" or "cosy"; it is being used to indicate that a context is being prepared for work so that the participants can go on to face experimenting with difference in a context that feels familiar. It is more than being friendly at the beginning to make people feel comfortable. With people who have come to experience initial friendliness by professionals as something to be suspicious about, then "warming the context" may include the therapist asking the family if they would prefer them to be more distant and professional than they have experienced so far. For example, "I was wondering if I had been challenging enough in the therapy so far?" Just as couples can get into stuck patterns in their relationship to each other, so can therapists with the people with whom they work, and some benefit may be derived from saying, "I thought about how we might change how we do the therapy sessions. What do you think?" For some therapists this would require them to "challenge their own coherence" (Pearce, 1989) if they saw themselves essentially as a warm and friendly person.

Coordinating resources

Between models of therapy ("Are you more of a doer, thinker or feeler?")

At any particular time in the evolution/story of a model of practice or in the work of an individual practitioner, therapists will be attracted/committed to, or "in love with" a particular form of practice, sometimes (usefully or otherwise) to the exclusion of others. The practitioner may believe that this is the way to do it. What they offer the client is a glowing and committed confidence in the way they work. Other practitioners like to offer a choice from within a range of ways of proceeding. This decision can be one that is taken moment by moment or one that affects the longer term. Either way, it significantly influences the creation and development of a relationship that can be therapeutic. Therapists can avoid starting off at cross purposes, and "negotiate between differences" (Frugerri, 1992) by asking questions to orientate themselves to the clients *general preferences*: "Are you more of a doer or thinker or feeler?" "Are you usually tempted towards thinking of reasons for what is happening or for ways out of what is happening?" "Would you prefer to address the problem first as it is, or in terms of what it might mean?" "When your life is going well/badly, in which aspect of your experience do you notice it first: how you feel, your ability to think, or what you do in your life?" "Over the first six sessions, which aspect of your experience do you think has been explored/changed most, and which do you hope to work on from now on?"

More specific questions might be: "In the videotape we have just been watching, which aspect of your experience were you most attentive to?" . . . "Is that what you would have usually noticed or might it be different for you?" "As you think about your life improving and your relationships becoming more loving, in the way you have just described, how might you notice this in what happens . . . how you feel . . . the thoughts that you have or how you are with people . . .?" "What aspect of the session led you to say that you 'felt better'—something you were feeling, doing or thinking?"

In order to enable the entertaining of difference, the following question may be effective: "If you were to step aside from thinking so much, what feelings do you think might emerge?" ... "What kind of differences might it make to concentrate on how you feel or what you do?" "So far you have said that you use these sessions to explore how you might act differently towards each other. How might it be if we used a session to explore what you mean to each other in the context of your future life together?"

Questions such as "As you begin to lose that feeling of despair, what thoughts are you able to entertain now, that you weren't able to when you felt so despairing?" and "How might you use those thoughts to do things differently in your day to day life?" could allow reflexive changes in experience to be evaluated.

Similarly, explorations can be made about clients' orientation to, and relationship with, problems, solutions, and resources; beginnings and endings, and "spreading the news" (Freedman & Combs, 1996) of their improvement.

Within a model (What are you more into . . .?)

The emergent popularity of narrative approaches to therapy (Freedman & Combs 1996; Parry & Doan 1994; White & Epston, 1991) and training (Kazan, Swan, & Law, 1993; White, 1992) has been immensely refreshing and inspirational to the field in general. Within the narrative approach a dominant/preferred narrative form seems to be "author and authorship", which is situated within a literary metaphor, generating a "language game" (Wittgenstein in Cronen & Lang, 1994) of "chapters", "rewriting life stories", and so on. This will fit very well with many clients. For some clients/ trainees other narrative forms will be more coherent with how they think about and talk of their lives. To avoid "passing each other by" (Pearce, 1989) it is important to coordinate the resources of the therapist with the narrative style, preferences, and resources of the client. Asking a client "What are you most interested in: films, books, plays, television, personal conversations, a particular hobby or sport, a job, dreams?", allows the therapist to use the themes, structure, and language of the genre to generate the conversation at this and future points in the conversation. It is not necessarily important that the therapist knows the particular genre, since the client can educate the therapist, who can then ask questions from the position of being curious.

The emotional language of the session

It is sometimes difficult to know how to respond to client emotions and to deal with the emotions experienced by therapists. Therapists can usefully and sensitively explore these decisions with clients:

"When you tell that story about what happened in your last marriage, you say it makes you feel so angry. Would you want me to be affected in the same way or could I choose to respond differently?"

"When you are telling me about this episode/time in your life what emotional response would you most like to have: for example, sympathy, outrage?"

"As you begin to cry, would you wish me to wait awhile, or keep talking with you as you cry?"

"You all have said how much happier you feel this past few weeks. Can I join in these feelings or would you like me to keep thinking about how you can avoid difficulties?"

Deconstructing clients' realities and creating a shared language

As a therapist sits with people and listens to the stories they tell and live in the sessions, different descriptions and distinctions (Karl, Cynthia, Andrew, & Vanessa, 1992) will come to his or her mind. A therapist will be affected by these descriptions and distinctions whether or not they ever speak them out loud. They might well share these with family members (distinctions in italics): "Do you *fight* like this at *home*?", "What effect does it have on you when your *daughter* speaks so *lovingly* to you?" "When you *argue* like this what do you *think* it *means* to each of you?" There may or may not be a fit between a therapist's description (naming) and the client's experience. The client may well act as if the therapist's description is an accurate description or explanation (Frugerri, 1992) of what is happening rather than believing their own view of events, thinking "the therapist knows best".

Questions such as "What do you call what is happening now . . .?" can bring forth the names/words used by the client to describe what is happening and so further conversation is more likely to be coordinated between therapist and client and increase the chances of it becoming a therapeutic relationship.

Further fine tuning can be achieved through questions such as: "What kind of . . . is this?", which is currently one of the most useful pattern questions to facilitate the deconstruction of emotions, acts, and descriptions that are taken for granted as being singular in their description, meaning, and effects. For example, an interviewee (client or therapist) says, "I feel so guilty when I do that." There are many possible responses that a therapist can make to this (time, frequency, location, effect, in relation to whom and to what) that act within the distinction of guilt as a singular entity. Asking the question "What *kind* of guilt are you talking about/experiencing?" helps the interviewee to make further distinctions. If the interviewee responds: "What do you mean, what kind of guilt?", the interviewer might reply, "Well, I was wondering if it is the kind of guilt that disables you from doing anything or the kind that enables you to act?" This kind of distinction-creating question can have the effect of introducing an important difference, specifically in relation to guilt. It can also have the more general effect of helping the interviewee and interviewer create other distinctions (Karl, Cynthia, Andrew, & Vanessa,1992) in entities that are unhelpful when thought of in the singular sense, such as tears, blame, love, stress, therapy, and so on.

This kind of process can be thought of as both *centring* the conversation within the client's initial description of their experience and introducing *variation* into that description. So it has the potential to be simultaneously familiar and different. Wittgenstein's concept of "centre of variation" (see Cronen & Lang, 1994) describes this well. Bateson's notion (1972) of "different but not too different" is also useful here.

Experience of the session/therapy

As a session of therapy or supervision gets under way, ideas begin to get generated by all the participants: interviewee, interviewer, and team members. Each participant is endeavouring to act coherently within their resources. Interviewers, especially, are likely to be empathically sensing (looking for) clues/cues from the interviewee to evaluate how the interview is going, and self-reflexively searching their resources to help the interview to go well. It is useful to develop a repertoire that includes questions designed to evaluate the process of the session, and the emerging nature of the relationships as it proceeds, rather than merely asking at the end.

These questions can range from simply checking out how the interviewee is experiencing the session so far to those with a more reflexive intent, designed to be generative of difference in the interview process and therapeutic relationship. For example, "How do you want me to participate in this conversation?" "We have been talking for a while now and I am wondering what you would hope that the team behind the screen have understood from listening to what we have been talking about?" "What kind of listener would you like me to be today?" *How do you mean?* "Well, so far I have waited until you have finished what you have had to say before I say something. I wondered if I might ask some questions to make sure I am understanding you in a way that you want me to?" "Are we talking about the issues that are important to you, in ways that are useful, at a pace that is OK?" "If this conversation/session/therapy were to stop now, what important issues would have been resolved already, and what issues would you feel we could have worked on further?"

Sometimes it is necessary to negotiate process interruption. For example, a man continually interrupted his partner every time she was in the middle of saying something. I said that I had noticed this, and he agreed that he had a tendency to alter what she said. I asked if he wanted me to go along with his tendency, or to interrupt his interruption (by touching his arm). He wasn't sure, but agreed to the experiment. After a while he found he was hearing things he hadn't heard before and decided to continue with the experiment in the session and then eventually at home. If he hadn't felt able to agree to the experiment we could have explored the strength of that interrupting tendency and how it might deprive him of things he might want to hear about. We could have negotiated that he sat behind the screen to listen to the conversation, or that the therapist videotaped a conversation with his partner, then, with her permission, the man could watch it (but without the remote control!).

In situations where a person is participating in an interview reluctantly, or has other reason for feeling apprehensive about the session, then if this reason can be elicited, a series of questions can be asked around the theme of: "How could the interview be organized/go so that you didn't feel that your experience was replicated or repeated?" "If it started to go that way would you be able to speak out?" "If the interview/sessions did go in a way that you experienced differently, what might be some of the effects that you would hope for in relation to the reason you are here?"

Sometimes it is difficult to know what effects are happening during a session and occasionally asking: "What have you heard yourself or someone else say today that may be important/useful to you in some way?" The responsibility for deciding what to select from all the things that have been spoken/done becomes relational (McNamee & Gergen, 1999).

Time and timing

A relationship between therapist and client(s) is more likely to become, and continue as, therapeutic when resources around the meaning and practices of time are coordinated (Boscolo & Bertrando, 1992, 1993).

"What is your relationship with time?"

In developing a relationship with a client's sense of time it is useful for the therapist to take the opportunity to explore their own relationship with time (this exercise could just as usefully be applied to any other aspects of this chapter). One way of doing this is to ask oneself the questions that are proposed below for clients to consider.

"When I say the word future . . ."

There is, within our field, a strong preference to look to the future (Boscolo, Cecchin, Hoffman, & Penn, 1987; O'Hanlon & Weiner-Davis, 1989; Penn 1985) since it is yet to be made and so is often more open to creative speculation. Therapists may have a favourite/regular time span they use to ask future questions. For example, "In five years time where would you like to see yourself . . .?" If this particular time frame fits with the client's own, then fine. If not, the client may feel a failure because they cannot conjure up an answer. The therapist may think of themselves as a failure or believe that the client has no sense of the future and so shouldn't be pushed any more, or that things are much worse than the therapist thought. Either way this impasse may hinder the development of a relationship that is therapeutic. Before asking this question it can be useful to ask, "When I mention the word future, how far ahead do you see?" Then construct the question around the client's sense of time. "So in (client's response) where would you like to see yourself?" Other aspects of time, past and present, can be considered in a similar way.

"How long did that hour last?"

One particularly useful idea is the distinction between chronological time and personal time. Who has not had the experience of an experience that lasted five minutes, by clock time, and yet seemed to go on forever? Conversely, many people will recognize the experience that actually took three hours yet seemed to be over in a flash. There are different languages and metaphors of time: fixed time/flexible time; public/private time; good time/bad time; quality time; just in time; in good time; time stood still; in no time at all. In working with a black person who had undergone a gender reassignment from female to male, we explored the range of "time zones" that he "lived in"; male/female; American black south; work time/play time and so on. Coordinating how he moved between these time zones became a feature of therapy.

The reader will be able to imagine a whole range of ways of exploring time as a context for the development of the therapeutic relationship. A useful question is to ask the client and oneself, "As we begin/continue to talk about this issue would you prefer to focus on the past, the present, or the future?"

Conclusion

Relational reflexivity is proposed as a practical, useful concept in coordinating the resources of both therapist and clients in creating, changing, developing, and ending therapeutic relationships. It can help clients to *orientate* therapists to use those abilities that will be most familiar to clients (not too different) and in negotiating when and how to use therapist abilities that may be *interventive* for clients (useful difference). It offers further distinctions on the general invitation to clients "How would you like this therapy to go . . .?" It can create practical invitations to co-create particular episodes, themes, whole sessions, and the general or particular direction of therapy. As therapist and client become used to this reflexive context for their relationship, then either can initiate difference. Clients may come to realize that they have the power to request or initiate changes in the therapy/relationship, and exercise this power in a variety of ways. Therapists learn how to invite the client to try something different without feeling that they are abusing their power. In an extension of Anderson & Goolishian's (1992b) work, therapists and clients may "play", in the context of their emerging relationship, with the idea of who is an "expert". In each therapeutic relationship, expertise may be thought of as being co-created through the coordination of the resources (expertise) of both client and therapist. Therapists and clients could take turns in being the "expert" in relation to particular topics. If therapists regard the position/identity of "expert" as being so uncomfortable to occupy, then it makes little sense to impose it permanently, and without reference to context, upon clients.

A few words of caution. Relationships, therapeutic or otherwise, cannot be made to work by planning alone, no matter how well done. Spontaneity, mistakes, humour, and misunderstandings are all part of the uncertain process through which relationships are created, sustained, tolerated, enjoyed, and end. No practice, including relational reflexivity, can be guaranteed to make relationships work. My experience is that relational reflexivity can become problematic if overused. Clients can become irritated or concerned if they experience the therapist as continually asking them what they want. They can experience the conversation as disjointed, or view the therapist as too hesitant, or lacking sufficient confidence. One father in a family with whom I had been keen not to make any cultural mistakes eventually told me, "We came here because the GP said that you knew something about children's problems, now please get on with it, and we will tell you if something is not right for us!" Too much relational reflexivity may also inhibit spontaneity and so can be used to evaluate the relational effects of spontaneous actions rather than trying to make sure that the spontaneous act will be appreciated before it happens.

I will end as I began, with an episode from practice that had a significant effect on how I see the process of developing a relationship that has therapeutic potential.

After a number of sessions I began to be influenced by the idea that the woman I was working with was avoiding the issue she said she wanted to work on (her childhood experience of sexual abuse). I wondered how to explore this idea as sensitively as I could, given our gendered differences, and my wish to create and maintain the relationship as therapeutic. I, self-reflexively, began to *think* of a question . . . *"Every time we approach that issue, you seem to change the subject . . . I am wondering why?"* As I began to *speak* the question I changed it to, *"Every time we approach that issue, the conversation seems to go somewhere else. Who do you think avoids it more . . . me or you?"* My thinking was still influenced by the idea that she was avoiding, but I wanted to be kinder by including myself in the question. She replied, *"You do."* I was taken aback, but eventually recovered sufficient curiosity to enquire, *"How? What do I do? . . . How do you notice me doing that?"* Thankfully she replied, *"Well, whenever I am close to talking about what happened you will say something like 'It doesn't have to be now . . . take your time', and so on."* In my wish to be sensitive I had acted superficially. The ways that I expressed my intention to be non-impositional meant that I had imposed my non-impositional stance. My desire to be respectful had led me to be reluctant to take any risks in the relationship, always seeking to be safe and certain (Mason, 1993). By engaging the client in the process of working the relationship out we were both able to change (me to take more risks in asking about the abuse, she in commenting on how I was in the session) and increase the likelihood that the relationship would become, and continue to be, therapeutic.

CHAPTER TWO

From system to psyche[1]

Justin Schlicht and Sebastian Kraemer

Theory underpins therapeutic practice, but, like the underpinning of a building, it comes to be taken for granted. We could not be free to eat, sleep, fight, argue, or love if we constantly feared falling into the cellar. There are times, though, when we need to tread carefully. As family therapists and psychiatrists we want to limit the constraints of theory, but that liberty comes only from the security provided by the ideas underpinning our work: systems theory, psychoanalysis, structural descriptions of families, intergenerational influences, and medical models of mental and physical illness. These are ideas that inform, but do not dominate, practice. Our goal is an informed spontaneity in which respect for our own experience is as important as respect for the patient's. Therapists know what they know, and patients, too, know what they know. When both are free to acknowledge this they may learn something new, the difference that makes a difference (Bateson, 1969).

The same may be said of "technique". Asking people to change seats *à la* Minuchin, or circular questioning *à la* Milan, are "techniques", which we may use but not rely on. As Carl Whitaker often said "If you're a black belt in Karate, and a man comes at you with a gun, what do you do? . . . You run like hell."

In this chapter we present clinical material as a basis for a dialogue between ourselves, in the hope that you, the reader, may join in the discussion. We add comments on theory and technique from systemic and analytic points of view.

SK

Sora was referred to me by a paediatric colleague. She was eleven years old and had temporal lobe epilepsy, but she was also bad tempered, immature, and wet the bed. Her fits were fairly well controlled by carbamazepine, but she continued to have apparent absences, when she was awake but not conscious. The epilepsy started when she was three after her family were attacked at their home in a war-torn country by armed men, who killed her paternal grandmother, one of father's uncles, and her teenaged sister, Dara, who was holding Sora at the time. The family went through several countries and finally arrived in Britain, a few months before this referral. There are six surviving children, aged from their twenties to eight. The eldest three do not live with their parents.

I invited the parents to bring Sora, and arranged for an interpreter. Father brought her, without mother. He is a fine looking man of about fifty with a charming smile. He spoke no English, but Sora had a few words. She told me that men with guns came and stole everything from the house. Father smiled benignly at this narrative, saying that she could not have remembered it, adding that Dara was killed by a bullet in the back, saving the life of Sora, then three years old, in her arms. I could not see any sign of father's grief, but Sora could not wait to tell me about her sister, the memory of whom "makes my body burn". She always wants to look at Dara's picture. I asked if mother could come another time with the photograph album and talk with Sora about her sister, but father says mother has diabetes and high blood pressure and should not be upset too much. Sora wanted to take one of the children's books in the waiting room, and I said no, but that I would get one for her.

I found this consultation incredibly moving. Working in very basic English, or through an interpreter creates a poetic sense; Sora's few words were well chosen. I thought that this consultation would be helpful, just because it felt so powerful.

JS: *Do you mean only that you were moved by it? If so, why should the session have been helpful? Certainly, I have frequently been surprised by the apparently "helpful" result of seemingly banal low-key sessions. Nevertheless, your feeling was important.*

SK: *I worry that I might sometimes be carried away by the process in the room, without knowing how much others are affected. Yet, as you say, the feeling is important, because we can never be just participant observers; we might be making things happen if we succeed in making sense of bits of information. Never before have I offered to buy something for a patient. I found* Noah's Ark *in a bookshop and gave it to her the next time, a month later. Father recognized the story, it is familiar in his country, too. Sora was very pleased. Mother still did not come, and I said I needed her to.*

JS: *I have often been tempted to give something to a child. With a story like Sora's it is hardly surprising that you felt that way. Nevertheless, the temptation is information worth considering as it so often awakens a memory, an echo of our own life experience. Have you wondered why you chose* Noah's Ark*? The story of Noah is a wonderful and apparently universal rescue myth. I was also intrigued by your statement that you "needed" mother to come to the session.*

SK: *I did not think of that. My only criterion was that I should not choose a parochial story such as the typically English ones or obviously Christian ones. That didn't leave me much to choose from! Needing mother to attend felt like little more than wanting to get both parents in the room for a consultation, as one might make an effort to engage fathers in therapeutic work in our culture.*

Sora said that her mother thinks a lot about her dead daughter. Father wanted Sora transferred to a special school, and I agreed with this idea. I said that Sora was alone in the family in expressing any grief for their losses, but I told them I knew that she was not the only one who felt it.

JS: *You state that you "knew", and such conviction, I think, inhibits the possibility of a different "knowing". For that matter how can you be so sure? Sora's problems may really serve to stop the family members actually feeling grief. But I dislike the dishonesty of the phrase, so often used by therapists . . . "I was wondering if . . .". Maybe you could say "Do you think that Sora is the only one who feels grief?".*

In that way you would hold on to your own idea while being curious, while, at the same time, allowing for the possibility of a new "knowing". "Curiosity is one of the permanent and certain characteristics of a vigorous mind" (Samuel Johnson).

SK: *I deliberately said that I knew. If this had been an attempt to be subtly strategic, it was very clumsy. No, I said what I felt because I thought that Sora's experience was being disqualified. I was indignant on her behalf. This reminds me of where I started in psychiatry—by reading Laing* (Laing & Esterson, 1964), *who was really not systemic at all, but he did observe how people's suffering could be enhanced by others' not wanting to know about it.*

JS: *As we talk I have come to realize some real differences between us. The position of knowing/not-knowing is crucial here. If therapists are on a spectrum between knowing and not-knowing, then I am at the "not-knowing" end, and you at the "knowing" end. This is very different from the issue of power, which so worries therapists. We agree, I think, that power is something we have to own; it comes with the job! It is important to accept that, and to deny it is dishonest. "I am here to help you help yourself", is the classic therapeutic double-bind, and I find it abusive. It is the abuse of power that is so damaging, but not the power itself. That power is a burden we must carry, and to which we must show respect* (see Hoffman, 1985).

"Knowing", though, is a different matter. I start from the premise that we can never truly "know" what another may think or feel, and I have too often been surprised by what a person says they think or feel to trust my own guess. To explain what we "know", however, limits the possibilities of discovery, and that which is discovered might be quite different from that which was explained.

But you say you "knew" that Sora was not the only one feeling grief. Does this different approach reflect our different professional paths? You have spent your professional life associated with the relative orthodoxy of the Tavistock (albeit as something of an "institutional maverick") while I have wandered about, enjoying being marginal, and suffering from chronic eclecticism, originally acquired at the Maudsley. There must also be more personal stories, which might be interesting to explore some time.

SK: *"Knowledge" is one of the sticks systemic therapists use to beat psychoanalysis with. Although "not-knowing" has a longer pedigree in analytic writing* (e.g. Freud, 1922e; Bion, 1970) *it is a common prejudice that analysts make up their minds on the flimsiest of evidence and force their convictions on the patient. It is not true.*

The next month I met mother. She wore fine printed cloth and golden jewellery. She is about ten years younger than her husband. Mother complained that Sora fights with her brother, and stares vacantly from time to time. But she also helps occasionally around the house as a good daughter "should". I thought more strongly that Sora was carrying a burden for everyone and therefore was not a popular member of the family.

Sora said: "I want my sister" but her parents explained to me that according to their understanding of the Qur'an one must forget the dead. My heart sank. They see Sora's persistent wish as evidence of bad faith, or of illness. I said that in order to forget, Sora first has to remember. Mother agreed that Sora could have her favourite picture to look at as much as she pleased, but drew the line at a framed portrait by Sora's bed. This would be too much remembering. The parents then told me that while they understood that the Qur'an gave no advice on how to grieve, it does allow the faithful to take medical advice. Sora meanwhile listened intently and drew a very nice picture of a painted hand, which she gave to me. Mother did not want to come next time though I begged her to.

JS: *Again that strong expression of your wish for mother to be there. As someone who has written so eloquently about fathers, have you suddenly discovered mothers? I am interested in the symbolism of the hand. In my experience families enjoy speculating about these things, though it sometimes takes courage to introduce the idea. I like Carl Whitaker's way of introducing these ideas to the family . . .* "Well you know we therapists, we can have crazy ideas about anything."

SK: *Yes, as a disciple of Whitaker's, I like to talk like that too, but I just said it was lovely because it was.*

I think my response above covers your comment about mothers. After all they usually turn up without fathers! But this man, for all his traditional patriarchal dignity, seems a very maternal figure for Sora. At any rate he is the one who takes her to all her appointments and champions her cause. I think mother is protected from having to deal with anything. That's where the patriarchy comes in.

JS: *Or perhaps father represents the family in the world outside the family, as I imagine would be the norm in their culture.*

SK: *In the debate—and the rapprochement—between psychoanalysis and systems, the father is always available to be fought over. Freud's ambivalence about his own father, who died in 1896, contributed to his formulation of the Oedipus complex at the turn of the century. He made the family triangle the heart of his psychology, but it was to be another fifty years before family therapists brought fathers (and siblings) into the consulting room.*

To deny the power of patriarchy is ignorant, but it is still so prevalent that it's easily mistaken for fact. After all, it has been around for at least 10,000 years, long before Oedipus (Kraemer, 1991). *Even in a traditional society like Sora's we can see how paternal power can be exercised without abuse. Though there is no doubting his control, he is also very affectionate and devoted. We are both fathers brought up as children in the 1940s and 1950s when few, including our own parents, questioned gender roles.*

There were several more meetings with just father and Sora. She was terribly grumpy and said that the other children picked on her. In these meetings, we often spoke of Dara, but my hope was that Sora would go to a special school where she would be in smaller classes and maybe could have some individual therapy. Here, it seemed, was a classic case of post traumatic stress disorder (PTSD). I thought I did not see her often enough to deal with this.

JS: *Mention of "post traumatic stress disorder" takes us straight back into the world of medicine. Medically trained therapists so often retreat into familiar territory when faced with ambiguity, intense feelings, and therapeutic impotence. Were you thinking of giving her citalopram instead of* Noah's Ark*?*

SK: *Yes, I looked up the literature on selective serotonin reuptake inhibitors in PTSD, but as they all lower the threshold for seizures, that was not a safe thing to prescribe. So I bought a book on eye movement desensitization and reprocessing (EMDR) for children* (Tinker & Wilson, 1999) *as EMDR is said to reduce the threat of the memory by practising specific eye movements while thinking of the trauma. I was told by a colleague, whom I consulted about this, that I would need to be trained. Reading a book would not be enough. So I didn't read it. But in pressing the parents to let Sora have her photograph I was using my authority as a doctor.*

Sora finally got a place at a special school, where her behaviour was not much better until the head made a dramatic decision; Sora was to be moved up two years, to a class of children slightly older than herself. Here she thrived. I continued to see her and her father at infrequent intervals and developed a way of dealing with her which was never to ask her father how things had been, but simply to welcome her and let her draw if she wanted and tease her when she grumbled, as she always did. Then she would smile a winning smile. A psychologist from a child and family clinic began seeing Sora at school each week. One of the key themes in this work (which I supervised) was Sora's developing beauty and sexuality, and her approach to the age at which her sister died so violently. Something of this was anticipated in the drawing of a painted hand.

The psychologist joined me in the family meetings each term at the hospital. For the first time we met two of Sora's siblings. They talked about whether they could ever go home again. "There are peacemakers trying to end the war", said father. It was just ten years since they had left. As if she had already left, Sora said "I didn't like it here" and then as an afterthought said some kind words about her psychologist and me. Mother missed her home, but was visibly upset when her son, using a map on the wall, started to piece together the family's journey, and the reason for it; the assassination of Dara, of father's mother and uncle. No one mentioned Sora's problems.

JS: *This seems to be a critical change when the focus has shifted from Sora to a more generalized expression of grief and loss. I hope this transition will free Sora from her awesome responsibility for the family.*

Sora says that she and her sister gaze at their dead sister's picture often, and feel sad. The psychologist said that Sora brought the picture of the Dara to the next session. In this portrait she is in Western clothes, without a scarf. Sora always wears a scarf in the hospital but also showed the psychologist pictures of herself in holiday in Europe without one.

JS: *Not surprisingly, my first response to your case was to remember a paper describing the "dazzle effect". Therapists can be dazzled by the stories that families bring with them. Their stories are sometimes horrifying, they may evoke disgust, anger, shame, and they can be far from our own life experience. You clearly express the impotence we feel as therapists when hearing these stories. You actually question whether you might have treated her as a classic case of post traumatic stress disorder. Such stories might drive us to retreat into the more secure territory of the medical model. But you didn't, and you bought her a Noah's ark instead of giving her citalopram, and you listened to the family's story. You didn't even try a bit of circular questioning, which might have done the trick! Were there, though, echoes of your own family? What was their experience of the holocaust? And where was Noah then?*

SK: *Well, of course there were, but that never occurred to me. In their twenties my father and his brother left Germany in 1933 as soon as Hitler came to power. Neither of them regarded themselves as Jews, but they were Jewish enough. In the 1960s my father found out that their father had died in Theresienstadt camp, fourteen days before I was born. I did not grow up with these stories, but they must have an impact. In cinemas I can never follow the story because I have no part in formulating it, but working with families and indeed writing on anything that interests me I have to find out how it all happened, going back generations—or even millennia—if need be* (Kraemer, 1991) *to make it coherent, at least for myself. I did not have history lessons at school after the age of thirteen or fourteen, which I regret. A major feature of all history, whether recorded or not, is migration and loss due to war.*

JS: *We are encouraged as therapists to be aware of our feelings, but not to express them too freely, particularly if those feelings are negative or hostile or angry. At the same time we set out to enable our patients to express such feelings, not as an end in itself, but more out of respect shown to each person. And yet, we deny ourselves the same respect, and behave as if non-verbal signals are only what patients do.*

SK: *Systemic therapists have in the past resisted using the term counter-transference, though it is the one that comes to mind here. The person or family asking for help brings with them expectations of help (or the lack of it) from previous formative relationships. The therapist is touched by these fantasies, which generate some of his own. This kind of primal communication is necessary in therapy, whatever words we use to describe it. A favourite systems concept, "curiosity" describes a necessary but not sufficient condition for therapeutic engagement. You can be curious but not affected emotionally.*

JS

Some years ago I was working in Sweden with a family in which the two stepdaughters had been sexually abused over a number of years. The stepfather was in prison, but was released each week for therapy. The girls refused to attend. I was struggling with two complex emotions: the first was that I could not understand why the mother was prepared to welcome her husband back into the family home, and the second was my anger and disgust at what the stepfather had done. They came to the fourth session, and the husband was very angry because his application for early release had been turned down. "It serves you right", I said, without thinking, "what you did was unforgivable." They were shocked, but it was only after my feelings were spoken that any work could begin, particularly since the way I felt was already part of what was taking place, but not negotiable until then.

SK: *The more desperate the case the more we need to be desperately candid. This is nothing new, but I think all therapists have to learn this for themselves. We start off trying to do it right, by imitating supervisors or heroes, but that's someone else talking.*

JS

Another story: when I was working in Sweden we had a close relationship with a family in-patient unit in Norway. On a visit there they asked me to see a family they had been struggling with for many months, and whom they had presented to a number of visiting therapists.

> The family was a farming family of two parents and three children, a daughter aged thirteen and two younger boys aged eleven and nine. The daughter was unable to move her legs or arms and needed help for all of her needs. As she was seen to move when asleep, and, occasionally, when awake and unobserved, her paraplegia was understood to

be a conversion disorder. The family was socially isolated, but this was not unusual in southern Norway. They spoke in a local dialect, but also used standard Norwegian, if heavily accented. Norwegian and Swedish languages are very close, and they can understand each other when speaking their own languages. We agreed to use Swedish and Norwegian, and for me to have occasional help as my Swedish was by no means fluent.

I decided to meet with the family and the therapeutic team together, and we had a lengthy discussion. After some time, I took a break and went for a walk by myself. I was puzzled but impressed by the intensive work that had been done with this family, which included a number of consultations that had already taken place before I came along. Following the advice of Carl Whitaker I tried hard to think of a story, song, book, poem, and could only think of *Sleeping Beauty*. Not surprisingly, the family knew the story, but seemed perplexed when I told it to them in my poor Swedish. Our meeting was then over.

The next day I met with the team and their colleagues who had been observing the meeting, and we reviewed the videotape of the session. To my initial embarrassment it became clear, very early on, that I had not understood most of what the family had said in response to my brilliant exposition of circular questioning, and that I had, in turn, understood very little of what they had said to me. Neither the family, nor my colleagues, with typical Scandinavian respect, had felt that they should comment on this during the meeting! The initial embarrassment changed to amusement.

Two weeks later the family cancelled their appointment as their daughter was out riding. One year later one of my colleagues asked permission to use the tape for teaching. The daughter, who was perfectly well, was adamant that the tape should be discarded.

SK: *A wonderful story. Therapists can do magic as long as they don't think they can. Imagine trying to be a stupid foreigner. One cannot try to make things like this happen, only to work out afterwards what did happen.*

They got to the consultation, that's the first thing, so were ready to be witnessed, if not actually to change. I have often felt that the family consultation is an anthropological event marking a transition (Perelberg, personal communication) *and that what one says precisely is less important than tone of voice, "body language", and all the things that contribute to a sense of occasion. A therapist who is impressed is part of that. The session can become a celebration of a forthcoming event that will change the family (such as a departure from home) but also a record what has already happened, but is too new to register in their "history". As they had had some previous consultations you must have been close to their last hope.*

You were probably quite respectful, because they were even more foreign than your usual clients, and you may even have been nervous. This adds to the dramatic tension. The sleeping beauty story helped I am sure but was the icing on the cake. They had visited the healer. Discarding the tape must be to do with wanting to save face and forget how stuck she was with her conversion disorder.

The Hungarian psychoanalyst Michael Balint (1957) *described the doctor's "apostolic function". Family change takes place all the time but can be marked by the therapist at moments of high emotion or meaning. Being white male doctors, now both over sixty, may make this easier for us but at the same time more open to the charge that this is a patriarchal attitude. Perhaps it is, but would it not be odd* not *to make use of one's training, role and gender? I am sure that, for example, a young female non-medical therapist must also use her own qualities to make something of these moments, too, if she is to be effective.*

JS: *Yes, I was nervous as I always am before a meeting with a family, and even more so if I am to meet an individual patient. Indeed, if I am not, I worry. In retrospect, and only in retrospect, the story seems to me to have more relevance than first appears to be the case. Many "princes" had been denied access to the princess because of the thick vegetation, and, in the story the family seem to be entirely accepting of the princess's state. The family would include the courtiers, or the therapeutic team. The prince who finally awakens the princess does so without a struggle, and with no great demonstration of strength. He just happened to be in the right place at the right time! The stories, tunes, metaphors, and poems, which come to mind at the time, need to be trusted. They invariably turn out to have a logic serendipitously related to the patients' experience, even if we do not "know" it at the time. Remember your choice of* Noah's Ark.

One tune that often comes into my mind before a session goes ". . . if I should take the notion to jump into the ocean, it ain't nobody's business if I do . . ." Similarly, if we ask ourselves to describe our therapeutic work metaphorically, we may produce some surprising

> *insights* (Schlicht, 1991). *Ask somebody else, and the result may be even more surprising! I am reminded here of Carl Whitaker's often repeated quote from Rabindrath Tagore:* "A mind that is all logic is like a knife all blade. It makes the hand bleed that uses it."

SK

A core idea in this chapter might be described as the search for therapeutic intimacy. This is a risky term for a risky process, but one which we believe is necessary for change. In telling each other clinical stories we have found some examples of this. That was not the intention at the beginning. Indeed, there was no clear aim, except to discuss our experiences of relatedness to families and individuals in them. If you set out to be intimate you may well get a slap in the face. It has to be a side effect of the primary task, which is to get hold of the drama by partly taking part in it.

Epilogue

JS

When Carl Whitaker had presented his work with a family at a conference one of the audience asked him how the family had "done". Whitaker replied "I don't know, but I'm doing fine."

At a party some years ago, a woman I did not recognize approached me. She looked angry and hostile. She said she had been wanting to speak to me since she had consulted me with her daughter some ten years previously when I worked in a psychiatric emergency clinic. She said that it had been a most distressing meeting, and that I had behaved cruelly, unprofessionally, and that I had insulted them both. The day before my meeting with them, the daughter, who was then eighteen years old, had returned from a happy holiday in Greece with her friends. Later the same day she became very distressed, tearful, and demanding. She repeatedly threatened suicide. I learned that she was in analysis as she had an eating disorder. Her analyst was on holiday. Her parents were themselves due to go on holiday the next day. The same events had happened on the eve of their holiday for the previous two years, and they had not been able to go on holiday. I began to remember the meeting, and also the fear I had experienced afterwards that I had behaved badly. I had said to the daughter that I thought she was a selfish young woman, and to the mother, that she was crazy to allow herself and her husband to be driven by such behaviour into missing their much needed summer holiday. I added that the daughter was old enough to look after herself.

The daughter then ran out of the room, crying bitterly, pursued by a very angry mother. I was left feeling bad, and desperately hoping that nothing terrible would happen. So my memory was as clear as the mother's, who then told me that, in spite of my appalling behaviour, her daughter was now married with two children, but that, *because* of my appalling behaviour, she had resolved, after the meeting, never to see a psychiatrist again. I further learnt that the parents had gone on holiday, but that it had been a most unhappy time as they were on the phone to their daughter at least every day. Their daughter has kept her promise, and has never seen a psychiatrist or therapist again.

Acknowledgements

We are grateful to the families who have given permission for their experiences to be recorded here.

Note

1. With apologies, and thanks, to Carl Whitaker

CHAPTER THREE

"Alice and Alice not through the looking glass": therapeutic transparency and the therapeutic and supervisory relationship

Maeve Malley and Alfred Hurst

Introduction

This chapter addresses the issues raised by working in a particular context, a London-based voluntary sector counselling and therapy agency for lesbians and gay men, and in a particular way—"in-the-room" supervision with all discussion in front of the clients. The experience of working in this way, in this context, made us aware of the effect that it had on us as therapist and supervisor and of how it seemed to be received by the clients seen during the two-year period that we worked together in this way. Some of the issues that it raised, though initially context-specific, were in fact general issues about power, knowledge and disclosure within therapy and about the nature of the therapeutic and the supervisory relationship. We discuss these issues from the angle of vision of the therapist, the supervisor, and what we surmise and were told about the experience of clients.

In-the-room supervision

While "in-the-room" supervision is not a new phenomenon within systemic practice (Gorell Barnes & Campbell, 1982), it is not a common way of working and is distinct from behind the screen supervision and reflecting team practice. This experience was distinct from the latter in that reflecting teams generally focus on the experience of the family, rather than the experience of the therapist, or the therapist with the family, and do not conduct their entire team discussion in front of clients, or confine supervisory input to this context. When we first embarked on this particular way of working we were not sure how it would be for the therapist or the supervisor, or indeed the clients, to confine our discussions about the work to this context. So, initially, it may have been a kind of experiment to see if we could talk about the things that seemed important to talk about, such as the therapist's approach, or the ways that the clients engaged with therapy and with the therapist, and the supervisory relationship—all in front of the clients.

It is not possible to know if we would have had entirely different conversations had we had additional supervisory discussions outside the room, but we can say that there never felt like a censoring of conversations, an unwillingness to raise issues of practice or theory in front of clients, or a sense that we had to tailor our supervisory conversations to the context. For me, as supervisor, this was undoubtedly affected by the fact that I was working with an experienced therapist whom I did not feel responsible for teaching. Since many of our experiences as supervisors are with therapists in training, this was a freeing context for me and one where I felt my primary responsibility was to help the therapist to be the best therapist that he could be in this situation. Since he had a great deal of experience in working therapeutically with lesbians and gay men, it also felt like a very secure situation in that it is remarkably easy to supervise a competent therapist in a respected and gay- and lesbian-friendly context—which is how the Project for Advocacy, Counselling and Education (PACE[1]) was experienced by a majority of clients.

The choice to work in such a visible way was not initially a conscious effort to promote therapeutic transparency, but was due to a combination of practical and political factors. The practical was the lack of access to rooms with a screen or video, which would have permitted the classic "screen/team" systemic approach, and the political was two-fold. First, that the agency in which we were working was transparent in that it explicitly employed only lesbian and gay male workers to provide services to lesbian and gay male clients. Consequently, the sexual identity of practitioners at the agency is not opaque; indeed, this is the reason that many lesbian and gay male clients choose to use this agency, because of the certainty of being seen by a therapist who is themselves an "out" (at least in this context) lesbian or gay man. Secondly, both the therapist and the supervisor in this context were very conscious of the possible issues for clients generally in their experience of the "screen/team" method (Reimers & Treacher, 1995) and particularly of the issues for a lesbian/gay male client group, who may have, often justified, anxieties about judgements made about them behind closed doors (Davies & Neal, 1996; Kassis & Matthews, 1987).

Enhancing therapeutic transparency

Acknowledging power hierarchies

Systemic therapy has increasingly considered issues of power and access to power within the therapeutic context, although it has tended to do so traditionally from a white, liberal, humanist, heterosexual position. While this can have its disadvantages, the fact that systemic therapy has been used primarily in Britain within a statutory sector context, rather than the private or voluntary sectors, has meant that it has had to grapple with the contradictions and dilemmas implicit in a largely middle-class, white practitioner base working with an often working-class, culturally diverse client base (Bor, Mallandain, & Vetere, 1998; Street & Rivett, 1996).

While the constraints and boundaries inherent in therapeutic provision residing within, and provided by, large and unwieldy bureaucracies have meant that the "my ball, my game, my rules" therapist position has yet to change radically in practice, systemic theory has been responsive to considerations of unequal power and access given to non-dominant societal groups or individuals where ethnicity, gender and culture is concerned. Normative judgements derived from the, by implication, desirable, though often illusory, patterns of white, middle-class, patriarchal, nuclear, intact family life are no longer so uniformly assumed to be reflective of realities in Nature and consequently seen as "right" or "natural". Systemic thinking, in common with psychotherapeutic modalities generally, has, however, been better, or less resistant in thinking of the profound effect upon women and black and minority ethnic peoples of these normative judgements, than in considering the equally dramatic impact upon lesbians and gay men (Jones & Gabriel, 1999; Leslie, 1995; Ussher, 1991; Vessey & Howard, 1993).

It is unrealistic to assume that it is possible for all clients to feel powerful, comfortable, and equal in the therapeutic context all the time—or indeed much of the time. By its very nature the experience of psychotherapy may be uncomfortable and contribute to clients feeling vulnerable. It is, none the less, desirable that clients feel positive about the therapeutic setting and the therapist, since it is this that seems to dictate a positive outcome for the client (Friedlander, Wildman, Heatherington, & Skowron, 1994; Lambert, Shapiro, & Bergin, 1986; see Alan Carr's chapter in this volume).

Supervisees, too, can feel vulnerable and disempowered within supervisory relationships. Making this relationship more public, visible, and accountable, assuming that it is a mutually respectful relationship, partially redresses the power imbalance between supervisor and supervisee, between therapist and client/s, and between supervisor and client/s, although the latter is a more oblique relationship. It is significant in this context, too, that the supervisor is a female and the supervisee a male, and both are respectively known by clients to be lesbian and gay. There would be an additional comfort and mutual understanding in sharing a non-heterosexual lens in their work together.

Self-disclosure

The concept of therapeutic transparency is necessarily fraught in that it can be seen merely as a cherished postmodern therapist illusion rather than as a reality of systemic therapeutic practice. One aspect of transparency is, of course, self-disclosure. There are real debates to be had about how, when, and why we, in our role as therapists and supervisors, answer or decline to answer questions about our own experience or feelings (Baldwin, 2000; Real, 1990). These choices may be based upon our theoretical orientation, our personal history, or our practice context, but the important point is that they are choices, not givens. Most therapists have a thought-out position on disclosure, but what we actually do or not do in therapy, or choose to disclose may reflect more about ourselves and our own assumptions than about what the client experiences as most useful. This makes the content and the timing of self-disclosure a significant aspect of both the supervision and the therapy. The effect on the therapeutic relationship may be strongly influenced by the client's response to the therapist's, or in this case also the supervisor's, disclosure or non-disclosure.

The supervisor's experience: part 1

Issues around self-disclosure were particularly central in this context where there were often areas arising in the supervision that were more or less familiar to me than to Alfred and vice versa. For instance, he describes working in a situation where his sero-positive status and his decision to disclose it made an enormous difference therapeutically, but was embodied in a situation much less familiar to me than to him. I have not had to face those particular dilemmas, and as a lesbian am less likely to have to do so.

There were at other times, though, situations when issues related directly to my own situation. For instance, a gay man discussing with his lover the age differential in their relationship—twelve years, the same age differential as with my own lover; or an Irish gay man discussing his family of origin context and the cultural conflicts he experienced in living in England as a gay man; or lesbian couples talking about sex, or debating if they felt safe enough to talk about sex. These were all issues on which I had to decide whether or not to introduce my own experience into the supervisory discussion and therefore by proxy into the therapeutic discussion. On the whole, self-disclosure by both the therapist and the supervisor seemed to contribute to increasing trust and safety within the therapeutic relationship.

Talking about sex, for instance, was also affected by the gender balance in the room. Lesbian sex and sexual practice has the dubious honour of being socially constructed as either non-existent or as possibly the single most erotic concept within the heterosexual male pantheon. Gay male sex, on the other hand, is more likely to elicit homophobic reactions or be characterized as non-erotic, non-emotional, and continual. Also, there is a prevailing mythology within the lesbian and gay communities that you can't stop gay men talking about sex, but can't get lesbians to talk about it at all. This is clearly more to do with societal gender stereotypes—men as hypersexual and possessors of proactive sexuality, women as asexual and only responding reactively—than reality. Whatever the reasons, it creates a particularly charged context for any male therapist, even a gay man, to initiate a discussion of the sexual relationships of lesbian clients or for a female supervisor to suggest that a male therapist could usefully raise the issue of sex with a gay male couple. Raising these social discourses around gay and lesbian sexual practices within the supervisory segment was particularly freeing for clients in the ongoing therapy.

It may have helped our clients, too, that we were able to display both our knowledge/experience in various arenas and our lack of knowledge/experience in others. In the area of lesbian and gay male relationships, where there are so few templates and so much anxiety about "getting it wrong" in various roles as parents, children, siblings, lovers, and friends, this may have been comforting to clients. We also had very different strengths, some of which may have been counter to traditional gender roles. Alfred has an almost "body therapist" awareness of working with clients in terms of how their thoughts translate into words, which translate into feelings, which translate into tension or tightness or awareness of where the feelings are held in the body. I am an extremely "heady" supervisor and therapist and so this kind of somatic awareness is not as easy for me, but I was constantly amazed and impressed by this way of working and how it worked for clients. This was a difference we talked about in the supervisory breaks and so clients saw different models of seeing behaviour and feelings discussed, without there being an agenda of "rightness" or "wrongness" about these differences. What we also had, of course, were Maeve/Alfred discussions, because undoubtedly the nature of the discussions was affected by our relationship and our fondness for each other, as well as by our roles. What we were unable to model was a same gender relationship, but what we did model was a collaborative, albeit implicitly hierarchical, relationship with a "reverse" hierarchy, or where the gender–power differential was, at least on the surface, reversed.

The therapist's–supervisee's experience: part 1

In this section I am going to start to tell my story, in a personal way, about my experience of being supervised in the room by Maeve while working with lesbian and gay couples. I aim to do two things: first, I hope to say what it was like for me, and second, to put my experience into some sort of theoretical framework.

I believe that for useful therapy and supervision to occur there are a number of conditions that are helpful for all involved. I find it interesting that the term "conditions" occurs so early on in my passage, as it leads me to an important theoretical influence in my work as a systemic therapist. This is, of course, the Rogerian core conditions of person-centred work— empathy, unconditional positive regard, and congruence (Rogers, 1951). I would say that I am a person-centred, systemic therapist rather than a psychodynamic one. I am hopeful that systemic therapy will embrace these terms as part of its theoretical framework rather than moving towards an increased emphasis on technique. I think that the distinction between these two different therapist styles is important and will determine the therapist's approach to self-disclosure of themselves to their client; that is, to be a blank screen or not.

A bit of background about myself. I generally work therapeutically with groups, either with groups of individuals on themes of sex and relationships, or with organizations on issues of process and development. I had a mixture of thoughts about moving to work with couples. I was at a crunch point in my journey as a therapist. I had recently completed my MSc in family therapy. I felt deskilled and uncertain about how I fitted in as a therapist. My clinical training seemed to emphasize technique rather than helping me to develop to be the therapist that I was, a therapist in the Satir model (Satir, 2000). For example, in my training I was told not to wave my hands about and to dress more formally than I was accustomed to. This, together with a heavy emphasis on heterosexual models, left me thinking that perhaps my life as a therapist was over. Fortunately, the writings of Carmel Flaskas reached me and affirmed my directions in thinking about emotions and the therapeutic relationship, and I went on to qualify, almost despite the techniques of my training course.

The supervisor's experience: part 2

In some respects the prospect of working in this way was as intimidating and as exciting as my original systemic training. The fear of my practice as a supervisor becoming visible and therefore of being exposed as inept or unhelpful, or just as doing it "wrong", was to the fore. Equally to the fore, however, was my excitement at the idea of supervision becoming more visible. I had felt uncomfortable about the idea of using a screen in an agency that works with lesbian and gay male clients. From my research with systemic therapists working with lesbians and gay men, and with lesbians and gay men using psychotherapy, and from my own experience as a client in psychotherapy, I was aware that there is still a reasonable expectation of the equation of lesbian/gay male sexual identity = pathology (Malley, 2002; Malley & Tasker, 1999; Milton & Coyle, 1999). The use of the screen, while useful and defensible in a number of contexts, is frequently off-putting to clients (Reimers & Treacher, 1995) and does introduce very graphically the idea of secret conversations and unseen others.

Since there were no real guidelines of how systemic practice managed the pragmatics of in-the-room supervision, (who sat where, who talks to whom when), we had to evolve our own practice. Before clients were booked in for an assessment appointment we sent them information about this way of working and a little information about ourselves: name, gender, age, ethnicity, training. We had relatively minimal information about clients before they came: age, gender, ethnicity, and a brief description of what brought them into therapy. The vast majority of the clients we saw over the two-year period were couples, most without children. They were extremely diverse in terms of national and cultural identity, in terms of age and class, and in terms of the issues they presented. All the clients referred themselves, though they had heard about the agency from a number of different sources. The agency operates a system of sliding-scale fees, dependent on income, with clients self-selecting the fee that they would pay. Although this may describe a self-selected, well-motivated, and possibly privileged population, in fact there are data that indicate that in one British sample of lesbians and gay men, this group may be much less likely to use statutory sector (i.e. NHS or Social Services) therapeutic provision and will in fact choose to pay for counselling or therapy, irrespective of their own financial, employment, or class status (Malley, 2002).

As supervisor, I sat behind and slightly to the right of Alfred. Consequently, since I was slightly out of the clients' direct line of vision they would have to turn to see me directly. I did not look at the clients for the vast majority of the time. Equally, I did not shy like a startled deer if they looked at me, but I discovered that since I was not making eye contact with them generally and Alfred was, they looked at him rather than me. My experience was that by not looking at the clients and not interrelating directly with them I tended to hear them differently. It felt as though I was somewhere in between hearing the content and the process.

My experience has always been that as therapist I will feel the emotional heat of what clients bring and feel how they relate to each other, whereas behind the screen as supervisor, I perceive the pattern and process of relating much more clearly, but have very much less sense of the emotional investment. My belief would be that this split is where mistakes can be made by therapist and by supervisor. Behind the screen I can be unnecessarily reductionist as a supervisor, without considering sufficiently where the main concern or feeling is located. The theory behind combining a therapist's and supervisor's experience is promising. Put the therapist's experience and the supervisor's experience together and a balanced picture of the clients and their ways of being should emerge. Instead, however, it can sometimes feel like a battle of views. This may be particularly marked or destructive if there is an explicit or implicit power dynamic in the therapist–supervisor relationship, a factor almost inevitably present in a training context, which is where people have their most consistent experience of live supervision.

As we became more used to this way of working, Alfred and I often focused either on contextualizing the issues, or on discussing how he was working with the clients, or how he felt about how he was working. The former point, contextualizing the issues, was particularly important in this situation. As noted earlier, lesbians and gay men do not have templates or models of how to be successful lovers, parents, children, or even friends. Aside from their own marginalized gay and lesbian communities, they have few role models in non-heterosexual coupling, and homophobic and heterosexist social opinion will predominantly judge gays and lesbians as unsuccessful in their relationships. Consequently, they may understandably de-contextualize their situation or internalize this social homophobia and judge themselves particularly harshly, or feel uncertain of their ability and capacity to have "good enough" relationships. This is not to say that we acted as some kind of uncritical cheerleading squad, but the systemic perspective was particularly helpful in terms of legitimizing and acknowledging their creative life choices and normalizing some recurrent difficulties. We talked about other lesbians' and gay men's experience, relevant research or writing or, as we discussed earlier, our own experience.

The therapist's–supervisee's experience: part 2

In this section I say more about my experience and add to the theoretical framework. Maeve has set the scene of how we sat and how we worked. Now, it's my turn to continue.

Unfortunately we do not have the clients' experience written by clients for this chapter. However, I am recording my experience, the therapist and the "supervision client". I make this point because I am not sure how clear the nature of the supervisory relationship is for the "therapy client", as the supervisory relationship happens largely behind closed doors. Systemic literature largely focuses on the client and therapist relationship, or the therapist and the supervisor, but rarely on the whole system, let alone the therapist's, and even more rarely the supervisor's, experience or use of self. As the therapist I am in the middle—both practising therapy and receiving supervision—or, in more systemic terms, I am having a relationship with both parties. The supervisor and I are engaged in the supervisory relationship and the couple and I are engaged in the therapeutic relationship.

It is important for these relationships to be made explicit as they provide a framework in the therapeutic system for transparency and define the roles and relationships within the therapy. The literature discusses the nature of the therapeutic system but the supervisory part of the system tends to be excluded, unless it is an article dedicated to the supervisory process (Moloney & Moloney, 1996).

Theory and the literature on the therapeutic relationship is beginning to have a greater presence within the field (Flaskas, 2002; Flaskas & Perlesz, 1996; Reimers, 2001), but extending these ideas to the supervisory process continues to be neglected and the landscape of systemic supervision remains under-theorized (cf. Campbell & Mason, 2002).

I decided to take this opportunity to work with Maeve at PACE. I knew PACE well because I had been involved in a range of capacities since 1987. I had met Maeve on a couple of occasions and had liked her. In short I felt safe. This is obviously an important factor for me as a therapist, but it is often overlooked, even by systemic therapists. Do I feel safe to be the therapist that I am? PACE is a safe place where lesbian and gay relationship and experience is not automatically problematized—a theme that clients frequently commented on in sessions and in their evaluations of the therapy. I will draw out parallels between my "supervisory client" or supervisee experience and the "therapy client" experience.

When working with a couple Maeve would be sitting in a chair behind me. She would greet the clients but that would generally be the extent of her verbal communication directly to them, except for a warm goodbye. I would then start the session in the normal way, hearing about why they had come and then the work together would start. Generally, at about two-thirds of the way through the sessions I would break the communication with the couple, turn my chair towards Maeve and we would start the supervision. After they had listened to our discussion, the couple were invited to comment on any aspect of what they had heard, or simply to carry on where they had left off.

My style as a therapist is such that I use my intuition about the couple, gained from being in their presence, as well as working with what the couple say, or do not say, to me and to each other. The work is entirely focused on them, but in building up the therapeutic relationship I might bring in my own experience. First, as already stated, they know that I am a gay man, they can see that I am white and middle-aged. They can also see many other things. I am not a neat dresser, I don't wear jewellery, I have both ears pieced and I don't have earrings, I speak with a middle-class southern accent, etc. I write this because they are all things that people may or may not notice and that may lead them to draw conclusions about me, factors that may influence what they think about me. I say this because I believe that in a systemic relationship—and really, I can't believe that any relationship is not systemic—all factors verbal or non-verbal, what you don't say as much as what you do say, have the potential for self-disclosure and are factors affecting whether a therapeutic alliance is built up or not.

Clients will also make assumptions about me, as I have about them. I am interested in this. In a straw poll I conducted with fellow students, I asked what a family therapist is like. The result was that they are white, middle-aged, monogamous, married, female, straight (as in heterosexual) and HIV negative. So, out of those factors, I am the first two only. I am not monogamous, married, female, straight, or HIV negative. Obviously clients can see that I am not female, but the other factors they might wonder about. When working with a couple where the issue is one of sero-discordance (different HIV status) it seemed important that I disclosed my HIV status. That is not to say that I disclosed automatically, or without thinking it through. Clients never asked me this, but then I have never been asked by anyone in my life outside of therapy either. Clients know how to behave! It is assumed that I will be HIV negative. If I allowed them to think that I was probably HIV negative, what would this be saying about my view of being HIV positive? I would be reinforcing the prejudiced views of society, as well as being dishonest in the therapeutic relationship. Does it matter where the therapist is coming from? I think that it does. For example, if I go to a financial adviser I want to know that he is experienced and probably qualified in this area. But more than that, I want to know if he is truly independent, or if he is working for the company whose products he is trying to sell. In the same way, I need to know where my supervisor is coming from. She does not have the same life experience, but I want to know the basis on which she makes her opinions or judgements. I believe that for the therapeutic relationship to develop, clients should be able to know something about where we come from as therapists.

In a relationship I want truth and honesty. However, I don't need to know everything and I believe I have the right *not* to self-disclose as much as *to* self-disclose. I decide the degree, according to the purpose and the depth of the relationship, but also according to how I feel in myself in the moment, and according to the needs of the client. I might sometimes introduce new information directly, or sometimes it is introduced in the supervision. I need my clients to be honest, I need my supervisor to be the same, and I therefore need to do the same. So, I might say that from the way the couple are speaking to me they seem to be assuming that I am HIV negative (or some other thing) and wonder about this, in terms of their issues or their relationship. I might do this with them or in my supervision with Maeve. This often opens different types of conversation with the couple about their views and assumptions of each other and of the world in general. The important issue is that the work remains client-focused while developing both the supervisory and therapeutic relationship. Developing these relationships in therapy and supervision does involve me and I am not neutral—nothing in my life is.

The supervision models the honesty in the client work. Maeve and I talk about our different feelings and reactions to what is going on in the room. Obviously she will often have different experiences, beliefs, or feelings than I do. This seems helpful to the work. Different views can be held and relationships continue, despite these differences. We were able to model ways of discussing difference, expressing feelings, challenging each other, and putting forward alternatives. Sometimes this involved talking about the different ways we have heard the same thing. This seemed particularly helpful in couple's work, where the battle is often about trying to show the therapist the "truth".

The transparency of the supervision means that our discussions demonstrated how Maeve and I heard things. I get involved emotionally in my work. I qualify this because it might sound unprofessional but I do not equate emotional involvement with "wrongness". Even losing control can have value in moments of emotional empathy with clients, crying or laughing together. A relationship that doesn't get things wrong or risk getting things wrong seems fairly unhelpful and unreal to me. In summary then, I would say that in-the-room supervision made my job as a therapist complex, but easier in some ways and more interesting. It meant that I could give myself to the work without having to take mental notes to bring for supervision. It meant that I was being given a safety net so that I could be me.

Conclusion

Out of a situation that at first we felt was not ideal, we developed a way of working that seemed particularly suited to the couples with whom we were working. It enabled us to be open about how we felt about the work with the couple, how we felt about each other and how therapy and supervision is about relationships. It was not always easy. Not all our clients and their situations were easy to empathize with, but the therapy seemed to develop in a rich way and the work was helpful both to clients and to us in developing our practice as a therapist and a supervisor. We believe that this way of working is stimulating and could be used with a range of client groups where change and a shared agenda for change are desirable, and where a sense of trust, safety, and transparency are significant for marginalized groups who have less access to mainstream counselling services.

Note

1. PACE is a North London agency in the not-for-profit sector, staffed by lesbians and gay men, working with lesbians and gay men.

CHAPTER FOUR

Working with men who use violence and control

Jo Howard

Introduction

The Southern Collective Against Violence and Abuse (SCAVA)[1] is an autonomous reference group that guides the development and delivery of two community health programmes for men who use violence and control in their intimate partnerships with women. Our decision to work as narrative and systemic family therapists with men in the Men's Responsibility Group (MRG) originated in wanting to develop a useful and meaningful response to women who had experienced family violence and who wanted to retain their relationships while hoping for the violence to end. Most of the men are mandated to attend the groups—either through the criminal justice or child protective systems or through their partners threatening to end the relationship unless the men address their abuse and violence.

This chapter describes ways our SCAVA collective, over the last decade, has attempted to develop and sustain effective therapeutic relationships with the men while privileging the accounts of the women and children. We use the voices of the facilitators and the stories of two men in the programme to explore the significance of relationship, gender, and feelings in building connections between violent men and their partners, and between group facilitators and the men in their endeavours to establish non-violent, respectful practices.

Identifying core principles of practice

Safety of women and children

The MRG programme includes twenty weekly group sessions for men (with male and female co-facilitators), with monthly follow-up sessions, individual meetings with the men and their partners when necessary, and group meetings with the women prior to the men starting the programme, six weeks into it, and at least once during the follow-up period. Men are invited to attend the monthly follow-up sessions for as long as they wish. The programme's core principle is that the safety of women and children is paramount. This means the men's progress is judged on reports from the partners, and at times, children, rather than their own reporting of change, given that men have been found to minimize the negative impacts of their violence and emphasize more positive changes than their partners following therapeutic intervention (Gondolf, 1993; Ptacek, 1988).

Men joining the group must sign a "no confidentiality" clause, providing the therapists with the details of their ex and/or current partners. The men are informed that the therapist will speak with their partners, but that they will not be told when, nor will they be given information about the content of what their partners say. Contact between the therapist and partner occurs at key stages during the group's duration, particularly when the man is first referred, about four to six weeks after the group commences and following the completion of the group. All groups are co-facilitated by a male and female therapist.

A feminist stance to men's violence

We adopt a feminist, sociopolitical stance that views men's violence as a gendered crime occurring in a patriarchal context, giving emphasis to men's sense of entitlement to power and control in their violent actions. We do not refer to those experiencing family violence as being in "violent relationships" (Goldner, Penn, Sheinberg, & Walker, 1990, p 356), but prefer language that clearly signifies the perpetrator as responsible for the violence— "men who use violence or abuse" or "men's violence to women and children". The challenge within the MRGs has been to acknowledge men's vulnerability in intimate relationships and their desire to be caring, respectful, loving, and lovable, while at the same time encouraging men to consider the role of patriarchy, gender inequality, power and control in their relationships and inviting them to take responsibility for their behaviour. That is, ". . . to notice how their desires for love, respect and intimacy are thwarted by abusive practices and sexist beliefs about relationships" (Augusta-Scott, 2001, p. 35).

Assessment and pre-group engagement

The assessment and pre-group meetings are a key mechanism in engaging with the men. This process can be confronting for the men for various reasons. First, many would not readily access "the helping professions" and are only doing so because they are mandated. Second, some of the men lack respect and have misogynistic attitudes to women but must be able to work with the female, as well as the male facilitator. Third, men know they will not automatically be able to attend the group although in reality very few men are rejected.[2]

The facilitator needs to bear witness to the man's story (Weingarten, 2000), to discuss what brought him to the group and his hopes and fears in attending. Some men may carry a belligerent attitude to the criminal justice system or their partner's decision to leave the relationship. Others may come with the desperation of knowing their relationships are tenuous and realizing that unless they change they will be alienated from their partner and children. The facilitator has to emotionally engage with the man to enable him to feel supported and be clear that taking responsibility is different from being blamed. The acknowledgement of the frustration, confusion, hurt, disappointment, and fear that men feel needs to occur while being careful not to collude with shifting the responsibility to his partner or past experience.

We contacted Angela after her husband Nick approached us to join the group, in response to Angela telling him she would leave unless his behaviour changed. Nick's understanding of the problem was that he "lost his temper". When he "lost his temper" he would yell, blame, and criticize both Angela and his six-year-old stepson and emotionally withdraw for days at a time, shutting himself in his room and refusing to speak. Nick would put his face close to Angela's and yell at her. He had pushed her and would kick obstacles and slam doors. Angela felt frightened and concerned that one day he would "snap".

Claire's husband Mark was court mandated to attend the group following Claire's taking out an Intervention Order against him. When he joined the group they were living apart. They have two daughters and a son. Claire was concerned about Mark's drinking as well as his physical and emotional violence. He had knocked her unconscious, broken her precious things, and intimidated her family and friends. Claire hoped that Mark would stop both his drinking and his violence, enabling them to reunite.

While the MRG has a core curriculum where topics such as "winding up and winding down thoughts", practising "other-centredness", and the friends and enemies of responsibility are discussed, the actual relationship between the facilitators and the men provides the vehicle to negotiate changes in attitudes and behaviour. And it is this early engagement phase that is significant in building relationships of trust and safety. Many men attending the group have experienced abuse and violence in their childhoods—although of course some have had loving and nurturing childhoods. For those not having had that experience themselves, it can be difficult to empathize with others, to be trusting and self-reflective in the process, and to practise "other-centredness"; all important qualities in adopting a greater sense of responsibility (Nyland & Corsiglia, 1998). The facilitators are in a privileged position to maintain their sense of caring and compassion for the men's past and present circumstances while holding the view that violence and abuse are not acceptable.

> Mark informed the facilitator in the assessment phase that his father has been alcoholic and his mother had left him in his father's care when Mark was eight years old. He spoke about being "sick of being blamed by every one" and that he "was always seen to be in the wrong". He

couldn't remember being cuddled or nurtured; on the contrary his memories of childhood were of looking after his mother after his father had hit her and avoiding his father following a drinking binge.

The facilitator was in a difficult position, having heard disturbing stories of Mark's violence from Claire. She recognized that if Mark felt he was once again going to be blamed, he would not return. She decided instead, in this individual session, to explore Mark's courtship with Claire, his thoughts and hopes about having children, the kind of relationship he wanted with them, and how he had hoped his life might be different from his father's. She was able to express concern and caring that things were not working out the way Mark had planned.

Mark's understanding of his violence was multi-faceted and reflected the coexistence of his sense of powerlessness and desire to control. On the one hand he believed that his violence was not his fault and that he had little control over his behaviour—"I can't help it, I just lash out without thinking", and Claire "drives me so crazy". On the other hand he acknowledged his attempts to control his partner and retain power over her through keeping her in line because he feared that she believed she was superior to him. Although his position on the use of violence did not shift in this first assessment, Mark—albeit reluctantly—decided to give the group a try because there was a stronger sense of wanting family connection than risking ending up alone.

Wanting to retain the relationship with their partners is the carrot that facilitators frequently use in order to build the therapeutic relationship with the men. The initial engagement process provides an opportunity to relate to the man as a person with ordinary needs and wants, and to explore aspects of his life "other than" his violent and abusive behaviour. Facilitators are highly attuned to the men's grief and distress, whilst attempting to not collude with or tolerate the violence and abuse.

One of the more difficult dynamics around engagement for the facilitator is to resist the temptation "to blame" the man for his violent behaviour—just as the man is likely to blame his own abused partner for his own violence. Holding back from blame while opening up a space to encourage responsibility provides an opportunity to explore whether the man's own sense of blame is helpful in moving him in the direction that he wants; that is, reunification with his partner.

Building a therapeutic relationship

A significant part of the building of the therapeutic relationship occurs before men join the group in the assessment phase and between sessions via phone calls, therapeutic letters, and individual meetings. The group focuses on educative sociopolitical and gender issues to do with taking responsibility for violence, and the men's own personal experiences are used to provide a lens into their children's and partners' experiences, though there is also room in the group for the men to be self-reflective about their own beliefs and feelings. Men who want to explore the impact of abuse on their own lives more extensively are encouraged to wait until there is clear evidence that they are taking responsibility for their violence. If individual therapeutic work occurs prematurely, it can be used as an excuse for their violence and result in a stronger focus on their own needs rather than those of their partners.

> It's not uncommon for men to make light in the group of their own experiences of abuse, even to make jokes about it. I use this opportunity to engage with the man. I will ask questions about why he may have responded in this way or explore what it is about how men are raised that encourages them to make light of serious and painful issues. When the men see that I care about what they have experienced and how that has impacted on them, it opens up a space to build trust and for them to see that as well as my taking a stand against their violence I am also emotionally supportive of what they have experienced. [Shane[3]]

The principle of encouraging "other-centredness" privileges the experiences of the women and children. Facilitators may be placed in a difficult position when men raise their childhood experience in a way that could justify or excuse their behaviour.

> When Nick spoke of the closeness of his family in Greece, the facilitators were able to encourage the men to explore what family connectedness, communication, and caring they hoped for in their own families and how the use of control, abuse, and violence circumvents this. In another session when one group member was sharing his sense of remorse for relapsing and verbally abusing his partner, Mark interjected with "You think that's bad, when I was a kid I'd get kicked for being home late from school." In this instance the facilitator chose to

> bypass Mark's comment and focus on the emotional experience of the other group member. However, in an individual therapy session with Mark the facilitator was able to explore Mark's comments and the context in which Mark had raised them. This led to a conversation that furthered the therapist's understanding of Mark's childhood and further cemented the trust and openness between them. The therapist was able to reiterate that although many men had had difficult childhood experiences the emphasis in the group was on enhancing the safety of women and children.

The development of the therapeutic relationship is emotionally challenging in the journey of seeking to embrace the humanity of the man who has committed these criminal acts. The knowledge that the men may not change their behaviour, or may make partial changes and then relapse, is held in coexistence with the belief that change is possible. Facilitators hold a stance that the men have the right to explore opportunities for change and be supported in this endeavour.

> You need to hold compassion for the men's situation but at the same time you can't be so empathic that you side with making excuses. You have to flip from his point of view but also hold the fact that he is an abuser. You have to hold on to what he's done but support that he wants a different way of being. [Eddie]

> I still struggle at times with holding the horror with the compassion, the humanity, their fear, and the things I like about them. In many ways this parallels the struggles the women have with experiencing the fear and horror of his violence and also of the human, likeable part in the man. [Michele]

The therapist must be able to tolerate any revulsion or dislike they have of the man, in order to work with him. This can be demanding and difficult. The therapist needs to locate what it is about the man that fosters these feelings. At times it is because the man challenges the therapist's own values and ethics, for example if he has been sexually sadistic or has made light of the impact of his violence. At other times it can be that something about a particular man triggers an emotional response related to the therapist's own life experience.

> Before I started this work I was apprehensive. Whilst I cognitively knew what to expect I had a level of fear, grounded in my own family of origin, that they might abuse me. I think also having had a history of working with women, hearing so many traumatic stories, meant my sense of fear in working with these men increased. I needed to think about my own history, of what drew me to this kind of work in the first place. I had to address the fear of men in my own life. [Michele]

> You must develop a relationship with the men where you see the men as separate from their violence. You must be able to believe that men do and can change. You must find some point where you can connect with them, where you can appreciate their humanity, where you can build mutual trust and respect. [Helen]

Different facilitators will also have different reactions to different men. One facilitator may see that a man is personable and making change, another may experience him as difficult to engage and resistant. The interface between a facilitator's lived experience and family of origin and that of the man's must be the subject of self-reflexivity, curiosity and insight.

While all facilitators found:

> Nick to be a reasonably personable man, with a quick sense of humour and active intelligence, Mark presented as stubborn and lacking in insight. Although he was able to name that his relationship was important, he immediately blamed his wife for his actions and for calling the police. It could have been easy for the therapist to see Mark through a description of "victim mentality" or "misogynist" and one of the women facilitators particularly struggled with trying to see "the other" in Mark that would enable her to meaningfully engage with him. In supervision she was able to make a link between her response to Mark's behaviour and to that of her mother, who was particularly prone to blaming. She recognized that at times she responded hostilely to Mark and was quick to blame him in return. The therapist met with Mark for an individual session between groups. This individual therapeutic contact facilitated Mark's sense that the therapist was there to support him and encouraged Mark to risk greater vulnerability, which in turn led to an increased appreciation of Mark's struggles by the therapist. In the first six sessions of the group Mark had come across as disruptive and belligerent. However, the group's ability to sit with Mark's distress and "testing out" behaviour and the facilitator's skill in

> not buying in to Mark's attempts at circumventing group process, led to Mark's increased capacity to listen to others and respect group process.

At times, weeks can pass without the men seeming to "get it". They attend the group but just don't seem engaged and appear to still be "outside" the group process. This can often mean that there is an undisclosed issue that is creating a barrier to being fully engaged in the group process. Brian, a married man in his forties, attended the group regularly and seemed bright and committed but there seemed a void there that the facilitators were not able to bridge. The facilitators felt frustrated with what appeared to be Brian's complacency, so named this in the group. Brian responded by requesting a private session. In this session he disclosed that he had been dwelling on his having had an affair with a woman several years before. He reflected on how his wife had thought she was "going mad" because he had continually misled her and denied her reality, putting the blame on her. This disclosure marked a critical turning point for Brian. He felt that the disclosure allowed him to move on but it also made possible a therapeutic alliance that had not been there prior to the disclosure. Facilitators may experience a man's disengagement or complacency as related to their own lack of skills or as a reaction to them personally. This can lead to feelings of failure, self-doubt, and incompetence by the facilitators, who have to be alert to the unsaid and unarticulated territory within the group that signals the blocks in progress to new understandings.

Men are invited to take responsibility for owning the group process and for encouraging responsibility and discouraging disrespect towards women. When there is a strong therapeutic alliance, men are more likely to feel strengthened to challenge other men and support them in their struggle against abusive practices. Most men eventually begin to take ownership of the group as they become more trusting of the process.

> At times the work is really hard, it's challenging and you wonder why you do it. But when I see men start to run with ideas and ways of thinking, when they start to challenge other men about their behaviours and attitudes, it makes you realize that the men do make changes and it is worthwhile. [Sally]

The group process can be emotionally and psychologically demanding, as facilitators must be on the constant lookout for "slip ups" from the men- blaming, minimizing, denial, and shifting responsibility. Facilitators are often confronted by the men directly or experience individual men's progress, or lack thereof, as frustrating and negatively impacting on other group participants.

While the process involves challenging the men, it is also important that men are supported in any small changes they take. Each group session begins with the opportunity for men to discuss their resistance to any invitations to act abusively or violently. We explore how the men were able to do this, what others thought about this and what it might mean if it continues.

> Nick was asked in his first meeting what worried him most about coming to the group. He was easily able to express his fear that his relationship would end. He spoke about his marriage only a year before and about how he hoped he and Angela would have children. Although he recognized that he "lost his temper" he also commented that Angela should "leave him alone" and stop expecting so much from him. The facilitator could have responded to the comments about Angela but decided to build the understanding and trust between herself and Nick as this would be the foundation for the more difficult work ahead. She did this by exploring his fears about the loss of the relationship, both from his perspective and that of Angela, and how each of them made life choice decisions.

The facilitator also explained that the group might challenge some of the ideas Nick had about how to deal with conflict and how to conduct a relationship. She asked him if he was ready for this difficult work, what support he might need to undertake it, and how he might cope when his ideas were challenged by the facilitators or other men in the group. These "readiness" questions, influenced by the work of Alan Jenkins (1990), help men to have a sense of what to expect and to acknowledge the difficulty in the work.

> Mark was far more difficult to engage. The first meeting provided him with an opportunity to "ventilate" about the system, his partner, and the unfairness of life. Mark made no attempt to hide his contempt for a programme he felt he was forced to participate in, and sat with arms

tightly folded across his chest. As with Nick, the woman facilitator needed to tolerate what Mark was expressing, but it took another meeting before Mark could identify that he was scared that Claire would leave him permanently. In the first meeting he was only able to say that he was angry about the next court hearing and how his wife might "get him" in court. It seemed that once he experienced the facilitator as empathizing with his situation, (which had not rightly been the case with his experience of the criminal justice system), he was then able to speak about his deeper fears.

> It's very different from other therapy and I tell the men this. We have to define the relationship clearly; for example the no-confidentiality frame and that we don't believe there are any excuses for abuse. It's also different because there's not so much an issue that the men have to like me. I remember working with a man who left the session saying "I feel like shit." I told him that's OK. We expect that in coming to terms with the effects of what you've done may leave you feeling this way, that this is part of the work in becoming "other-centred". [Eddie]

Feelings as "other-centred"

Although family therapy acknowledges the importance of utilizing the feelings that arise in the process of therapy as a means of joining or engagement (Minuchin, 1974; Smith, Osman, & Goding, 1990), the SCAVA model places greater emphasis on the men's awareness of the feelings of others rather than their own feelings. Our experience in working with men who use violence is that there is a preoccupation with their own feelings—jealousy, hurt, rejection, loneliness, entitlement, defensiveness, self-centredness, blame—but very little outer-directed feeling, particularly caring and empathy, towards those with whom they intimately relate.

> In the early stages men tend to say things like "Work got on top of me" or "She puts too much stress on me". Later on most men are able to recognize that they can experience stress or pressure without resorting to violence. One woman partner told me how her partner would sit there, not hearing when she'd try to talk about her day, but now he actively listens and asks questions. [Helen]

Feelings in the facilitators arise in the process of individual or group therapy. A man may make a derogatory sexual comment about his partner, another may tell a "funny" story which amuses most of the men in the group but in fact is experienced as distressing to the facilitators and other men whose attitudes and awareness have begun to shift. It can be a particularly difficult challenge for male facilitators who are invited to join in with "blokey" humour. The facilitators may feel disgust, frustration, or anger but choose to address the comment in the context of the safety of women and children. In some ways the facilitator holds the feeling, as if felt by the partner, through asking questions like: "Does saying that about your partner fit with respect and consideration, or with disregard and misogyny?" or "You tell that as if it was a funny story—how do you think your wife experienced that incident?"

Certain feelings are encouraged in the therapeutic process—guilt, sadness, regret, shame, concern, and empathy. For instance, a therapist may ask Mark to imagine what his children may have felt when they witnessed him abusing their mother. This encouragement of "other-centredness" is a strategic position taken by the therapist who is always on the lookout for opportunities to encourage the client towards practices that stand in contradiction to entitlement, self-righteousness, and abusive power practices.

Questions of gender—who should work with men who use violence and how should they behave

The sharing of experiences, and the linking of women's experiences with the experiences of other women, was an important part of the women's refuge movement (Laing, 2001). The arguments for this have centred on the reclamation of women's space and knowledge, and that women could be listened to, believed, and find they were not alone. The arguments for women working with men who use violence have been less clearly articulated and it is generally assumed that male therapists are well placed to work with violent men. Much of this assumption is based on the belief that male therapists have a greater opportunity to engage with these men, and offer themselves as male role models, particularly in relation to their shared, lived experience as males. There is also an assumption that male therapists are better equipped to challenge men and deal with confronting attitudes, although women facilitators do report that men will try to test the female facilitators more than the men. While some behavioural change programmes only use male facilitators, we have found that a gender mix is useful.

> One night the usual male facilitator was sick and we couldn't get another male replacement. So the two female facilitators worked together. Even though we were at week eight where the men had seemed fairly settled, the men behaved atrociously. They really acted out—telling sexist jokes, laughing about violence, and really challenging us. We were worn out by the group's end. [Sally]

Some therapists have argued that it is important to develop therapeutic models in violence work that emphasize the positive aspects of women's qualities, such as nurturing and connectedness (Knudson, 1997). It is not the place of women facilitators in the MRG to offer a response to men based on gendered assumptions of how men should behave differently, but rather as a challenge to men's assumptions about how women are, or should be.

The MRG process assumes a gender–power differential within the relationship between male and female co-facilitators that is made overt *and* minimized. This gives an opportunity for the men to witness a model of social and relational interaction based on respect and striving towards equality. This is achieved through inclusive practices such as sharing the programme development, assessment of men and partner contact, and checking in with each other about fairness and equity of the facilitation process (Rodnight & Wright, 2002). Male facilitators practise deferring, rather than arguing with, the women facilitators, and asking questions rather than dictating or having an "all knowing" stance. The male and female co-facilitators model "reasonable" and "genuine" gender relationships to the men, and attempt not to reinforce attitudes that are inherent in relationships where men use violence and abuse.

Women facilitators in other men's programmes have raised concerns about their relationship with male facilitators, such as feeling undermined and having less authority or voice within the group, and that even when male facilitators espouse values of equality and cooperation they can tend to dominate the facilitation of groups and consult with male colleagues rather than their female co-facilitators (Frances, 1996; Hughes, 1997; Hughes & Weiss, 1997). The challenge is to avoid mirroring patterns within abusive relationships. Women are more likely to experience being the "moral conscience" within the group, particularly if the male facilitator aligns with the men in any components of the work. Without support from her counterpart, she can more easily be duped into taking responsibility for the men or becoming the emotional "dumping ground" for the group. A core SCAVA principle is that if any disagreement arises between the male and female facilitator in the group, the female's point of view overrides that of the male. This sends a message to the men that it is acceptable for men to take a "one down" position and to privilege a woman's viewpoint.

Having a woman in the group counteracts the silence and secrecy inherent in family violence; it is a statement that this is not "secret men's business". The participation of women facilitators enables women to speak of their own experience as women living in a patriarchal world. Pease (2001) argues that change for men will only be possible when men understand the impact of their privilege and power on women's lives. The inclusion of women facilitators gives a woman's voice to the group, particularly in relation to the men's understanding of the effects of violence. The women facilitators can, at times, act as a conveyor of feelings for the men's partners and children and maintain accountability to them by voicing women's experience that can often remain unarticulated through fear in the context of intimate violence.

> Sometimes the men are a bit suspicious. They think because I'm a woman I might take their partner's side. And in a sense I do, but I still need to hold an openness to the men's experience. The men in the group may engage more readily with the male facilitator. This process is addressed through sharing the facilitation roles and modeling respect and cooperation. [Michele]

Conclusion

The building of therapeutic relationships with men who use violence and abuse is complex and multi-faceted. This relationship cannot develop without an appreciation of the man's feelings and experience, yet the therapist must tread the difficult path of joining with the man while maintaining a clear focus on the impact of his violence on those he claims to care for. The paradox that most men readily blame their partners and children for "causing" the abuse yet so easily react to feeling blamed themselves must be acknowledged and held as part of the therapeutic process.

> Nick is viewed as a "star" by the facilitators. He completed the twenty-week sessions and continued in the monthly follow-ups. He and Angela attended conjoint therapy and he continued to see a therapist individually. Three years later he still attends occasional "monthlies" and has spoken to new men joining the group about the trials and tribulations of undertaking this work. He and Angela are together and have a fourteen-month-old girl.
>
> Mark's participation in the first six sessions was characterized by blaming and aggression. However, after the sixth session Mark seemed to be able to sit back and listen to others and dropped his macho stance a little. The facilitators attributed this change to the individual session that occurred after the sixth session, where the therapist was able to explore Mark's childhood experience but also revisit the difficulty of the work and the invitations men experience to be tough, rowdy, and, as Mark put it, "not like a poofta".
>
> Mark completed the twenty weeks, missing several weeks at a time. Although Claire saw that Mark was trying and had made some changes in his thinking, she did not return to the relationship. However, she believed that his participation in the group meant that Mark was more in touch with the children's needs and was able to be reasonable about the Family Court settlement. This led her to feel more relaxed about Mark having contact with the children. Mark was referred to a drug and alcohol counsellor about half-way through the group. He reported that his drinking was more contained and that he did not drink while the children were in his care.

It is difficult to ascertain just how much the therapeutic relationship and group process and connectedness contributes to men's change. It seems that men's desire for change is a key factor in their success and that some men are more prepared than others to relinquish their power, control and previous ways in order to maintain their intimate relationships. A strong therapeutic alliance can foster this desire for change and enable men to take the risks to challenge abusive and violent ways. We continue to learn . . .

Notes

1. I am indebted to the consultation and feedback from SCAVA members and facilitators Eddie Gallagher, Helen Wirtz, Sally King, Shane Weir, Michele Wright, and Dr Ron Schweitzer from the Inner South and Monash Link Community Health Service, Melbourne, Australia.
2. It is more usual for men to be asked to consider their motivations for joining, rather than being rejected outright. This may occur if a man appears to be more interested in appearing to be "doing the right thing" to achieve a positive legal outcome rather than his partner's well-being, or if he has severe mental health or substance abuse issues that may impact negatively on group process. The MRG philosophy stresses inclusiveness, rather than exclusion.
3. Named quotes are from facilitators who were interviewed by the author about their experience of running the MRGs prior to writing the paper.

CHAPTER FIVE

Not getting lost in translation: establishing a working alliance with co-workers and interpreters

Hitesh Raval and Michael Maltby

Introduction

An interpreter is booked with one day's notice by a practitioner in order to carry out a mental health assessment with a client from an ethnic minority referred by her GP. The interpreter arrives prior to the client's first appointment and the practitioner meets them both for the first time in the waiting room where they are talking animatedly. As the interview progresses it becomes evident that the client is becoming increasingly uneasy. The interpreter does not seem to be asking the practitioner's questions verbatim and at times appears to be having additional exchanges with the client. The interpreter and the client both become more agitated and the practitioner is confused and uncertain about what is happening. There is no time at the end of the session for the practitioner to explore his concerns as both he and the interpreter have other appointments to keep.[1]

How do we begin to understand something of the process of what has happened? Would it have been possible to do this piece of work differently? What steps could have been taken to make this first contact more productive and to develop a more effective working relationship between all the parties involved?

This chapter aims to address issues related to how the role of language interpreters is constructed within a mental health work context, and how this can influence the quality and effectiveness of therapeutic engagement. We make a case for viewing the therapeutic alliance as going beyond the traditional boundary of practitioner and client/s (e.g., Clarkson, 1995; Flaskas, 1994), so that the interpreter is seen as an integral member of the therapeutic system. The chapter explores how practitioners can develop a better understanding of the process issues impacting on their work when an interpreter joins the therapeutic system.

Constructing the role of the interpreter

Having an interpreter present in a consultation with service user/s changes the boundaries and relational dynamics of the therapeutic work. How this is managed is dependent on the range of views held by the practitioner and the interpreter about the interpreter's role. At one end of the spectrum is the view that the only legitimate role for an interpreter is that of word for word translation (Marcos, 1979). Other roles include cultural consultant or broker, advocate for client or community, link worker, and bilingual co-worker (Raval, 2003). However, it has to be recognized that even the task of translating demands a very high level of skill and bilingual competence if it is to be carried out effectively. The personal contribution and impact of the work on the interpreter also has to be acknowledged, and rather than seeing this as a hindrance to the work (Solomon, 1997) this can be thought of as informing the therapeutic work.

We would view a bilingual co-worker as a colleague who brings a particular range of experience, skill, expertise, training, and cross cultural understandings to facilitate a process of translation that enables two or more people not sharing the same language to fully access each other's world of meanings and experience. To adopt this position requires a shift in how we construct the role of the interpreter, and how we utilize the personhood of the interpreter in understanding the relational patterns that become a significant part of the therapeutic encounter. We need to pay attention to the interpreter's family, work, and societal context if we are to understand something of the process that is taking place in the therapeutic encounter. We have to acknowledge that the issues being brought up by the service user will inevitably impact on the interpreter, as well as the interpreter's emotional reactions to the client sometimes being a reflection of how the client is feeling.

Viewing the interpreter strictly as a neutral conduit prevents us from developing this richer understanding of the process that may be impacting on the therapeutic work. At a practical level, viewing the interpreter as a co-worker leads to some important considerations about how this relationship needs to be established and negotiated to operate effectively. Without any prior contact there is no opportunity to discuss the parameters of the work and agree how any issues that might arise can be addressed. Without allowing some time for debriefing and reflection after the session, the possible need to clarify and make sense of aspects of what has taken place can be lost. If a co-worker relationship is desirable it needs to be built and sustained, not just left to chance. The remainder of the chapter highlights some of the issues that need to be addressed in this process.

Establishing a shared understanding

As a co-worker we have to give recognition and credit for the skills that interpreters bring to their work. Co-working relationships develop over time, as does developing a familiarity with each other's work. Frequently, mechanisms for booking an interpreter from an outside agency do not allow for this to happen easily (at least within the UK). Ideally, a co-worker model is better suited to therapeutic work where the interpreter is employed to work specifically within a service as a bilingual colleague. This allows for practitioners and interpreters to develop a shared understanding of the work setting and the cultural context (Raval, 2005; Raval & Smith, 2003).

If one of the legitimate roles of the interpreter is that of a cultural adviser/broker, or as an advocate for the local minority population, it becomes important that such roles have been clarified before starting a piece of work with a client. The interpreter or bilingual co-worker may have much to offer the practitioner if given the chance to offer such cultural consultation. At a preliminary meeting the practitioner and interpreter can have a helpful discussion about broader community considerations or specific cultural issues that may need attending to when seeing the client for the first time. The interpreter may advise the practitioner on managing particular sensitivities or cultural norms with the client. The discussion may also address the issues pertaining to the cultural specificity of certain mental health concepts, or ways in which questions need to be phrased, so that concepts that are unfamiliar to the client, or not directly translatable into another language, can be attended to. The practitioner can use the preliminary meeting to:

- Explain his or her approach to therapeutic work
- Provide a rationale for the types of questions that will need to be asked at the first appointment
- Clarify the aims for this first meeting with the client, and
- Decide what is going to be possible to cover on this first occasion with the interpreter.

> A school referred a young person on the verge of permanent exclusion. As part of the planning process a preliminary meeting was set up with a bilingual co-worker to discuss the possibility of jointly taking on this piece of work, given the bilingual co-worker's broader remit of working with children and families from particular community groups. In the role of cultural consultant the bilingual co-worker was very helpful in providing a context for the challenges facing the community group that the young person came from. The roles that the bilingual co-worker was willing to take on also included being an advocate for the family. The discussion also focused on agreeing ways of working together. As part of the planning it was envisaged that a meeting was likely to be needed at the young person's school.

Often confusion can arise when the respective roles have not been negotiated clearly or successfully. Interpreters need to be helped to gain an understanding of the therapeutic models informing the practitioner, and aided to develop a shared working understanding of why the practitioner goes about his or her business in particular ways that at first may seem alien. Taken for granted ways of working for the practitioner may be unfamiliar to the interpreter and may actually be culturally inappropriate with a particular client group. There may be a need to have a conversation about the use of taken for granted categories such as "depression", which may not easily translate into another language at either the literal or metaphoric level. Gaining access to details of the client's mood may require a five-minute conversation between the interpreter and the client, with the practitioner having to manage this time in an observer role. It is important that the preliminary planning and discussion with the interpreter can grapple with the complexities of language and cultural metaphors that will need to be worked across, and within, language translation in a creative way. There also needs to be a clear understanding of what the aims and possible outcomes of the consultation actually are.

Developing trust in the co-working alliance

One of the common issues that arise in this type of work is that of building up trust. Different therapeutic models have emphasized the importance of creating an environment where, particularly at the earlier stages of the therapeutic encounter, constructive steps are taken to facilitate trust or joining with the client or family (Flaskas, 1994; Goldenberg & Goldenberg, 1996; Perry, 1993). Yet, going back to our first example, what ways are open to the practitioner and the client to build up trust or a working alliance when access to what is being said can easily be lost? If there is only a summary translation from which to make judgements about what is being translated or left out and how this is being conveyed, confidence can be eroded. Quite often practitioners describe a negative spiral involving a sense of losing trust in the interpreter and a fear that they are losing control and confidence in their own work with a client (Raval, 2002). This may lead them to intervene in more directive and simplistic ways or to abandon certain therapeutic aims, and this can impede the clinical effectiveness of the work (Raval & Smith, 2003).

It is time well spent prior to starting a piece of work to have a discussion about each other's perspectives, to decide how much flexibility the practitioner and interpreter feel would be needed to allow the interpreter to render a meaningful translation, to set ground rules about how each would feel able to maintain their respective roles, and to create a structure that allows for open dialogue should difficulties arise. The interpreter needs to be given time to explain to the practitioner how he or she normally likes to work, what has worked well in the past, or to explain to the practitioner new to this type of work how the process of translation can best be facilitated. The practitioner has to be open to learning from the interpreter. There may need to be a discussion about how confidentiality is going to be explained to the client, and how the interpreter is going to be able to negotiate his position with regard to this if he is from the same community as the client, or is having to help the same client in a number of different health or social care contexts. The client will quickly sense if the relationship between the practitioner and interpreter is strained, which will have an impact on the client being able to build up trust with either of them. Such preparatory work is very important if the practitioner and the interpreter are going to create a containing and trusting context in which the work can take place.

In a co-worker model, establishing trust between the practitioner and interpreter could be seen as an important precursor and contributor to the building of trust with the client. The client needs confidence in both the practitioner and the interpreter and the way they relate to each other could be seen as offering a relational model to clients through the way that they interact (Raval, 2002).

> In the example introduced earlier of the young person facing exclusion, it soon became apparent that the parents held the view that their child did not have mental health problems, and that the difficulties were due to the unjust way in which the school had handled the situation of their child having been racially taunted and bullied over a prolonged period of time. As the meeting at the school progressed the parents' discomfort at hearing mostly negative things about their child was becoming more noticeable. At this point the bilingual co-worker indicated to the meeting that she was taking up an advocacy role for the parents, and intervened by requesting to talk with the parents outside of the meeting. This intervention required trust on part of the practitioner in the bilingual co-worker's professionalism and skill. On returning to the meeting the bilingual co-worker was able to express the parents' concerns, and shift the focus of the meeting to look at strategies for preventing the young person from being excluded. This led to a helpful discussion about the school's general policies and mechanisms of

managing racism and bullying initiated by pupils, and what further steps were required to develop a workable approach to manage this situation in the future. At this point the parents began to engage with the attempts that the school were trying to make to tackle the broader issue of school bullying and racism.

Establishing a safe environment

Many mental health frameworks consider the idea of having a number of constant people and having some degree of stability in one's life as being important contributors to positive adjustments and functioning when faced with challenges in life (Byng-Hall, 1999; Marris, 1996). The psychoanalytic tradition places particular emphasis on the importance of a predictable structure and constancy to the therapeutic setting. It views therapeutic work as allowing the client to experience and develop an understanding of his or her relational patterns and experience in the context of the consistent and boundaried relationship that develops between the therapist and the client. This can be viewed in terms of the metaphors of containment (Bion, 1963), holding (Winnicott, 1991), or a secure base (Bowlby, 1988; Holmes, 2001). In all therapeutic approaches there is some recognition that the therapeutic relationship must feel safe and reliable enough to facilitate meaningful disclosure and to contain the risks inherent in managing change. If one makes the case that the interpreter can play a significant part in this encounter then the interpreter's role and understanding of this become important aspects of establishing and maintaining an adequate therapeutic environment.

Some of what is usually seen as being important in providing safety and constancy for the client can be difficult to preserve when working with interpreters. Typically, many practitioners draw on interpreting support from agencies external to the service setting. There is often insufficient planning, or resource constraints that work against being able to book the same interpreter all the time when seeing a particular client or family. For clients, it must prove difficult to form a trusting and containing relationship with the practitioner and the interpreter when they have to start afresh at each appointment with someone new and unfamiliar. The anxiety and sense of disruption that practitioners sometimes report when working with interpreters may well mirror the insecurity and uncertainty also experienced by the client and the interpreter. Even if at one level the client may have a notion of being "held in mind" by the practitioner, this relationship is inevitably disrupted if the same interpreter cannot be available for all the contacts with the practitioner. The sense of continuity of the work can all too easily be lost. It therefore becomes important to have the same interpreter with a client. Again, this is where services that are able to employ dedicated bilingual co-workers, or provide sufficient support structures to ensure that the same interpreters can be booked in advance, are more likely to produce a positive experience of the therapeutic encounter for all concerned.

Having the same interpreter for ongoing therapeutic work can help to maintain a sense of continuity and containment, which is lost when there is a different interpreter every time that the client sees the practitioner. It then becomes possible for the practitioner and interpreter to have useful discussions about the emotional impact of the work in the debriefing time that needs to be scheduled to support the work. They may need to understand and talk about what each is feeling about the client, whether they are picking up different aspects of the emotions that are being experienced by the client, and what steps they may need to take in order to prevent being placed in polarized positions by the client. Often interpreters do not receive supervision for their work, and this may have to be negotiated on the interpreter's behalf so that they have a separate safe environment in which to reflect on the emotional impact of their work. There is greater likelihood of the client feeling safe enough to talk about personal issues when there is a greater level of integration and collaboration between the practitioner and interpreter.

Negotiating inclusion

Many practitioners describe an experience of feeling excluded and left out when working with interpreters. This feeling also mirrors what many clients experience in their daily life when having to be so reliant on others to communicate with people. Where briefing and debriefing is built into the work, the rationale for this, and the form it will take, has to be made explicit to the client, and their view sought. The approach of having discussions in front of the client offers another alternative, though this would need to be done where both the practitioner and interpreter are familiar and trained to work in this way. If such a feeling begins to dominate then it is not too surprising that practitioners begin to experience their work as getting out of control, or a sense that the interpreter has taken over the session. There are important and powerful feelings that need to be carefully considered here that once again may be mirrored in the way the client can feel about the interpreter–practitioner relationship as well as reflecting wider issues of inclusion–exclusion at a social level.

At a practical level the interpreter may need time to develop engagement with the client, be able to translate in ways that are accurate, and to render the full meaning of the questions that the practitioner would like answered. For example, with bilingual co-workers whom we have worked with on a regular basis, we have seen the role of the practitioner as that of facilitating a dialogue without feeling the need to have all the content translated. Working in this way has made it possible to ask the bilingual co-worker to explore issues for the client in a more general way, and then being able to take a step back to monitor process issues or develop our thinking about what is going on for the client. We may ask the bilingual co-worker to ask some questions about the client's difficulties or a specific issue (e.g., "could we find out how the client feels about that situation"), and allow a conversation to take place between the bilingual co-worker and client about this rather than expecting a translation of everything that is being said by the client. A short summary of what is happening to the client may at times be more useful than a conversation frequently disrupted by the need to have everything translated. Often the bilingual co-worker will require a longer discussion with the client in order to obtain adequate and meaningful information that can be used by the practitioner. What effect can this have when we are more used to having direct communication with the client? It can, of course, easily lead to a feeling of being left out. Rather than seeing this as what the bilingual co-worker needs to do their job, we may easily experience the bilingual co-worker as doing the job that we should be doing.

Therapeutic work relies heavily on language as the main tool with which we do our work. It is through careful listening, understanding of associative meaning and thoughtful interpretation that we come to know our clients. We also strive to find the right form of words to communicate back to the client something of our understanding and our observations about what is taking place in the therapeutic encounter. When working with interpreters we have to find different ways of being able to do this with the aid of the linguistic and personal skills of the interpreter. We need to elicit the help of the interpreter, who is experiencing the impact of what the client says more directly, to help decipher meaning at both a verbal and non-verbal level.

We also need to appreciate and understand the emotional impact of the client's narrative on the interpreter, as well as the impact that the practitioner and the interpreter are having on the client. Perhaps those moments when the practitioner is not required to be actively engaged in the conversation provide opportunities for reflection and formulation of the client's difficulties in ways that are not possible in direct conversation with a client and that include awareness of the interpreter's responses. Time spent in debriefing after seeing the client can then become important in terms of having an open conversation with the interpreter that can go some way to understanding the feelings and emotions that were present in the room and lead to a joint reflection on the process and outcome of the session. If these are not understood and talked about, the meaning of subsequent contacts with the same interpreter and client may become increasingly opaque. If they are considered, this can then create the opportunity to enlist the interpreter's skills to creatively communicate the practitioner's understandings back to the client in a more deeply processed way.

In considering this issue, the experience of the client should not be neglected. Any dialogue between the practitioner and interpreter that excludes the client may have corresponding effects to those that exclude the practitioner. The need to work within a dialogical framework that includes the client will depend heavily on the interpreter's capacity to convey something of the meaning of any in-session exchanges between the practitioner and themselves and of openly acknowledging the purpose of any out-of-session contacts that the interpreter and practitioner may have.

Some ways of addressing such issues could be through using the briefing or debriefing time to develop shared ideas about how to understand the client's difficulties, or to consult the interpreter on the most culturally appropriate and effective way to implement an intervention. If the practitioner and interpreter are comfortable about having a discussion in front of the client (summarized by the interpreter) about how they are able to understand the client's difficulties, the client may feel more able to engage as an active participant rather than a passive receiver. There is always a chance, in this triangular configuration, of one individual feeling excluded. This is particularly true for the client and practitioner but also for the interpreter, who may find the responsibilities of conveying communications accurately leave little time for their own reflection. Such felt imbalances increase the likelihood of defensive splitting. The practitioner has to be attentive to this process and the issue may have to be spoken about explicitly. For example, we have found it can be helpful to acknowledge at the outset that there are times when people may feel left out and to talk about ways in which this is going to be managed should the need arise.

> When working with an adult client the gender and age of the interpreter were quite important in helping to create a safe therapeutic environment in which the work could take place. Having the same interpreter was important in containing the client's distress, and helping the client talk about their distress. In the earlier part of the work it was important for the practitioner to seek out the interpreter's perspective about the cultural appropriateness of the practitioner carrying out this piece of work, given the gender and cultural differences between the practitioner and the client. As the client became less questioning in the sessions about the practitioner's ability to hear, and withstand the emotional impact of, the client's trauma, it became more important to use the debriefing time to attend to the emotional impact of the work on the interpreter. For the interpreter the greatest distress was caused not by hearing about the client's past trauma, but by their similar current family circumstances and the day-to-day struggles they both faced.

Negotiating power and influence

Collaborative approaches have moved many systemic practitioners away from overtly directive approaches, where the aim was to diagnose the problem and intervene, to those that are more attentive to agendas set by the client (Anderson, 1992; White & Epston, 1990), but ultimately certain forms of power still reside predominantly with the practitioner, whichever model of work we use and however we try to balance this out with the client. Many interpreters may feel they do not have a great deal of power in relation to the practitioner. The practitioner has the responsibility to ensure that both the interpreter and the client are enabled to feel empowered. When meeting for the first time the client needs to be informed that, should they have concerns about working with a particular interpreter or practitioner, neither the practitioner nor interpreter would be offended, and that steps could be taken to find another worker and/or interpreter for the client. Where such a request is part of a collaborative working culture it is often possible to talk about such issues in an open manner that allows the client to have their concerns addressed, and the same interpreter and practitioner to continue with the work.

Practitioners need to ensure that the interpreter does not feel intimidated by their professional status or become silenced in the work. It could be argued that viewing the interpreter as a mouthpiece is one way in which they are silenced from being able to share their views and opinions about the work. For example, what if the interpreter feels unable to say to the practitioner that the question just asked of the client is completely inappropriate culturally or at a given point of time during the consultation? Is the interpreter empowered to question or reflect on this, or should they withhold any such observations?

The practitioner also has to have a conversation with the interpreter about issues related to social inequalities that exist for them within the community in which they live, and that might have an impact on their work with clients from the same community. The practitioner and interpreter may need to have sensitive conversations about the discrimination or racism that is experienced by the interpreter in his or her daily life, and how this impacts on the way they are able to do their work. Many people who work as interpreters are often highly qualified professionals from their country of origin, but unable to gain access to similar employment in the country to which they have migrated. The practitioner may need to think about how to draw on the interpreter's prior work experience when the person's competence is not only that of an interpreter.

Clients may also be feeling a lack of power in the context of an unfamiliar setting where they may be able to get help for their difficulties. The client may think that the interpreter is more powerful than they really are. Again, there is the basic issue of power for the clients in not being able to access the help they need directly in a language that they can converse in, and being able to have the confidence to represent themselves without having to be represented by another person. The practitioner has to develop ways of setting up the consultation in ways that ensure that the client is able to voice any concerns or dissatisfaction with either the practitioner or the interpreter. Issues of confidentiality will need to be discussed, particularly if clients are worried that their difficulties will become public knowledge by virtue of the interpreter being part of their local community. The client may think that the interpreter is too closely allied with the practitioner's work setting and culture, and may have reservations about the interpreter not closely adhering to the client's cultural beliefs and values. There may be many such conversations that need to take place before a client and interpreter are able to feel that full and unimpeded use can be made of the therapeutic encounter. If power issues are not addressed it is likely that the work will be undermined.

> We return to our example of the young person who was facing the prospect of being excluded from school. During a session following on from the school meeting, the conversation moved to the young person talking about their experience of being racially taunted. This was the first time the young person had been able to talk about their distress in such a direct way. The bilingual co-worker intervened by giving a culturally appropriate personal example of having been teased as a child; this carried weight for the family as they shared the same cultural heritage as the bilingual co-worker. The intervention took the form of a family story of a cultural tradition where people are given a somewhat derogatory nickname, though this is usually done in an affectionate, tongue-in-cheek way. Often the family may use this nickname without the person knowing this. The bilingual co-worker described how he had felt upset when first overhearing his family using this nickname. This story engaged the young person, who wanted to know what the nickname had been, and opened up a conversation for the whole family

where the parents spoke about their experiences of racism for the first time. Hearing the parents speak seemed to free the young person to move out of the role of victim and own her part in what had happened at school.

Embracing difference and diversity

Another process that can happen when carrying out therapeutic work with the help of an interpreter is to retreat to what we are most comfortable with when faced with uncertainty or unfamiliarity. For example, practitioners have reported feeling less able to utilize reflective interventions and having to rely on more practical interventions when working with interpreters (Raval, 1996; Raval & Smith, 2003). Working across culture and language entails working with clients at many different levels of meaning and value to make sense of life experiences. Given some of the types of experiences that can take place, as described earlier, one can see why the work can sometimes be reduced to a very practical or literal level rather than risk becoming antagonistic.

We have found it helpful to take a position where we seek to understand and work with as many of the different perspectives and life experiences that are making up the client–interpreter–practitioner system as possible. These perspectives contain the possibility of both enhancing the work and limiting it. The way in which the therapeutic work is contextualized has a significant bearing on this. When part of the work is about making use of the diversity that is present in the therapeutic encounter, it then becomes possible to make this more explicit and work with it in the room. The focus on trying to understand how and why this system is working well and whether it is meeting the needs of the client or not, becomes an important part of the work that has to be done. This can be done through making the discussions about diversity and difference more explicit in the room and in the discussions that take place independently between the interpreter and the practitioner. For example, unless concerns that the interpreter or client may have about the stigma of mental health intervention are addressed, there is less likelihood of a successful outcome.

Kaufert (1990) proposes that working with interpreters involves a process where the cultural beliefs, life experiences, and explanations that enter the therapeutic encounter have to be negotiated. Part of the task is to reach a working consensus where the practitioner, client, and interpreter are able to find a shared way of understanding the "problem" and ways to solve it. This may take a while, as different levels of consensus are needed before it becomes possible for there to be sufficient agreement in how the "problem" can be understood and what may be the best ways of solving it.

When such a reflective space is not made available within the context of the therapeutic encounter, it is easier to retreat into familiar positions. If the reflective conversation is not made possible, there is a greater danger that polarized positions will be taken up, and that the work may be narrowed down to offering practical help as this may, on the surface, appear more tangible. The challenge of working with interpreters is to create and allow those reflective spaces and conversations to occur in order for new positions to become available.

Conclusions

Although we have challenged the view that interpreters working within therapeutic contexts can be seen only as language translators, their need for skill in this regard should not be underestimated. Both their accurate and creative use of language is crucial to the construction of shared meaning within the therapeutic relationship. In many cases the option of adopting a relatively neutral and unobtrusive role may be both professionally and clinically appropriate for interpreters, and lead to effective work being undertaken. However, we have tried to demonstrate that the assumptions of this model of working are incomplete and do not reflect the potential complexities of the practitioner–interpreter–client system across the diversity of situations that frequently arise. By construing the interpreter as a co-worker, their potential contributions to the therapeutic process at a personal, cultural, and directly therapeutic level can be more adequately acknowledged and conceptualized. This in turn can lead to the therapeutic encounter being harnessed in a way that can be of greater ultimate benefit to the client. Clearly, adopting such a position may have practical, resource, and training implications that will also need to be identified and addressed.

Note

1. The case examples used in this chapter are fictitious amalgams of clients we have worked with and care has been taken to disguise these where an example has drawn on actual pieces of work.

CHAPTER SIX

Intercultural: where the systemic meets the psychoanalytic in the therapeutic relationship

Lennox K. Thomas

The therapeutic relationship is a creation of the therapist and the client or patient. It is the constant factor in all therapies. Just as the wheels of a railway carriage must fit the rails in order to pass along them, so the way in which the therapeutic relationship is constructed can facilitate the progress of the therapy. The therapeutic relationship can also be a place where race, class, and other prejudices can be subtly played out or, alternatively, where the meeting of difference can be fruitful and enlightening.

Different schools of therapy have a variety of ways of seeing and using the relationship, sometimes considering the personality of the therapist as determining the nature of the relationship. Some therapists combine more than one, or even two, schools of therapeutic thought. Social workers in the 1950s and 1960s, whose contact with clients extended beyond the strictly therapeutic, found a way to use psychoanalytic theory to understand emotional states and repeated patterns in their clients' behaviour while being clear about how they managed the real relationship (Ferard & Hunnybun, 1962; Irvine, 1956a,b). The work of Bowlby and Winnicott provided an opportunity for therapists and social workers to pay attention to the effect of the environment on the individual and the relational experiences during development. Recent writers in integrative psychotherapy (Clarkson, 1995) have taken a more contemporary and realistic view of the therapeutic relationship in which the traditional transferential relationship is only a part.

Working therapeutically with people from cultural and ethnic backgrounds different to our own brings a particular challenge to therapists. Intercultural therapy is a meeting place where it is possible to have a legitimate dialogue between various people. This new look at diversity and the relationships in therapy follows on from the wave of feminist writers who brought a critical and new perspective to systemic and psychoanalytic therapy (Gorell Barnes & Henessy, 1994; Mitchell, 1974; Perelberg & Miller, 1990). Working therapeutically with black and minority patients has brought about writers who might not particularly gather under an intercultural banner (Dupont-Joshua, 1998; Evans-Holmes, 1992; Fletchman-Smith, 2000; Rose, 1997; Tann, 1993), and others who would (Kareem & Littlewood, 1992; Thomas, 1992, 1995, 2002a,b). Some have addressed minorities in clinical work and theorizing and others have examined the existing practice models and found them wanting.

This chapter will trace contributions to understanding the therapeutic relationship in intercultural therapy, exploring the cross-over of the psychoanalytic and systemic that emerges in intercultural work. As a backdrop, I begin with some personal reflection on psychoanalytic ideas, and then move to a discussion of the experience of intercultural therapy with a particular family (the Pond family). This discussion serves as a springboard for a fuller outline of the attention to the systemic and intrapsychic in intercultural therapy, the experience of transactions and transference in therapy and therapy systems, and the issues of the preparation and personal development of therapists for intercultural therapeutic relationships.

From models of the mind to interactional behaviour

A move from a one-person psychology

Freud's structural and topographical models of the mind gave us tools to understand complex human behaviours. Moreover, his models gave us an ability to place this complexity within a framework that allows it to be thought about, with the potential of being understood by the therapist and the patient. The problem with the use of the transference is that the reality of past relationships is viewed solely as the patient's commentary on the quality of the many-faceted relationship, with the therapist thereby subordinating any real relationship.

Early British family therapy adopted styles that bore the hallmarks of psychoanalysis and this was not surprising because many therapists who were working with families had early beginnings in individual psychodynamic or attachment work (Box & Thomas, 1979; Byng-Hall, 1985). The recent moves for a rapprochement between these different therapies is thus also not surprising. While there are generations of systemic therapists who feel no such familial ties with psychoanalytic theory, there are many who do. The early tensions that existed seem to have given way to a renewed interest in what the two therapies have in common, if anything. There has been an interest in developing therapeutic styles derived from analytic theory that could be used with families (see, for example, Carr, 1989). Other work has sought to adopt and adapt aspects of psychoanalytic concepts and theory (Flaskas, 1992; Larner, 2000). The more recent writers have considered the uses of some ideas from analytic technique in a systemic framework. In as much as family and systemic therapy can see the value of older established therapies, psychoanalytic practitioners have seen the value of systemic techniques with both individuals and families.

Coming from a child-care and clinical social work background, I first trained in marital and family therapy before psychoanalytic therapy. During all of my therapy trainings I found myself the only person of African Caribbean background. It was as a means of survival that I tried to find reading material that made some reference to ethnicity and culture. As a social worker I was well accustomed to the synthesizing of ideas in order to use what was helpful. The task of social work has always been broad, requiring a varied repertoire of skills, and it is perhaps for this reason that the profession has been able to call on many frameworks. Early British family therapy was very attractive to me because it offered new and exciting ways of working with families in the Probation Service. I found myself drawn to working conjointly with other professionals who were involved with the family. I had laid great store on the early discipline of family therapy to help me to find a way to work with my multi-cultural client group. Being able to sit in the room with more than one person without the brief of gathering a social and developmental history from each person present was liberating. Attending to the communication and the relationships between members of the family in the room was interesting.

The shift from an enquiry into an individual psychology to observing a multi-person interaction was not an easy one for workers schooled in a classical adult psychoanalytic model such as British clinical social work had become. There already existed in the analytic framework differences between therapeutic techniques that focused attention on a one-person psychology (following the lines of Freud's two models of the mind), and a two-person psychology (developed in the light of Melanie Klein's work (1937, 1957) on the infant's early relationship with the mother). Winnicott, Bowlby, and social workers James and Joyce Robertson went on to make the child and its primary care-giver the focus of their work. Winnicott was able to help focus attention on the importance of the relationship of the child to the family and John Bowlby's work on attachment theory (1951, 1958, 1969) has always been valued by those working with children and their families.

The difficulty of change has been well documented in the social sciences (Cooklin, 1999; Menzies, 1988). Many psychoanalytic therapists working with individuals and families have been able to benefit from the work developed by systemic thinkers. This way of working helps the therapist to work with the appearance of third persons in the material without seeing this purely as a manifestation of transference requiring interpretation that parallels the relationship between the therapist and the patient. More recent forms of brief, time-limited psychodynamic therapy are more active and share more with a systemic model. A great deal can be learned from systemic therapy, which advocates a *not-knowing* position and seeks to understand the person in their social context.

The Pond family

Mrs Pond, a senior teacher employed in a local school, rang up the local family consultation service to find out if there was anyone there who could see her nineteen-year-old son Greg with the rest of the family. The Ponds lived in a wealthy north of London suburb. Mrs Pond said that her son had been very depressed for the past six months and that neither he nor anyone else in the family knew what had made him so unhappy. She said that he was attending college and had always been very bright at school but found it very difficult to make friends, so unlike his sixteen-year-old sister, Abigail. Her husband, she said, was convinced that their son would come out of it in his own time. He had told her that as an adolescent he was no different from his son and had caused his parents a great deal of concern. She added that Mr Pond has problems with a stomach ulcer and was working himself into his grave (he was a scientist in the understaffed pathology department of the local teaching hospital).

Greg had been taken to child guidance at the age of seven; he was introverted and highly strung. He apparently hated seeing the therapist and told his mother that he did not want to see anybody now. Mrs Pond said that her son would come if it were possible for them to be seen by a black therapist. She added that she was East African Asian and that her husband was white British. Greg, she explained, had taken to calling himself black and telling people at college that his parents were from East Africa. Tearful on the telephone, Mrs Pond said that this did not bother her, but she felt that all of these things must be hurtful to his father, not wanting to take anything from him in a way.

The therapist told Mrs Pond that because of work commitments the black therapist might not be able to see them, but her son's preference would be borne in mind. With this Mrs Pond was reassured that Greg might make the effort and wondered if he had put forward the idea of a black therapist as a ploy not to come to the consultation centre, not expecting them to have had a black therapist. Mrs Pond said that they would await an appointment, and that her daughter was very supportive of her, and that without her she did not know how she would cope with her son and her husband.

Mr and Mrs Pond, Greg, and Abigail attended for their first appointment and were met by Rose, a white English therapist, and Salaam, an Ethiopian therapist. Both women explained to Mrs Pond that Rose was the person to whom she had spoken on the telephone and that Salaam was a member of the team who would be working with the family. This seemed to ease Mrs Pond's discomfort and the therapists facilitated the introductions, explaining how they worked. The therapists Rose and Salaam acknowledged that they were aware that a request had been made to see a black therapist and were interested to know if this had been discussed in the family. Rose said that she was interested in the issues of difference and ethnicity and was happy to engage with the issues when they arose.

Mr Pond said that he was pleased that they were able to see his son so soon and was aware of the long waiting times for services and that it did not matter to him what colour they were. Greg looked at his sister Abigail and then to their mother, who said that she, too, was glad that they were able to see the whole family. Greg was first invited to comment on if and how he thought that the meetings might be able to help him and his family. He said that he was not happy at home and had not been for a long time—he added that he was seen as the family scapegoat and that his parents' problems have now become his and weigh him down. Asked by Salaam if he thought that this might change, he said that he hoped that it would. Abigail thought that the meetings would be helpful but that they, the family, needed to stop themselves from being mean to each other when they were at the sessions.

Mrs Pond said that she would be interested to hear what Greg thought their (the parents') problems were, but felt relieved that they were now here and that she was not constantly caught up with what was going on in her family. Mr Pond said that he felt that Greg had been hostile towards him for some time and had called him a "sad old white man" during a family row after he had encouraged his son to go out to the cinema because he was so down in the dumps. He said that he was hurt and did not feel that he understood his children any more, feeling that they were almost like strangers who had taken up lodgings in the house. Abigail told her father that he would understand them if he bothered to talk to them.

Mr Pond was silent and Mrs Pond told the therapists that her husband worked very long hours recently and that he was covering for the staff shortages at the hospital. Greg said that as usual mum was covering for him so that nothing more was said to upset things but the fact remained that his father regretted marrying an Asian woman and would now like them all to disappear. Both Mr and Mrs Pond had joined in the conversation and Mr Pond said that his son was not himself and was saying anything that came into his head. Greg, quite upset now, said that his father's family had no contact with them, probably because they were prejudiced and they were ashamed of them. Abigail said that it was time that they all spoke their minds because everything gets hidden but that it does no one any good. Mr Pond said that he was upset at first but thought it best that the family came back the following week.

In the team meeting Rose asked Colin, a one-day a week clinical trainee, if he had anything to say from a black perspective. He said that first, he was not black, he was of mixed parentage, and could not represent a black perspective, but that his experience as a child was not too different from that of the Pond children. He added that they needed to be actively curious about what happens to race in the family.

On their return, Mr Pond said that the intervening week had been the worst of his life. He said that his children had said things that were very hurtful to him, but after some thought he realized that he had not faced up to many facts in his life. He had felt that his children were drifting away from him and wondered if he chose to use his work as an excuse so that he did not have to face his obvious redundancy in the family. His wife, he said, was all the children needed, she was a wonderful mother and coped with everything. They did not seem to need him particularly over the colour thing that so affected Greg in the junior school. Mrs Pond became tearful and said that she saw what was happening but felt that every attempt that she made to help them to get closer as a family did not work out. Abigail told her mother that she was partly to blame for allowing dad to get away with everything, not being around, behaving like a white stranger in his own home, and not even appreciating mum's family who were the only extended family that they had. Abigail said that although she seemed happy-go-lucky she, like mum, worried about the family. She added that her Asian cousins had such a happy, close family life and that she wished that her family were like that.

Rose turned to Salaam and said that although racial and cultural difference gets touched on in the meetings, the significance to the family did not seem to get discussed. Mr Pond said that Greg and Abigail talked about the racial and cultural differences in the family all the time but he could not understand why because they have everything and he and his wife made sure of this. Mrs Pond said angrily "You are forever telling them how lucky they are but you cannot seem to talk to them about how they might feel as mixed race—your son is busily trying to ignore the white side of himself, and you have for years tried not to see the Asian in us." "It has been so hard to get through to you, dad", Greg said, and added that he did not even know that mum had really noticed how he and Abby felt. Mrs Pond was in tears and Abigail was attending to her. Mr Pond seemed lost for words and Greg said it was the first time that he had noticed that his father probably did not fully understand what they were talking about and he felt for him because he did not walk about in their skin to see what they saw and feel what they felt.

This second family session marked the beginning of successful work with the Ponds and a good working partnership between Salaam and Rose. The Ponds are not alone as a family in their difficulties of not being able fully to conceive of each other's feelings and needs. The mixed racial heritage of the children and the fact that they live in a majority white society with little support from the white side of their family had set up for Greg, in particular, ideas about his parents' marriage and his father's lack of regard for them. Whether or not this was the case, Mr Pond experienced himself as surplus to requirements in his family. Mrs Pond felt that she was caught in the middle with Abigail and Greg feeling rejected because they were not white and presumably not like their father. Getting difference talked about in families can be difficult not only for therapists to do, but also the families themselves.

Rose and Salaam were able to talk about the different feelings that they had about the family. Salaam, also from East Africa, shared a culture that was similar to that of Mrs Pond. While she was sympathetic to Greg's situation, she hoped that he would be open to communication with his father. Salaam felt that her culture and her generation expected that parents and elders should be respected. Rose did not feel that she was similarly affected by the work with the family. She talked in the team about feeling uneasy in sessions and feared that Mr Pond, whom she found difficult to like, might try to make an alliance with her as the only other white person in the room. The fact that the family was able to make use of the therapy was in part thanks to the professionalism of the therapists, who were able to remain united and dedicated to the task of helping the family, and to family members, who, each in their own way, were finding the situation at home intolerable. For Rose and Salaam, the work with the Pond family had helped to strengthen the team's confidence in working cross-culturally.

Working interculturally

Rather like the Ponds, it has taken some time for the family of psychotherapy to be able to have conversations about difference. It has been difficult to talk about black and white even when this has an impact on the clinical work, and this particular difference is often hidden among the other multiple and sometimes improbable difference that one might encounter in therapy. Psychoanalysis had turned a corner when it was possible to talk about the relational aspects of development and about the facilitating environment and the impact of postmodernist ideas on family and systemic therapy. The part that our ethnicity plays in our daily lives and how we are all "raced" and differently valued in society is still yet very much unsaid in therapy. The book *Exploring The Unsaid* by Mason and Sawyerr (2002) has been a ground-breaking publication in British family and systemic therapy, advancing practice ideas for working cross-culturally. Similar writing in the USA (Boyd-Franklin, 1989; Boyd-Franklin & Hafer Bry, 2000; McGoldrick, 1998; McGoldrick, Pearce, & Giordano, 1982) played an important part in bringing British family therapy closer to engaging with the issues. The ability to work across the difference of racial and cultural boundaries is inescapably the way for us all in multi-cultural communities.

Most of the therapeutic relationships that I have as a therapist are intercultural. I rarely share similarities of culture or background with patients and of necessity over the years I have tried to find ways to get our differences and what they might signify talked about in therapy. Sometimes this can be done briefly, unless it is an issue of substance for the family or individual that has played a part in bringing them to therapy. There has been a slow but steady flow of papers in British family therapy publications about working with minority ethnic populations (Lau, 1984; Miller and Thomas, 1994; O'Brian, 1990; Woodcock, 2001). In the paper "A systemic approach to trauma", Woodcock (2000) moves from a discussion of the traumatic event to advancing some thoughts on the impact of the event and its relation to the attachment styles of those he works with. His use of attachment theory seems interesting and helped him to understand and work with families where more than one member was affected by a traumatic experience. Although notionally coming with psychoanalytic antecedents, attachment ideas seemed to have fitted seamlessly into the writer's systemic practice. Might it be that the experience of working with unfamiliar client populations will bring out the need to find different ways of working, which in turn might bring together the different ideas and frameworks of systems, psychoanalysis, and other therapies?

In thinking about ways of working with minority ethnic patients at Nafsiyat Intercultural Therapy Centre, Jafar Kareem wrote:

> At Nafsiyat we aim to offer a form of dynamic psychotherapy which is not necessarily tied to one theoretical orientation but which derives its strength from various analytical, sociological and medical formulations. The object is to create a form of therapeutic relationship between the therapist and patient where both can explore each other's transference and assumptions. This process attempts to dilute the power relationship that inevitably exists between the "help giver" and "help receiver". [Kareem & Littlewood, 1992, p. 16]

There is now a substantial body of literature written by British-based black and minority ethnic professionals and others about practice with black and minority ethnic patients. Much of this writing has come from therapists associated with the work of the late Jaffar Kareem and The Intercultural Therapy Centre, Nafsiyat. Although trained as a psychologist and psychoanalytic psychotherapist working in child and family psychiatry, Kareem found that his patients' minority backgrounds and immigrant status often played a part in their selection of family treatment as a method (Kareem, 1988). The significance that is placed on family and extended networks in other cultures was always taken into account when therapy was offered. So, with its roots in psychoanalysis, the work of the Intercultural Therapy Centre worked systemically. The therapists did not want to work only with black and minority patients, but also aspired to develop a useful model, or at least a collection of principles, to work interculturally. Being able to work effectively across cultural and racial boundaries is in part about a communal experience of people from many backgrounds and cultures being able to value difference and the contribution that this makes to human understanding.

Intercultural work is a meeting place for me where it is possible to have a legitimate dialogue between the various aspects of ourselves. Kareem believed that as well as engaging the intrapsychic and inter-relational, it is where we can take account of our social and communal experiences. Similar therapeutic styles in

Australia and New Zealand have thrown up their own way of understanding the particular experiences of working with indigenous and marginalized peoples in their land (see the Dulwich Centre Newsletter, 1993). Intercultural therapy has been a place where my systemic and psychoanalytic interests can work well together, where both western-informed juggernauts can run along almost in parallel with other ideas. It was comfortable to work in an environment where the issues that surrounded us were more than black and white. There were people from a rich collection of language and backgrounds. As well as having an interest in cultural sameness and difference, staff were encouraged to explore their own racism and to consider their place in the racist social pecking order.

Kareem believed that the challenge of being able to explore our own racialized experiences and our own investment in holding on to racial and cultural stereotypes would help to make the consulting room a safer place, but also a place where patients could do their own exploration, often in order to help them to make sense of their existence in the land of their colonizers. Many ideas were overturned in the early days and orthodox ideas were challenged, annotated, creolized, and even dismissed. Often the test was whether or not the classical ideas were universal across "non-western" cultures. If the concepts or ideas were culture bound, usually to white western cultures, and did not have the ability to travel, then they were considered as not helpful (Kareem & Littlewood, 1992). Structural approaches to family treatment implied a position of people within families and led therapists to think about the position of black and minority ethnic families in the structure of British institutions. Theory was never considered to be bigger than the therapeutic task and that theory was a western view to suit its population, often within an exclusionary zone that paid little or no attention to a race, class, and power critique.

Psychoanalysis has been able to shine a light on the intricacies of individual psychology and helped to understand some of the distortions of the ego. We often encountered in work with minorities the experience of the "proxy self" (Thomas, 1995). Systemic theory, with the embracing of second order ideas, has been able to turn the lens on the therapist as observing participant and has brought a new light to shine on the therapeutic relationship.

Transactions and transference

The effect of powerful feelings transmitted from person to person, and person to therapist and back, can be acknowledged in our work with families and individuals. The fact that other forms of therapy have come to rely on this does not make this information any the less helpful and usable. What we experience as therapists as a result of being with a family or individual might have to be reconfigured in order for us to make sense of (and work with) the transmission of emotion to ourselves, teams, and supervisors. With monotonous regularity, teams fall apart over powerful issues, sometimes arranging themselves on one side or another of an issue and re-enacting existing or unspoken splits in families.

Alan Carr (1989) discusses the idea of counter-transference and its use to therapy teams to help them understand and work with families where child abuse has taken place. I have found that the most valuable aspect that I have gained from my training in clinical social work has been the development of my skills to understand and use transference. Good supervision teams in training cohorts can provide a useful space for exploration if they are safe and have spent time working through some of the anti-discriminatory issues as a foundation for discussing their own family life and how their clinical work might have an impact on them. For growth of trust in teams to take place, these issues of difference and context are not only important for the safety and survival of members, but also for individuals to be challenged in their personal learning. If we are not able to hear and learn about our colleagues' sexuality, disability, gender, and race, and the part these played in their development and family experience, then we will not be able to help clients who present these issues in therapy. I would go further to say that therapists who are unable to work with these issues have a potential to do more harm than good.

One way of exercising self-protection is by the patient retreating behind a mask or proxy, so that the therapist engages with a false representation of the patient (Thomas, 1995, 1999). The true, socially devalued self is hidden and protected, not often engaged with in the therapy until it is safe to do so, if at all. The personality structure that has been developed to survive with a disability in an able-bodied world, or being a disadvantaged minority ethnic or black person in a white supremacist world, or a lesbian/gay man in a heterosexist world, is one of accommodation. People need to experience a therapy that is in the context of their oppression.

Until therapists are able to fully understand the extent to which the politics of power affects minorities and devalued people in the therapeutic relationship, providing helpful therapy will inevitably be limited. The contribution of intercultural therapy to an understanding of proxy identities in the consulting room was first developed in order to work with black and minority children who have been raised in majority white societies. The use of proxy selves in therapy as a protective move is not limited to black and minority ethnic children. This concept has a far wider application for others who occupy a "distinct" socially inferior classification. The ability to work through the use of the proxy self is as important an issue for minority community therapists as the working through of racism is for those of majority and dominant cultures.

Preparation and personal development

Even if family and systemic therapists cannot cleave wholeheartedly to the ideas of transference and counter-transference as described by psychoanalytic writers, these concepts are important. It would be helpful to find a way to be able to differently configure them in order to explore some areas that might be hidden in family and systemic therapy. Some other therapeutic modalities consider it most important for the therapist in training to spend some time on personal development so that this part of them, which is used as an instrument in the therapy, can be well explored and exercised. In our multi-cultural world, it is important that therapists can deal effectively with deep-seated attitudes and beliefs that are predicated on race and beliefs of superiority. Early family therapists were as likely as psychoanalytic therapists to use individual therapies, sometimes accompanied by a therapy group, as a means of personal development. Intercultural therapists have also adopted this model. After the move away from psychoanalytic frames of mind, family and systemic practitioners have been left to make their own choice, with courses often having little to offer as structure or guidance.

Unlike many other modalities of psychotherapy, family therapy has not had what has traditionally been called its training therapy. The family genogram (Lieberman, 1980) has been tried as a possible means of getting fledgling therapists to be able to tell a story of their life and family as well as getting an understanding of what they might unwittingly or otherwise bring to their clinical work with families. This was intended to help trainees to be in touch not only with what the family said about itself as a unit and a social organization but also with its views about other groups of people outside the family (Miller & Thomas, 1994).

In our multi-cultural world it is as important that we as therapists can understand and talk about our families as it is that we can understand and talk about our different social contexts and how this might impact on others. The difficulties that we encounter when attempting to work with difference is not at all surprising because of the prejudice, social stratification, and social ordering that we might have inherited from previous generations of kin. It is an issue for all therapists that we are aware of how we use our power and influence in therapeutic relationships. Therapists from psychoanalytic, systemic, and intercultural schools need to know how we are coded in relation to how we speak, our gender, skin colour, and social class. As a matter of exploration we need to know what meaning this has for the families and individuals that we work with. The issues of social context in the therapeutic relationship have been largely neglected by psychoanalytic trainings and they have much to learn from systemic and intercultural therapists. Reflective therapists will be interested to know when their own difference can help families to engage with these issues in ways that help them to talk and engage with the therapy, as well as helping them to tell their personal stories.

Conclusion

Family and systemic therapists and therapists working psychoanalytically can draw on ideas from each other's framework unselfconsciously without the fear of buying into a grand theory. There has been a long tradition of therapists using ideas that have not strictly come from their own tradition for the very reason that a new or unfamiliar idea works well at the time for the therapeutic task at hand. British intercultural therapies developed in order to work with diverse populations and, perhaps for that reason, privileged finding ways that might work rather than honouring one tradition alone. The pragmatism of meeting the needs of people who came to be seen as individuals and families, often with common problems, led to developing ideas of working across many barriers. As well as finding helpful models that themselves did not exclude or discount cultural experience, such a way of working had to be able to engage with the reality of racism and the resulting assaults on identity and self-esteem.

CHAPTER SEVEN

Before and beyond words: embodiment and intercultural therapeutic relationships in family therapy

Rabia Malik and Inga-Britt Krause

Social constructionism has provided a valuable framework for a social perspective on science. Its followers have questioned, and even been irreverent of, scientific theory and results. Nevertheless, approaches that are commonly referred to as social constructionist constitute a broad genre (Williams, 2002) rather than a clearly unified body of theory and they may also implicate different theoretical, ethical, and political points of view and possibilities.

To some extent this depends on the question of what it is that we consider to be socially constructed. Are we talking about language, texts, meaning, culture, the self, the person, relationships, knowledge, or emotions? And by "social construction" do we mean that any of these entities need not be the way they are, that they are not inevitable in their particular form, or that they are not determined by the nature of things (Hacking, 1999, p. 6)? Alternatively, do we mean that the forms that these entities take are the results of particular shared conventions for making sense and understanding the world? In the one case, we seem to be raising the issue of whether or not "anything goes". In the other, we seem to suggest that, once up and running, conventions themselves exercise restraint, so that all making-sense must move in a hermeneutic circle

(Taylor, 1981) because there is no means of understanding anyone with whom you do not share the same conventions.

What, then, if we consider relationships between persons who, through their personal history or the history of their social relationships, do not share common conventions in language, meaning, culture, convictions, ideology, and beliefs? Such a case includes most relationships between ethnographers and their informants, relationships between strangers from different cultural backgrounds, and intercultural therapeutic relationships.[1] In considering intercultural therapeutic relationships, as therapists we know that unless we choose to operate as authoritarians or oppressors it is not the case that "anything goes". Yet, we also know that intercultural communication and comprehension is possible, even though this may be a special case of social construction not allowed for, or elaborated upon, in social constructionist theoretical frameworks.

In this paper we begin by considering the dilemmas that social constructionism raises in understanding modes of communication that go beyond words. We refer to these as embodied modes of communication and we consider the centrality of these modes of communication in constructing intercultural therapeutic relationships. We then describe some experiences (we call them images or snapshots) derived from our therapeutic work with clients from Rwandan, Pakistani and Bangladeshi backgrounds and tease out various strands in our thinking about embodiment in relation to these experiences. In order to do this we draw on a number of theoretical sources from different disciplines, a predicament that we think is inevitable when attempting to connect process to content in cross-cultural relationships.

Embodiment

We agree with writers such as Flaskas (2002), Pocock (1995, 1997), and Lannaman (1998) that social constructionism cannot provide an adequate framework for systemic psychotherapy without incorporating some notion of common human constraints and in this way qualifying its own premise. What kind of constraints might these be? Lannaman notes that although not restricted to language and discourse, social constructionism tends to concentrate on these aspects of communication and on the synchronic and visible aspects of their co-construction (Lannamann, 1998, p. 298). One consequence of this has been that material and embodied aspects of persons, and especially of those persons who do not have power and control, have been rendered invisible.

To this we want to add that social constructionist approaches in family therapy have also tended to downplay (and have therefore rendered invisible) other aspects of social lives such as history, the unconscious, and those patterns of habits, routines, social rules, and etiquettes that Bourdieu has referred to as "habitus" (structures) or "doxic" (knowledge) (Bourdieu, 1977), and of which we may be unaware. This is despite the fact that these aspects are equally the results of interaction and communication between persons and therefore as imbued with meaning as language and discourse. As Lannaman notes, social constructionism *can* accommodate these recursive social processes but this raises the question of how to avoid reproducing and reifying the split between subjective (socially constructed) worlds and objective (generative) worlds that characterizes so much of western modes of thought, but which is not universal to all epistemologies. These questions are particularly acute for intercultural therapy.

The physical body is one fairly obvious constraint on human activity. Bodies are biologically and socially constituted (Douglas, 1966, 1970). Much of who we are, our sense of self and self identity is inscribed in our bodies and forms the context in which other modes of communication are rooted. As Shilling (2003) argues, while biologically our bodies share many common natural features—bones, muscles, flesh, blood—they differ in the function they serve as social symbols and as personal resources. Thus, at once our bodies are symbols of our human nature, our social positioning and standing, and our individual expression. Through them social divisions become embodied, and through them we exercise our human agency and act on the world. Indeed, they are the vehicle through which we come to experience the world. Understanding these constraints of the physical body not only provides a route for addressing experience, but can also constitute an anchor for cross-cultural relationships and ethical and non-discriminatory intercultural therapeutic practice. We have reached this position because we have both noticed that therapy with clients from non Euro-American backgrounds frequently moves forward as a result of processes in the therapy room in which the human body, physical objects, or embodiment feature in some way. This, we think, has important implications for the relativism implied in "strong" versions of constructionism that we have puzzled over and for intercultural therapeutic relationships.

In relation to the body in systemic psychotherapy we make two assumptions. First, the body is both a physiological entity and culturally constructed. The body–mind divide and the relative concealment of the body from most forms of psychotherapy is one such cultural construction, and one that is not shared by people in many societies with different ideas about illness and healing than those generally held in Euro-American psychotherapy traditions (Csordas, 1994; Kapferer, 1991; Laderman & Roseman, 1996; Malik, 2000). Second, the body is intricately linked to, and implicated in, experience. It is this that Csordas has described as embodiment and that he defines as "an indeterminate methodological field defined by perceptual experience and the mode of presence and engagement in the world" (Csordas, 2002, p. 241).

Images or snapshots from therapy

Involving touch

> Some years ago one of us (BK) watched through a one-way screen the following sequence during a therapy session.[2] The therapist, an African-American man, was meeting with a Muslim family from Rwanda consisting of a mother, her sister, and three daughters. There was also a team of therapists watching through a one-way screen. Before the session, the African-American therapist had greeted the Muslim, Swahili-speaking interpreter in the waiting room in front of the family by shaking her hand in a friendly manner. The interpreter was clearly disconcerted but shook the therapist's hand in return. Several of the colleagues behind the screen reprimanded the therapist for this during the break, pointing out that this was against Muslim practice. You do not shake hands in a greeting and women certainly do not shake the hand of a strange, non-related man. The therapist conducted a sensitive and interested interview and by the end of the

meeting the mother in the family, who was a thoroughly traditional woman, got up, walked over to the therapist, took his hand and shook it. Her daughters followed her example.

Involving food

Rashida was a twenty-two-year-old Bengali girl who was referred to see RM. She had been abused by her brother at the age of twelve and, when she disclosed the abuse some years later, she had been cast out by her family, who felt she had dishonoured them. Rashida had been suicidal and had attended individual therapy for a number of years, which she had found helpful. When she came to see RM the focus of their work had been on Rashida's identity and relationships. Rashida had an ambivalent relationship with her Bengali culture and she missed her mother and sisters terribly. Over a period of time she reinitiated regular contact with some of her family members, but struggled with negotiating her identity with them. Rashida and RM decided to have a therapy session with Rashida's eldest sister at her home. In the beginning of the session, Rashida asked RM if she would like some tea. RM agreed and accepted her hospitality. While she was making the tea, Rashida's sister called out to her, instructing her to boil the milk and water together and not to make tea in an "English way". Rashida laughed and said, "They think I am too much like a *goori* [white person]." She brought the tea over and offered RM a cup first and then her sister. She then brought over a tin of biscuits and placed them next to RM. RM picked up the tin of biscuits and offered them to Rashida's older sister before taking one herself. Rashida's sister took a biscuit and started to tell RM how Rashida did not respect the ways of the community. For the remainder of the session they talked about the community and what they both liked and disliked about it from their different points of view

Involving clothes

The Naseer family self-referred to RM and had specifically requested to see a Muslim therapist. Mrs Naseer was an Irish Muslim convert, with six children, and was experiencing difficulty with her eighteen-year-old daughter. She had separated from her Moroccan husband following domestic violence. As the first session drew near RM began to reflect on the significance of her Muslim identity for the family. On the basis of her conversations with Mrs Naseer on the telephone, RM had expected the family to be strict Muslims and the women, at least Mrs Naseer, to be wearing *hijab* (a veil). As RM did not wear the *hijab* herself and did not feel confortable wearing it for the session, she decided to cover herself by wearing a shawl instead. When the family arrived, all of the women apart from the girls below age ten were wearing *hijab*. During the session RM and the family talked about what had brought them to therapy and how they could be helped. Towards the end of the session RM recalled with the family how they had requested to see a Muslim therapist and wondered if she looked like the kind of Muslim therapist they had in mind. Mrs. Naseer immediately said that she had been surprised that RM did not wear *hijab*. RM asked the family about what they thought made somebody a Muslim, was it something visible or invisible. This theme became the focus of much of their subsequent work together.

Involving images

Rehana was a twenty-nine-year-old Bengali woman who came to see BK as an initial step to engaging in therapy with her family, which consisted of her, her husband, a son aged ten, and a daughter aged two. Her parents and younger brothers lived near her and her in-laws lived in another English city. Rehana was born in the UK and the therapy took place in English. Rehana was not sure about coming to therapy. She had been referred because she was depressed and the psychiatrist who had referred her also felt that there were marital or family problems. Rehana talked about her life, repeatedly minimizing the problems, saying that she had been depressed but who isn't? She had had problems but who hasn't? She did, however, admit that she would like her husband to be more attentive. BK listened, saying only that she had read the letter from the referring psychiatrist but that she usually tries to put this knowledge aside and hear what clients themselves want to say. Rehana then went on to tell BK about having had an arranged marriage in which love had grown, but that she had also had an affair and that her husband did not know. This had caused her a great deal of anguish. She said that she did not know whether the psychiatrist had written about this in the referral letter. BK said that indeed she had read about the affair in the letter and then asked how Rehana had coped with these understandable and tumultuous feelings. She described how obsessed she had been, how she could not think of anything else but her lover and how she had found out that he had another girlfriend. BK said that in her language (Danish) and in English as well we say that "love makes you blind" and that she did not know whether this was what you said in Bengali. Rehana looked at BK for a little while and then said, "You know, I am going to tell you something I have not told to anybody. This man practiced *jadu*[3] on me for a very long time. It was disgusting." BK asked questions about the *jadu*. Where did he place it? How did it stop? Did her husband know about the *jadu*? Rehana said that it had stopped because she and her husband moved house. Later, while getting up, she said, "It is finished I am a family woman now, but now that I have known that kind of love I want to have it with my husband."

Commentary on the images of embodiment

We see a common thread from our therapy sessions, involving the body, embodiment, bodily movement, talking about the body, and images relating to the body. The example of touch is perhaps the most straightforward example. In this the body is clearly implicated in engaging with the world and other persons. Touch breaks barriers. In touching there is a sense that we are doing something together, that we are experiencing and being experienced, that we are intimate with each other. This experience of intimacy is perhaps almost genetic, as is suggested by research pointing to the important role of tactile stimulation for healthy child development (Montagu, 1978). It is also worth noting that such stimulation is relatively absent in Euro-American societies compared with child-rearing practices in other societies, where infants are in more or less constant physical contact with carers (LeVine *et al.*, 1996). Similarly many different kinds of healing incorporate touch such as in the laying of hands, blowing, massaging, etc. (Csordas, 2002; Kapferer, 1991), or the use of physical objects or symbols (Levi-Strauss, 1963) as a central focus in the therapeutic encounter.

There is, we suspect, a great deal of variation in how much family therapists touch their clients. Most of us probably follow our own cultural etiquette and this rarely brings us into physical contact with our clients and then perhaps only through some sort of ritual, such as the shaking of hands in greeting like our African-American colleague did when he met the interpreter. In the more activist family therapy approaches, such as those of Minuchin and Satir (Minuchin, Wai-Yung, & Simon, 1996), the therapists tend to be more interventionist and directive and this may involve physical touch if only fleetingly (for example, during an enactment). Even when an intervention does not involve touch, the structural therapist may direct clients to make physical movements, such as the changing of seats or standing up. In these approaches, the therapist is deliberately strategic about whether or not he or she is central in the therapy.

It was this almost invasive aspect of the therapist as expert, and its implications for assumptions about reality, that was criticized from a constructionist point of view by Anderson and Goolishian (1988), Hoffman (1988), and others—this may also have been what was in the minds of the therapists who reprimanded our African-American colleague. However, there is more to the image of the Muslim woman shaking hands with our African-American colleague. After he had conducted a patient and culturally sensitive interview, the mother returned his gesture of openness and intimacy. She engaged with her body and she expressed this as a kind of mimesis, by repeating the greeting in a manner that she had seen the therapist employ.[4] In this, the mother was no doubt exploring differences, but was she also revealing something else? Something that was expressed through her stretching out of her arm, through her touch, and perhaps through the forcefulness of her grip? Was this her reality in some form, just as the shaking of hands in greeting belonged to the cultural and emotional reality of the therapist? Or was she mimicking the therapist, who was mimicking those who taught him how to follow etiquette? The incident seemed to indicate that the mother chose to shake the therapist's hand and that something new was happening. This was a physical movement.

In the image of the offering of food we saw a combination of a physical movement and an exchange of objects. We tend to think about physical objects as being in a different category than persons. This is a heritage from our world of commodification and dualism. Physical objects can be extensions of persons imbued with meaning, obligations, and agency.[5] Perhaps the nearest we can get to this continuity between persons and things in Euro-American traditions is in objects of art. However "ordinary" things can take on such qualities, too. We need look no further than to gifts and presents in order to see how such exchanges not only create relationships and thereby obligations and expectations, but can also be instrumental, such as when they evoke in us memories and emotions from other contexts of our lives. In all societies persons have relationships with each other via the things that they exchange, buy, and give to each other (Mauss, 1954).

Universally, such processes and relationships are created and expressed through the giving and taking of food. Who you eat with and who you do not eat with demonstrates commensuality, because food (and in particular cooked food) comes into contact with the physical body of the persons who have it or prepare it (Levi-Strauss, 1970). Food and the process and interactions around eating are therefore excellent vehicles for the expression of embodied social relationships. Rashida's offering RM tea can be seen as an example of this. The tea and the method of making it was symbolized by Rashida's sister as an arena for the expression of cultural differences and for difference between the two sisters in their approach to the cross-cultural context in which they were living their lives. Rashida made tea "English" style. Yet Rashida's way of preparing the tea, her style of offering it and the order in which she distributed it was also imbued with more traditional ideas about relationships and embodied respectfulness. In turn, RM's offering of the biscuits to Rashida's sister before she took one, was a kind of mimesis reproducing and replicating meanings about relationships. We consider that this mimesis facilitated a respectful connection between RM and the two sisters, in the context of which different ideas about the importance of community and social relationships could be talked about.

Like food, other "things" are imbued with meaning when they are used, manipulated, or adorned in an expression of the self and personhood. Vygotsky suggested that such objects or symbols could come to be assigned meanings, in such a way that they act as mediating devices (Vygotsky, 1978). Mediating devices stand between the person and social and cultural conventions in the same way that tools have stood between human beings and the environment in human evolution. Through their use both are altered. We may say that their use leaves an imprint both on the body and on the physical and social environment. As the meanings that these objects are assigned are socially constructed and collectively produced, they may act as tools of agency, shaping the self's experience, cognition, and affect. Mediating devices thus become pivots of repeated meaning that may be conscious and voluntary or unconscious and forgotten. They become part of subjective experience as well as a way of expressing that experience.

Clothes are a good example of this subjectifying process. RM's wearing of a shawl in her first session with the Naseer family can be seen as acting as such a mediating device, reminding both the family and RM herself of the religious and gendered meaning of modesty and covering up. This communicated to the women in the family not just something cognitive or visual, but also a notion of the shawl as a thing and of what it feels like wearing it, how wearing shawls has implications for one's movements, posture and sexual modesty. Although RM's experience of covering may have been different to that of the women in the Naseer family, it provided a sufficient connection or shared experience to open up a discussion about what makes one a "Muslim"—outer visible signs, or inner hidden signs.

We have emphasized embodiment as a mode of experience as well as engagement and in line with this the continuity between bodies and minds on the one hand and objects and persons on the other. We now want to suggest that although we use separate analytic categories such as cognition and affect, in our descriptions these categories, and especially the duality they suggest, do not do justice to the experiences we are discussing here. The language that we are using does not seem to be able to capture the unity we are trying to convey. Csordas writes about "embodied knowledge" or "somatic modes of attention" (Csordas, 2002, p. 253) as a way of addressing this problem. In these he includes intuition, imagination, perception, and sensation. For the psychotherapists, this position offers more promise as a way of understanding how therapists connect to persons as whole persons, that is to say, to bodies as well as to minds. For example, it provides a more unified framework for the therapist–client relationship and for such processes as intuition, transference, and attunement, which may begin by the therapist becoming aware of a physical sensation in her own body.

The sequence involving Rehana talking about her love affair is an example of this. The encounter involved somatic modes of attention in both BK and in Rehana, because of the power of the physical imagery of blindness to connect cross-culturally. Rehana's story about being deeply in love in a socially and culturally inappropriate context evoked in BK a human theme. This was the theme of contradiction between feelings and desires experienced by a person and the rules and obligations of social relationships. Describing Rehana's feelings and how she understood her predicament up to this point would not have conveyed her experiences adequately. Expressing the contradiction through the image of being blinded by love created a much closer resonance with Rehana's feelings and thoughts and the meanings that she herself attributed to the events she experienced. Rehana then was able, almost freed, to address the human theme of unrequited love in a culturally specific fashion, explaining how her lover had taken possession of her by using witchcraft. There was one human predicament but two culturally constructed images. In turn, the physical imagery was a result of both therapist and client listening with their bodies and their minds. We suggest that this is also the way people generally in all cultures and societies listen when they want to engage and connect with others.[6]

Embodiment and therapeutic relationships

While the literature on "use of self" in systemic therapy has alluded to, and has begun to elaborate on, the nature of the therapeutic relationship (Flaskas, 1997; Hardham, 1996; Real, 1990; Rober, 1999), much of the focus has been on a cognitive experience or the "internal dialogue" of the therapist (Rober, 1999; Hilderbrand & Speed, 1995; Real, 1990). Relatively little attention has been paid to the body as an aspect of the "self" or to somatic modes and their social construction. Through the images derived from our therapy sessions we have tried to demonstrate experience as a more unified and more holistic phenomenon. This has been noticed by other systemic psychotherapists. For example, some accounts describing an impasse or a turning point in the therapeutic process have used somatic, sensory, or bodily terms, such as "an intuition", "a gut feeling", "a hardening", "a melting" (Layton, 1995, p. 57). Rober (1999) and Haber (1994) stress the importance of the therapist taking into account what is evoked in himself or herself, as what in the first instance may not be understood may be a clue to the "unsaid". We have suggested that this begins as an embodied sensation.

What, then, are the implications of turning our attention on to the bodies of therapists and clients and the embodied processes implicated in their relating? One implication is that we must go beyond language both in our thinking and in our techniques. There is scope for a development of a whole repertoire of using ourselves, what we wear and how, how we sit and stand, how we interact with our clients, what imagery we invoke, whether or not we use objects and things, and whether or not we touch. But this also requires that we go beyond cognition and language in questioning our own assumptions because bodies themselves are cultural and political.

It may seem to be a paradox that intercultural therapeutic work, along with therapeutic work with violence and power, highlights the need for our theoretical framework to include some kind of notion of a reality outside language. This has to do with experience. Not with whether or not we can know another person's experience, but whether or not we can accept experience as real. Flaskas addresses this as a question: "In abandoning a core interest in the idea of an external reality, do we risk minimizing the power of the human experience of reality and realness, and what might this mean for the process of therapy?" (Flaskas, 2002, p. 54). In intercultural therapy the acknowledgement of human experience of reality and realness is all we can hope for as a basis for our work. Attunement and understanding follow from this. We think that our four images from therapy showed different ways in which the therapists validated the experiences of their clients by making themselves available through being attentive to somatic themes. The handshake may have been a mistake, but it nevertheless cut across stereotypes to experience, while both the sharing of biscuits and the shawl that RM was wearing "stood in" for a bundle of meanings, many of them somatic, which could not have been communicated so easily in words. Similarly, the image of "blind love" was a powerful cross-cultural connector because it evoked the body and the image, or the idea of not being able to see could be experienced as real by both therapist and client.

Another implication of focusing on the body is that it draws attention to the body as part of the self and, therefore, also as an aspect of the living subject. This seems so obvious that the point hardly needs making. However, implicit in this is also a duality between subjects and objects that, as Csordas argues, easily slides into a distinction between body and mind, and between the self and other (Csordas, 2002, p. 255). Intuitively we know that our bodies are not objects, but when it comes to other bodies, and in particular other bodies that are very different from ourselves, bodies that at first sight may have a different skin colour and a different gait, a different smell, and may be inscribed with a whole set of ideas, habits, and routines that are different to our own, it may be a different story. Such bodies are easily objectified. Indeed, stereotyping, discrimination, racism, and violence are processes of objectification in which one party relates to the other as subject to object. In such instances the body *becomes* objectified through a process of reflection filled with social and political content (Dalal, 2002; Krause, 2002). This leads to domination and discrimination rather than intersubjectivity as a basis for therapy. While we recognize that intercultural therapy requires constant vigilance in relation to personal assumptions and political awareness, we also suggest that as a framework for therapy embodiment offers a starting point for a focus on the reality of experience both inside and outside the therapy room. This is because embodiment emphasizes the body as one aspect of a perceiving and engaging subject and from a cross-cultural perspective this avoids relying on a predominantly Euro-American body–mind dualism as a theoretical paradigm.

Summary

We have argued for the inclusion of the body and processes of embodiment in the repertoire and approaches in systemic psychotherapy. While we consider this important for the development of theory in systemic psychotherapy, we particularly argue that embodiment as a framework is vital for the development of equitable and culturally sensitive intercultural systemic psychotherapy. This is so not only because in many cultures and societies language and texts are not privileged over experience, interaction, and behaviour, but also because the idea of embodiment conveys a domain that is open both to experience and to mutual recognition. In this sense the body is real, even though the meanings associated with it are socially, culturally, and individually constructed and therefore may vary from person to person.

From the point of view of theories of social construction, embodiment as a theoretical framework therefore highlights two important qualifications. First, it points to those aspects of social being that not only may be outside language but also outside awareness and consciousness. In this sense, the body and practices of the body are old patterns of meaning in part distilled and condensed from past ongoing social interaction—and it is in this sense that the body is socially constructed. Second, it points to the body as an aspect of the selves of therapists and clients. While this aspect may be outside an individual's awareness, it is none the less a requirement of training that the therapist is someone who is skilled in becoming aware of her own sensations, feelings, and emotions. Damasio refers to these as embodied thoughts (Damasio, 2003) and as therapists we recognize these as the basis for intuition, motivation, empathy, and transference.

It is the fact that these processes are human processes, and not that we share or can anticipate the contents and the meaning of them, that indicates the commonness between us and our clients from other cultural and social backgrounds. Thus, rather than being *in spite of*, it is instead *because* there are some broad and general constraints on meaning, thought, feeling, and interaction that communication and comprehension across cultural differences is possible. Embodiment is one aspect of existence in which we experience these similarities and differences and this is why embodiment as a framework has much to offer systemic psychotherapy.

Notes

1. Following Kareem and Littlewood, we use the term intercultural therapy to refer to "the effective therapeutic intervention and facilitation by a member of one ethnic group in the decisions, choices and subjectivities of a client of another" (Kareem & Littlewood, 1992, p. 11)
2. This sequence has previously been discussed in relation to taboo in Krause, 1998, Chapter 6.
3. *Jadu* refers to black magic or witchcraft in which special substances, sometimes including body parts of the victim are placed in special places near the victim.
4. Taussig has described the mimetic faculty as "the faculty to copy, imitate, make models, explore differences, yield into and become

Other" (Taussig, 1993, p. xiii). Minuchin also describes mimesis as a therapeutic technique (Minuchin, 1974, p. 129).

5. There is an extensive body of literature on this topic starting with classic text *The Gift* by Marcel Mauss (1954).
6. We are here following the phenomenological approach of Merleau-Ponty (1962, 1964).
7. We consider that this is a more fruitful starting point for intercultural therapy than the psychoanalytic notions of projective identification, transference, or the attachment framework, because this approach retains notions of social construction as a central assumption. This is not to say that psychoanalytic and psychodynamic approaches cannot incorporate a phenomenological one. Such a project has, for example, been suggested with some success by Farhad Dalal (Dalal, 2002).

CHAPTER EIGHT

Sticky situations, therapy mess: on impasse and the therapist's position

Carmel Flaskas

Foreword

Let me begin this discussion of impasse with two descriptions of practice already published within the family therapy literature.

The first piece of practice

Peter Rober (1999)[1] writes about a first session with a family with a rebellious teenage son, a mother, and father. The mother begins to cry before she even opens her mouth, and the father is bristly and abrupt in his first interactions with the therapist. The therapist continues to try to engage the father, becoming more irritated with him as the session goes on, as the father becomes more rigid and blaming of the son, and more adversarial towars the therapist. Later, when talking with one of his colleagues, Peter explodes in an angry outburst against the father, and when he hears himself doing this, he is struck by the proportions of his rage towards the father.

The second piece of practice

I have written before about my work with a couple, whom I had already seen with their children as part of a piece of work focusing on one of the mother's daughters (Flaskas, 2002).[2] It is a blended family, and following the successful conclusion of the family therapy, we embark on couple work focusing on some of the parental differences that had been raised in the family sessions. In the privacy of the couple work, the therapeutic net widens, and the wife's unhappiness and disappointment with her husband, and his anger about this, very quickly come to be placed on the table.

I had built a strong working relationship with both of them in the family work, but now the therapeutic relationship moves into a new territory. The sessions now become dominated by the husband's resistance to his wife's expressions of her unhappiness. She is very fluent and, both within and outside the sessions, he goes on a verbal strike. I become taken up with efforts to engage more with the husband, and if you were to have asked me where I thought the difficulties lay in my work with them, I would have said in my engagement with the husband. Yet, after a few such sessions, I have a dream about the wife, and in my dream I see that she is mad. This dream comes too late. The couple does not come back to the next session—it is the husband who rings, very distressed, to tell me this, and he says that it is his wife who does not want to continue the work.

Introduction

Impasse is part and parcel of everyday therapy practice and, not surprisingly, it is a main refrain of supervision. This chapter explores the therapist's position in the experience of impasse. It begins with a description of impasse and the emotional and interactional constellation that can gather around it. This leads to a discussion of different ways in which impasse may be understood—in terms of stuck narratives, and as a challenge to curiosity and the capacity to think. These themes move across narrative and systemic and psychoanalytic understandings, which are then gathered up in a discussion of the task of maintaining empathic connection and emotional containment. Although they form no coherent whole, none the less all these ideas underscore the importance of therapist reflection, and the importance of both thinking about and using our position as therapists during impasse.

Describing the constellation of impasse

To think of therapeutic impasse as a description of times when the process of therapy becomes stuck serves as a rough beginning point for my discussion, and yet this very general description covers a number of different kinds of experience and it is also shorthand for an emotional and interactional constellation that can gather around the family, the therapist, and the therapeutic relationship.

Stuckness can occur in all phases of therapy, within sessions and across many sessions. It can occur in engagement and become a barrier to the development of a good-enough therapeutic relationship, and a therapy that begins well can easily become stuck during the family's struggle with change. Transitory stuckness within sessions is simply part of the ebb and flow of the therapeutic connection between the therapist and family, and in this sense it should not be highlighted as especially problematic. A particular sequence of stuckness within one session usually becomes problematic only if it becomes entrenched across sessions, or if it routinely emerges and disrupts the therapy. Having said this, though, I should also point out what as therapists we perhaps know only too well: the process of relational, behavioural, and emotional change does not occur in neat predictable unidirectional blocks, and precisely because therapy is a very human endeavour, periods of stuckness are often simply part of the territory of change.

It is useful to have the idea of "impasse" in our heads as therapists because it helps us to be more attuned to problematic stuckness, and this attunement is in turn useful for two quite pragmatic reasons. The first is that therapeutic failure is generally prefigured by impasse. Let me be clear that I am not arguing here that impasse *causes* failure. Indeed, we would need to be in the serious grip of therapist omnipotence to claim a direct causal relationship between impasse in therapy and therapeutic failure. Failure is rarely addressed in the family therapy literature, though in two articles that have done so, its complexity is underlined (Kaffman, 1987; Spellman & Harper, 1996).

In thinking about failure, one can also turn to the research undertaken across thirty years related to generic factors in successful therapeutic outcome. This research is well represented in the collection by Hubble, Duncan, & Miller (1999a). They note the "big four" groups of factors that seem to make the difference: the strengths and capacities that clients bring with them and the circumstances of their lives outside the therapy; the therapeutic alliance; clients' capacity for hope and their expectation of change (the "placebo" effect); therapeutic models and techniques (Hubble, Duncan & Miller, 1999b). Many of us are by now familiar with the findings that clients' strengths and the circumstances of their lives seem to account for 40% of the outcome variance, followed at 30% by factors relating to the therapeutic alliance, with clients' hopefulness and models/techniques accounting for about 15% each. I am quoting this research again here to make the point that in the same way that therapy success is multi-factorial, therapy failure is multi-factorial. And although as therapists we have influence within a 45% ambit of the factors related to therapy outcome, it is still "just" 45%.

"Just" 45% is, none the less, very precious and, regardless of whether impasse prefigures failure or comes to represent a movement forward in the messy process of change, it is important to note that impasse is always felt in the therapeutic relationship and it always affects the therapeutic relationship. It also always challenges the therapeutic relationship, as well as challenging our skills and techniques and our understanding. During impasse, a constellation all too easily develops that threatens the therapeutic alliance and can both compound, and become embedded in, the very difficulties the family is bringing to therapy. The nature of this constellation is the second reason why it is useful to be attuned to impasse.

I will map this constellation, though I am aware in doing so that my map badly collapses the particularity of the experience. It also makes impasse sound rather abstract, which it is anything but, for it is often tough emotional territory. If we think that one of the emotional tasks for therapists is to be able to tolerate the experience of failure, another is to be able to tolerate the frustration, uncertainty, anxiety, dread, blame, anger, shame, guilt, pain, and hopelessness that can quite quickly begin to coalesce in various shades of emphasis when families become stuck yet again with the difficulties that seriously concern them. For the family, being stuck in the difficulties is often only too familiar, but in therapeutic impasse they are stuck in a place (therapy) where things are supposed to change and with a person (the therapist) who is supposed to be helping. The emotional territory of impasse is, for better or worse, shared by families and therapists, though it goes without saying that it is almost always far more painful and difficult for the family.

To write of the therapeutic task in impasse of tolerating this constellation is maybe an unreal dictation of what a therapist "should" do. Yet it certainly does help as a therapist to develop a higher threshold of reactivity, to have some buffer that allows us to appreciate the family's experience without reacting against it or joining in with it, and without either acting out or reacting against the fantasy we have about what the stuckness and mess means about ourselves as therapists. So it is nice, in situations when a parent relentlessly attacks a child in a session, to resist rescuing the child and redirecting the blame (ever so professionally and relentlessly) to the parent. Or to resist embarking on an escalation with the family about exactly who did what to whom (and it most certainly wasn't you). Or feeling so inadequate that you lose the capacity to string two sentences together. Or becoming increasingly pleasant and fake-therapeutic as chaos and hell breaks loose around you. Or to resist suddenly converting to religion in the middle of a session, and then start praying for a real therapist to walk in the door.

Of course I'm joking—but only in part. In the impasse constellation, it is very easy to find yourself in an anti-therapeutic sequence with the family, which potentially compounds the impasse and embeds the family's difficulties, even though the sequence within the therapeutic relationship is at the same time a reaction to (and sometimes a reflection of) the family's struggle. However, it is really too neat to say simply that one needs to learn to tolerate the emotional territory of impasse, for such a high plane of differentiation is neither humanly possible, nor would it necessarily be a boon to the therapeutic process. It is true (in Bowenian terms) that part of learning to be a therapist is learning to hold on to your position as a therapist and your separateness from the family while maintaining your therapeutic connectedness with them. However, it would be impoverishing of the potentials of therapy to think that this means emotional cut-off or retreating to the distance of the therapist-as-expert position. But if we give up the rather bankrupt strategy of reprimanding ourselves as therapists when we become involved in the emotional mess of impasse, what can we do to hold on to the "therapeutic" part of the therapeutic relationship?

This question is in part the subject of the following sections, but before finishing here, let me summarize the description I have been giving so far. Impasse is problematic stuckness during the process of therapy. It is part of the messy and discontinuous process of change, although therapeutic failure is also often prefigured by impasse. The emotional territory of impasse is usually difficult, and sequences that are driven by blame and/or shame are common both within the family and within the therapeutic relationship. For this reason, at times of impasse, one is vulnerable as a therapist to contributing to anti-therapeutic sequences in the therapy relationship. Overall, it is useful to think of impasse as an emotional and interactional constellation involving both therapist and family.

On narrative closure, curiosity and the capacity to think

To describe impasse as an emotional and interactional constellation is in itself one way of understanding it, but now I want to explore more specific ways in which this constellation may be understood, again staying with the focus on the therapist's experience and the therapist's role. Impasse may be theorized from different angles—in terms of narrative closure, or as a challenge to the therapist's curiosity and capacity to think. The first angle fits more with a narrative frame, while the second ranges across systemic and psychoanalytic ideas. As you might expect, some elements of these understandings will overlap while some will conflict, and so for this reason I will discuss them separately before addressing the way in which these understandings relate to the task of maintaining empathic connection and emotional containment during impasse.

On narrative closure

Narrative ideas offer one way of framing the experience of impasse as a closure of narrative for both the family and therapist. For the family, the stuckness may be experienced as an unsafe confusional zone, or alternatively it can lead to the hardening of a particular story about the difficulties, with each of these options very effectively foreclosing possibilities for change. As a parallel process, the therapist may become overwhelmed and then disempowered in the therapeutic role, or alternatively become wedded to a specific way of understanding what is happening for the family that closes off the search for therapeutic possibilities. If you like, from this narrative frame, therapists become stuck with their own version of a dominant story that cuts them off from the experience of the family's dilemma, and decreases their own flexibility and creativity in meeting the challenge of impasse.

Though the relativist tendency of postmodernist thinking discourages the identification of what constitutes a "better" story, I would argue that it is hard to work with families and not have in your head some idea of what might constitute a better/more therapeutic/more liberating story. David Pocock (1995), in his discussion of the possibility of the coexistence of modernist and postmodernist ideas, identifies some features that constitute "better" stories, and I think that many therapists recognize in his list some of the implicit criteria that guide their own practice. Pocock suggests that better stories are stories that are more congruent, more "object-adequate", more encompassing, more emotionally holding, more shared, more emotional, more conscious, more just, more provisional, and more hopeful (Pocock, 1995). These guidelines may inform our understandings of the process of therapeutic change in general, but they also have value in thinking about what might need to shift for both ourselves and the families in our struggle with the narrative closure of impasse.

The challenge to curiosity and the capacity to think

The idea of narrative closure may sit alongside other ideas from systemic and psychoanalytic thinking. For while narrative closure draws attention to what is happening to the story, the systemic idea of curiosity is angled more towards the conditions of meaning-making and story development. The idea of curiosity is most closely associated with Milan therapy (see Cecchin, 1987), having as part of its evolution the earlier Milan idea of neutrality (see Selvini Palazzoli, Boscolo, Cecchin, & Prata, 1980). The notion of the therapist's position of curiosity now signals the therapist's openness to meaning, and particularly to the construction of meaning that recognizes the integrity and sense of the family's dilemma and possibly the integrity of the presenting problem itself as an expression of the family's and/or individual's struggle.

Curiosity is, in one way, an orientation toward this kind of understanding. Used well, it should open space within the therapy for the development of new meanings. However, through the human act of relating within the therapeutic relationship, the therapist's curiosity should also be experienced by the family as evidence of her/his commitment and interest and desire to understand—curiosity, then, should be "experience-near", not "experience-distant". If used in this way, it becomes as much a tool for empathic connection as it is a tool for inviting new meanings.[3] Although curiosity has its background within the Milan framework, it has become part of a more general configuration of theory and practice ideas within family therapy. For example, one sees a strong commitment to the therapist's curiosity in the techniques of narrative therapy, and Harry Goolishian and Harlene Anderson also very deliberately developed the allied idea of the therapist position of not-knowing in their therapy framework informed by postmodernist and social constructionist ideas (see, for example, Anderson, 1997; Anderson & Goolishian, 1992b).

There is also resonance between the family therapy notions of curiosity and not-knowing and ideas from psychoanalysis. In Glenn Larner's exploration of this wider resonance, he writes of the tension of knowing-not-to-know, and explores the historical shift in psychoanalysis from a primary interest in an individualized concept of mind, to an interest in the relational context of knowing and being known, and indeed the relational concept of the capacity to think (Larner, 2000). Larner singles out the work of Wilfred Bion, which has been particularly important in this shift as well as influencing broader therapy discussions (see, for example, Bion 1967, 1970; Symington & Symington, 1996).

Bion's notion of containment within the analytic relationship, and his ideas about the space for thinking that the analyst tries to create through her/his immersion in the analytic work, have been translated for use in wider therapeutic contexts. These ideas are tied very closely to his understandings of the emotional and relational processes of the capacity to think. As I've noted elsewhere (Flaskas, 2002), Bion's ideas suggest that trying to find and hold the capacity for thinking both requires and achieves emotional containment, and it is a meeting of conscious and unconscious experience. One could think of the developmental metaphor of a baby's "ordinary" experience of unlanguageable distress, which comes to be lived through and made bearable by the physical holding of the parent, who is also emotionally holding the baby by trying to make some meaning of the baby's experience, and having the baby and the baby's experience "in mind" (Flaskas, 2002).

Thus, we can add to our understandings of impasse the systemic idea that the therapist loses curiosity, and that this affects the capacity to generate new meanings and narrative development, as well as affecting the family's experience of the therapist as someone who is trying to understand. A different, though strongly resonating, description from psychoanalysis would point to the loss of the therapist's capacity to think during impasse, which in turn connects to the therapist's capacity to feel contained and be containing within the therapeutic relationship.[4]

On maintaining empathic connection and emotional containment

If narrative ideas point to the crisis of storying during impasse, and if the systemic and psychoanalytic ideas are angled more towards understanding thinking and our capacity to generate meaning, how do these all ideas relate to the task of maintaining empathic connection and emotional containment?

The ideas of curiosity and the capacity to think link quite closely in their understandings to the emotional constellation of impasse. As discussed, within psychoanalytic thinking the capacity to think is integrally related to the processes of holding and emotional containment, and I have also argued that curiosity, at least when it is practised and thought of as "experience-near", should be a powerful tool of empathic connection. It is very possible that we are talking here about two sides of the same coin. Yet having said this, when I am stuck myself in impasse with clients, often what I hear first in my own frustrated or rattled internal discussions is how removed I have become from the family's experience, and how I have "lost touch" with them and their concerns. I am not sure whether it is just that it is easier to notice the failure in empathic connection first, or whether this is a more primary process in the experience of impasse—at any rate, it is often more frequently the "presenting edge" of the therapist's experience of impasse.

Conversely, I am not sure whether the first port of call in shifting yourself as a therapist is to free the story, which then allows you to be more emotionally in touch with the family, or whether you start by becoming more in touch with what may be happening for yourself and the family, which then allows you to free your thinking. With any luck, of course, it can be both.

Larner essentially opts for the idea that it is both, for he suggests that within therapy, the narrative that is being constructed itself acts as an emotional container for the therapeutic relationship. In a peculiar way, Stephen Frosh (1997) gestures to a similar idea even though he does this in the context of a strong critique of the limits of narrative ideas. He writes of working with a family that has been through a tragedy, and says that the main part of the work is not the development of a new narrative as such. In this kind of situation, he says, to the extent that narrative helps, it does so by flagging the therapist's continuing attempt to maintain meaning, to understand, in a situation in which meaning seems to have gone from the family's world (Frosh, 1997).

In a third, but quite different, contribution, Peter Rober (1999) gives a very rich discussion of impasse and the therapist's use of self. He uses social constructionist rather than narrative or psychoanalytic ideas, and frames impasse as a break in the circle of meaning. In his discussion of the therapist's use of self during impasse, his reflections move flexibly back and forth from the therapist's emotional responses and thinking to ways of using these reflections to develop different meanings and orientations to the family.

In impasse, then, there may be no either/or between continuing to think and develop narrative on the one hand, and trying to stay emotionally connected on the other. The activity of thinking and languaging and making meaning, and of trying to wonder about what is happening for ourselves and our clients, is one way in which we also try to stay emotionally connected. In short, in impasse we can use the power of the convergence between languaging and relating to others, and value as well the power of language to name and "hold" our emotional experience. Although the postmodernist influence within family therapy has highlighted the power of language to construct experience, it may be impoverishing to confine our understandings of language to (just) the power of construction. Language constructs experience, but at the same time it also represents and symbolizes experience. Thus, there is no need for an either/or between construction and representation, and it may well be that the powerfulness of the human communication of language lies precisely in this convergence. It is for this reason that the processes of thinking and languaging are themselves related to emotional experience and the ability to both feel contained and be containing.

Conclusions—on reflective practice and the use of self

This chapter has explored impasse with a view to generating understandings about the therapist's position during impasse. It began with a description of impasse as problematic stuckness in the process of therapy and therapeutic change, tracking the significance of the emotional experience of impasse for both the family and the therapist. The fear of failure frequently accompanies impasse and can trigger intense feelings of blame and shame, which in turn makes the therapist vulnerable to anti-therapeutic sequences in their work with the family. In moving to a different level of description about the emotional and interactional constellation of impasse, the chapter then explored understandings offered by narrative and systemic and psychoanalytic ideas, in particular the ideas of narrative closure, and the challenge to curiosity and the capacity to think. These understandings were then tied back to the task of maintaining empathic connection and emotional containment.

So what might all this mean about the challenge of impasse and the therapist's position in the interactional constellation of impasse? At the very least, the discussion strongly supports a plea for reflective practice during impasse, and for an orientation towards impasse that uses the messiness of our involvement. This means the development of a discipline of reflection that challenges ourselves about own stuckness during impasse. Supervision should also invite this kind of reflection, though sometimes people speak of "internal supervision" as a way of recognizing that this process does not necessarily need the external context of supervision. Rober (1999) uses the metaphor of "inner conversation" as a way of distinguishing this "internal" therapist reflection from the "external conversation" with the family in the therapy, though he also notes that the "inner conversation" that the therapist has with her or himself, or in the presence of colleagues, or in supervision, will itself begin the process of moving to more external forms.

The discipline of reflection or "inner conversation" can take a number of forms. We can notice and put words around our own emotional responses, assuming that these responses make some kind of sense even if they are in the immediate time unhelpful in maintaining, or are even damaging, the therapeutic relationship. We can try to make sense of our emotional responses in light of the family's struggle and their emotional dilemmas, and in this way actively work toward bridging our experience to the family's dilemmas. We can think about the family's fear of failure, their experience of hope and despair, and the ripples of the fear of failure within the therapeutic relationship. We can force ourselves to reflect on the interactional effects of both our emotional responses and the ideas we are becoming stuck with, and to question our own role in problematic sequences within the therapeutic relationship. When we hear in our own thinking an inflexibility and closure in the way in which we understand the family, we can generate within ourselves alternate and equally plausible ideas about the family's dilemmas that enable us to be in alliance with their experience and not either enmeshed with it or in opposition to it.

In short, we can use narrative and/or systemic and/or psychoanalytic ideas to help us orientate respectfully to both our own stuckness and the family's stuckness and to challenge our limits of empathy and the effects of our own ideas and behaviour in the therapy.

Through this reflection, I would argue that we are first emotionally containing ourselves as therapists, and that this is an essential step in working toward re-establishing a containing environment in the therapy. I would also argue that we are using and not censoring the richness of our own involvement in the impasse. Moreover, regardless of the particular understandings we use to kick-start our thinking, the process of thinking about our own involvement should be used to orientate us back to the family and their dilemmas. It is to be hoped that the process of freeing our own thinking and emotionally containing ourselves helps us to put the "therapeutic" part back into the therapeutic relationship. It can also often "buy time" in the therapy relationship, which is not to make any grandiose claims about ensuring success. Sometimes, though, it is within our power to avoid therapeutic failure, and buying time can be important.

Many further questions flow from this discussion, in particular about the relationship between the therapist's internal reflection and the "outer conversation" of the therapy, the specificity of each practice experience of impasse, the openness of the therapist to the family's experience and to her or his own way of using self, and the broader repertoire of skills required by the therapist in meeting the challenge of impasse. The discussion offered in this chapter may be used as a beginning point, to draw attention to the usefulness of the therapist's experience during impasse, to confirm an orientation towards reflective practice and the use of self, and to note the diversity of ideas that may be drawn on in making sense of, and staying connected with, both the family's and our own experience during the emotional and interactional constellation of impasse.

Afterword

The first piece of practice

> When Peter Rober hears himself explode to a colleague about the father in the session, he becomes much more aware of how problematic the interaction with the father had been, and how out of touch he had been with the father's experience. In the middle of his ranting to his colleague he says something like "That man is so rigid he doesn't live any more—he's dead but he just doesn't realize it." Peter goes into the next session, and directly raises how bad he felt about how things had gone in the first session. The father begins talking about how he had felt that Peter had been provoking him. This discussion is surprising but quite free, and respectful on both sides. The father then begins to talk about the changes in himself over the past few years since he has had a very unstable and serious form of diabetes. He says he doesn't enjoy life any more, that he tries to hold on to life but feels as if he is dead already, and that he just can't bear emotions any more. This is news to the mother, the son, and the therapist, and it becomes a very different kind of session.
>
> One hears in this honest description of practice a readiness to use the messiness and involvement of the self of the therapist—rather than

censoring his anger towards the father, Peter uses it as a source of reflection about the interaction in the first session, and what he might need to do to repair it and try to create a more understanding space. Impasse is avoided, and in the father's response to the invitation to allow himself to be more understood, more sense can be made of the therapist's response. Indeed, negative though the therapist's anger had been, it showed a joining of a different kind with the emotional realities in the family, and it allowed a much more solid and real connection to be built in the therapeutic relationship and a fuller and more compassionate story about the father and his dilemmas.

The second piece of practice

My work with the couple gets seriously stuck and there is no happy ending to this piece of therapy. The counter-transference of my own identification with the wife means I effectively lose my curiosity and empathic connection with her, as I come to be taken up with trying to engage the husband. In the fluent reasonableness of the wife's complaints, I do not sufficiently listen for what is not said, and where exactly she feels she is in all this mess. And yet the stuckness that happens in the therapy also mirrors the couple's struggle—the husband's mainly silent anger at his wife's disappointment dominates the emotional space, her experience becomes distant, and neither of them are left feeling very good.

And so I come finally to have a dream about the wife. Of course my dream is about myself—dreams always are—and there are no prizes for guessing who the mad woman is! But it is interesting when at least our unconscious begins reflecting on some puzzle we have about how we are fitting with our clients' dilemmas. Too late I think "what on earth might be going on for the wife?" and recognize that my engagement with her experience is far more fragile than my engagement with her husband's experience.

I know that strictly speaking you are meant to end with a success story, but failure is often preceded by impasse, as it was in my work with this couple. Even in failure though, impasse can show the richness of the therapeutic system and therapeutic joining. But although therapeutic impasse presents real dangers, it also presents opportunities for using the richness of the therapeutic relationship, and the messiness of our involvement with our clients' struggles.

Notes

1. Rober (1999) explores this practice example in an excellent article on impasse, and some of the ideas in this article are discussed later in this chapter. See pp. 223–225 for his discussion of his work with this family.
2. I explore this practice example in a discussion of counter-transference and empathy and the therapeutic relationship (Flaskas, 2002). See pp. 154–155 and pp. 169–170 for the original discussion.
3. See Perry (1993) for a very good discussion of empathy and systemic practices.
4. Transference, counter-transference, and projective identification are other relevant psychoanalytic ideas, and they offer a very useful lens for making sense of anti-therapeutic sequences and unconscious experience during impasse. However, I have not prioritized them for discussion here, as I have explored them elsewhere (see Flaskas 1996, 1997, 2002).

CHAPTER NINE

Systems of the heart: evoking the feeling self in family therapy

David Pocock

Near the end of the first year of a psychoanalytic individual therapy, a male patient, ill for most of his adult life with depression, anxiety, and bodily pains, explains that he really doesn't mind the forthcoming holiday break. Instead, it is in his words "a perfect arrangement", since he can spend more time with his children. A few moments later he draws his knees up to his chest to cope with intense pains in his abdomen. He feels that the most comfortable position for easing the pain would be to curl up on the couch on his left side, which would mean turning his back to me. This feels impossible to carry out since he fears I would feel so rejected that I would never forgive him and our relationship would be permanently damaged. A year later, he is still unaware of any difficult feelings when this break comes round but is less physically affected. Instead, I find myself feeling tetchy and needled. Exactly two years further on, the patient—by then mostly free for several months from physical pain—is so enraged at the prospect of me leaving him that merely the sound of my breathing triggers his intense irritation.

Over those four years his irritable bowel syndrome—a matter formerly between his body and his doctors—has slowly but progressively been replaced by something new in his relationship with me: the capacity for anger and rejection and the discovery that these feelings do not destroy

> my interest in him. We come to understand that I sometimes irritate him since, among other reasons, I am not always available when he wants me. He feels more alive when he has these feelings and comes to realize that, of the two states of mind, he mostly prefers to be alive and angry rather than sick, depressed, and compliant. Over subsequent months he begins to find that this new capacity to feel anger and to reject means that he can discriminate between things that he likes and things that he doesn't like. These choices increasingly define him as a person and soon another feeling is added to his repertoire that he describes as joy.

Where has this emergent aspect of the patient—his capacity for anger and rejection and feeling alive—come from? To what extent has it been made in the therapy and to what extent has it been found? If found, then where did it go and why is it back?

I am starting with this highly abbreviated case example in order to begin to illustrate something more easily seen in the longer time frame and narrower focus of individual psychoanalytic psychotherapy but constantly experienced in the immediacy and complexity of family therapy: that what the feeling self can be is continuously negotiated within the context of the relationship with others and that what the relationship with others can be is continuously negotiated by the feeling selves.

I am using this awkward term "feeling self" reluctantly. I am doing so to emphasize the ordinary human capacity for feelings and the way that the self is regulated, both internally and in relationships, on the basis of which feelings come to be experienced as acceptable in both domains. I would prefer simply to use the term "self" throughout, but this seems currently too much identified with the more cognitively framed relational or narrative self of contemporary family therapy (Gibney, 1996). In other words I fear that "self" can't at present be relied on to carry the additional meaning of thoroughgoing emotionality.[1]

In this chapter I briefly re-examine concepts of self-in-relationship, drawing on perspectives from systems, relational psychoanalysis, object relations, attachment, infant research, and social constructionism. I use these ideas to elaborate two notions: first, that each self in the family therapy room (including the therapist) is involved in a profound moment to moment negotiation of the nexus of relationships between selves and, second, that each self is simultaneously adapting to this between-ness through processes of self-regulation.

I am using the term *ethos* (modified from Bateson, 1972, and Krause, 1993) for this dynamic product of meeting selves. Ethos is seen here as that which is made by embodied minds operating within the greater between-ness of culture. It is co-created by the participant selves at all levels of interaction, including those outside of consciousness. It encodes the negotiated range of acceptable and unacceptable feelings and the associated behaviours of the participants. Ethos includes conserved patterns and regularities as well as novelty and constant re-appraisal. This is not just an issue for therapy: when two or more people are relating—no matter how briefly—they are negotiating ethos.

My use of this term, to a greater or lesser extent, has a family resemblance to some other terms: "intersubjective" (Benjamin, 1999; Stolorow & Atwood, 1999), "joint action" (Shotter, 1993), "analytic third" (Ogden, 1994) "cotransference" (Orange, 1995) and "shared family holding" (Scharff & Savege Scharff, 1987). But it is the negotiated emotionality of between-ness that I wish to emphasize. In short, ethos is the emotional micro-culture of everyday relationships.

While each self in interaction makes up and changes aspects of the ethos by moment to moment participation, the ethos in turn acts as context for who each participant self can be at any moment through processes of self-regulation or longer term adaptation. Within a therapy setting, the self of the therapist, like all others present, both helps to make the ethos within the ethos-selves system and is simultaneously affected in the possibilities of who he or she can be by the ethos. It is through awareness of these possibilities—especially by the therapist noticing pressures for emotional self-regulation—that potentially important new ideas about the family system can develop.

Theoretical intersections

Postmodern ideas of a relational, narrative, or dialogical self that is empty—other than that which is made through relationship—are usually positioned in opposition to the autonomous self which, the argument goes, is identified with modernism (Gergen, 1991; Rosenbaum & Dyckman, 1995). The postmodern self is in the ascendant in family therapy and a major part of its popularity is the considerable optimism for change that it implies. It may feel churlish to gainsay an idea capable of generating such hope, but there are other voices in family therapy, not so much defending the modern autonomous self (which in any event, at least in psychoanalysis, is mostly a straw man) but doubting that the fully relational self sufficiently encompasses the experience of being human (Flaskas, 2002). Frosh (2002) for example, sceptical of the extent of claims for re-storying, notices the remarkable tenacity with which some sense of personal identity is held on to—for example, that even damaging self-denigration is preferred to the terror of self-dissolution.

Alongside this apparent polarity of the relational and autonomous self is a small but emergent collection of ideas in family therapy from therapists trying to hold the tension between post-modernism and modernism rather than allowing its collapse into opposites (Flaskas, 2002; Larner, 2000; Pocock, 1995, 1997). Flaskas (2002), in line with Frosh, argues that there are limits to the fluidity of self and explores a dialectic between the interior–autonomous self and the relational self. Paterson (1996) covers similar ground and sees autonomous and relational selves as opposite sides of the same coin.[2]

Resisting the split into modern and postmodern gives a wide border zone in which ideas from many sources can be allowed, spaghetti-like, to intersect and drift apart. In this uncommitted place, theoretical integration and the coherence of one's therapeutic model are lower orders of priority than thinking potentially useful thoughts and using these in as helpful a manner as possible in the unfolding of the work. That said, if we believe that our experience of the world is made up of what-is-there-and-what-we-make-of-it then it is worth paying particular attention to ideas that, despite their different origins, seem to converge. This is, of course, a social process of creation but, with reality never far away, it is also a social process of discovery.

From these convergences my sketch of the inter-relationship between self and ethos can be drawn quite simply. The human baby, as a consequence of the evolution of a large brain, is born developmentally early and therefore in a state of considerable need of protection, food, warmth, and the everyday cherishing that we recognize as part of ordinary parenting. The infant is no passive recipient of such care but is capable of communicating a wide range of strong feelings such as joy, love, and contentment when its needs are met and distress, rage, and despair when they are not. A reasonably attuned, reliable, and containing response to these communications gives rise to a secure attachment that sustains the infant through the lengthy and potentially anxiety-provoking period of dependency. A feature of secure attachment is for a child to be able to express freely—within a given cultural context (Gergen, 1991; Krause, 1993; Rothbaum, Rosen, Ujiie, & Uchida, 2002)—a wide range of feelings. The autonomous secure parent is able both to respond to these as signals of need and to help bear the feelings for the infant when they threaten to overwhelm the young mind (Kozlowska & Hanney, 2002).

This, so far, familiar account has the child's development somewhat passively embedded in the care environment—a child seed thriving or withering depending on the qualities of the parental soil. What needs to be added is the extent to which the infant from birth has the capacity to co-construct the care environment to try to maintain an optimum between its needs and the parental resources available for meeting them. Feelings are not then simply products of the self but attempts to connect—or to regulate connection—with another (Orange, 1995). The infant is able to be proactive in co-constructing the environment by the capacity for self-regulation (Beebe & Lachmann, 2002). Feelings that cannot be tolerated (contained) by the parents may need to be removed from the relationship in various ways by the infant so that child and parents can find tolerable ways of going on being.

Contemporary accounts of attachment support the centrality of this mutual process of adaptation to form a reliable attachment strategy that makes the best of the parental resources available and avoids the worst (Crittenden, 2000; Kozlowska & Hanney, 2002; Sloman, Atkinson, Milligan, & Liotti, 2002). Indeed, in disorganized attachment styles, associated with severe unresolved parental loss and trauma, it seems to be the impossibility of establishing any kind of reliable adaptive ethos that is so disorientating (Green & Goldwyn, 2002).

While many forms of parents–child ethos may be good-enough, more extreme mutual adaptations in which infant feelings are cut off (Bentovim & Kinston, 1991) somatized (McDougall, 1989), or pushed outwards through projective identification (Box, Copley, Magagna, & Moustaki, 1994) may lead to a depletion of the child self. This may make itself known as unwanted compensatory behaviour that may form part of the presenting problem. For example, in the situation of an unsupported depressed parent the infant may regulate the extent of his or her neediness by experiencing need itself as bad and the ethos between parent and child may be that of mutually negotiated low levels of demand and supply. Only when a second child is born—perhaps into a more supported and robust family environment—might the first child be freer with its rage.

A baby may learn to avoid rejecting a parent (not wanting what the parent wants) if, for the parent, this triggers walled-off traumatic memory of feeling unwanted (Kingston & Bentovim, 1981; Bollas, 1987). This otherwise manageable ethos might then prove difficult for a child in establishing a strong sense of identity (what-is-me compared with what-is-not-me). In a more complex situation a son may initially live comfortably within the family ethos of not minding the loss of a father who was violent to his mother. However, the cost may be that the son manages the pain of not being with his father through becoming like him (Goldner, Penn, Sheinberg, & Walker, 1990). Angry challenges[3] to the mother may then trigger overwhelming emotional memories of the father for both, leading to uncontainable levels of destructive rage. Here the ethos may become dominated with an enactment of feelings in relation to the father's violence and the parental care aspect of the ethos may break down into continuous disruption and disrepair.

In the case example at the beginning of this chapter, the patient's mother had been brought up in a family where extreme violence and rejection were commonplace. The relationship between her and her husband was distant and hostile and, understandably, she seems to have been depressed and overwhelmed. The father seems to have taken little interest in the care of his son. One crucial aspect of the early ethos established between my patient and his mother, as far as can be understood from his experience, is that provision of care was contingent on him managing not to mind lengthy periods of being left alone as a baby. Any protest on his part was met by retaliation through abandonment or threats of abandonment and he became entirely compliant although frequently ill. It seems not to have been sufficient for him to keep his feelings to himself but a more extreme self-regulation seems to have been necessary to help maintain a survivable ethos between he and his mother, which was to cut off from consciousness all ordinary feelings of anger and rejection. Instead, these seem to have been sequestered in the body through somatization.

There is an important point to make here—that the boundary between the conscious and dynamic unconscious mind of each subject is recursively linked to the intersubjective (Stolorow & Atwood, 1999). The choice of who we can be and what we can think and feel are not then simply ours to make consciously but instead is shaped to a considerable degree unconsciously in the context of ethos. The tipping point for this fluid boundary between conscious and unconscious is the perception of emotional acceptability or non-acceptability. In systems of the heart the safer we are the less we have to hide from others and ourselves.

Ethos and the therapeutic relationship

In individual, couple, or family therapy a new ethos is formed when the therapist joins and participates in the emotional life of the session. New possibilities for being arise when participant selves experience a therapeutic micro-culture in which blame and condemnation of strong feelings and the behaviours that enact or replace such feelings are eschewed in favour of a search for emotional understanding (Orange, 1995; Pocock, 1997). Aspects of the feeling selves of the participants, kept out of mind in the interests of adaptation, may be evoked when the therapist makes him or herself available to be affected and to think in the newly forming ethos of the therapeutic relationship (Box, Copley, Magagna, & Moustaki, 1994). In Shotter's (1993) "knowing of the third kind" it is the capacity for people to influence each other "in their being" that forms the basis for other kinds of joint action. In systems of the heart, participants are not just partners in conversation but engaged in mutually moving and being moved with the totality of themselves (Hoffman, 2002; White, 2000).

I have a strong memory of one family session from ten or more years ago when working as a member of a team behind the screen. I don't recall the reason for the referral and almost no factual details other than that the referred problem related to a daughter. What has remained in my mind is a visual memory of a tanned, fit, and relaxed-looking father and, in striking contrast, a mother and two daughters looking ill, unkempt, and depressed. Every aspect of their presentation, including the meaning they gave to their difficulties, supported this healthy/ill divide between the father and the others. Only the referral letter from the GP gave a different picture—that the father had some months previously been diagnosed with a serious and, most probably, terminal illness. Everyone in the family knew this fact; they knew we knew this fact, and yet the overwhelming feeling was of the impossibility of speaking of this openly with the family. To do so felt, among the team members, akin to killing the father. But more than this, completely against the grain of our therapeutic knowledge, was a powerful feeling that his illness was entirely irrelevant to the difficulty for which they were seeking help. Now I would say that the family ethos required the promotion of father as healthy by every means possible including self-regulation through loss of health and distracting symptoms in other family members and, above all, through a need to stay silent to maintain the irrelevance of the issue. In the family–team ethos we were also struck dumb.

In this extreme case it was not difficult to be moved. But I wish to suggest that the therapist is moved in all therapeutic encounters. The difficulty may come in noticing this and finding potentially useful meaning in it. Some of the most useful moments come at the beginning of a first meeting but can easily slip away in the preoccupying business of settling into the session. Collectively and individually family members will have been anxiously anticipating this meeting and conscious and unconscious fantasies will begin to gather in relation to the meeting itself and particularly in relation to the therapist (and/or team). The therapist will undergo a similar conscious and unconscious process fed by his or her prior experiences and whatever information is available at referral stage. Ethos begins from the first mutual glance in the waiting room. It is built out of these preliminary fantasies but modified in the enormous complexity of meeting each person through feedback processes of confirmation and discomfirmation and the gathering of new fantasies and feelings.

There is, in other words, an awful lot going on and a great deal for the therapist to hold as competently as possible. It is, therefore, a difficult time for the therapist to attend to disruptive feelings that are the consequence of participating in the newly forming ethos. These disruptions often work against the attempts of the therapist to be competent and so there is a natural tendency to not give them thinking space. And yet it is in this ruffling of the therapist that understanding can begin.

> I was already feeling somewhat rattled before meeting Amy, aged thirteen, and her mother for a single session to assess urgency. I had been searching for the case file and it had turned up only five minutes before the appointment, giving me time only for a cursory reading of the referral letter and no opportunity to reflect on the information. When I introduced myself in the waiting area I was met by broad, anxious smiles from both mother and daughter. It felt like an unusually long walk to my room and they chatted brightly to each other behind me, which seemed to add to my tension. I couldn't seem to steady myself through my usual introductions and rituals of starting the first session and felt both incompetent and disengaged.
>
> Within a few minutes matters went from bad to worse when it dawned on me (accompanied by a small surge of panic) that I had forgotten the name of the daughter and, try as I might, I couldn't bring it to mind. This is not unprecedented but what was particularly unusual in me was a great reluctance to own up. This was partly professional pride—I didn't want to look as inept as I was feeling—but my forgetting also felt unforgivably uncaring. After several minutes in which I hoped fruitlessly that the mother would mention her daughter's name I decided to come clean. "I'm so sorry, this is stupid of me but I have forgotten your name." This, too, was somewhat unusual. I wouldn't normally put myself down since this might require someone in the family to feel sorry for me and inhibit their freedom to feel about me as they wished.
>
> There was, however, an immediate easing of tension at this point. I felt more my usual self and was able to think. In the ethos developing between the three of us, my self-regulated feeling of incompetence together with the confession of ineptness helped, I think, to free mother and daughter from anxiety that they would be judged. Having revealed that I was no paragon of competence the emotional climate between us became more accepting and we all seemed somewhat restored.

Amy explained that she had been feeling very low for no obvious reason. She had been getting into a lot of angry confrontations with teachers at school and had been excluded on five occasions in the last year. She also confessed with considerable shame that she had been cutting her arms. In exploring the history of the difficulties, her mother quickly explained that Amy had no problems at junior school but things quickly started to go downhill as soon as she started secondary school. I explored what else might have been happening around this time and the mother told me that Amy's grandmother had died. They had, according to the mother, a close relationship. Soon afterwards Amy's elder sister returned to the family, bringing her young son, and several months after that Amy's mother began a new relationship and, shortly afterwards, he too joined the family.

I noted all these losses through death and displacement but noted some special emphasis on the grandmother and asked Amy how she felt the loss of the grandmother had affected her. She began to cry quite freely but, when her mother looked at her, the mother too filled up with tears and suddenly Amy stopped herself crying and the mutual anxious smiling behaviour of the walk up the corridor was reinstated. I realized at that point that I had been organized to assume that the death of the grandmother was a loss only for Amy. I hadn't registered at all that it was the mother's mother who had died. I pointed out my misunderstanding and said to the mother "So that was a great loss for you also." She agreed and looked sad. I was aware of Amy anxiously monitoring her mother's expression and I began to consider the extent to which Amy had begun to take responsibility for her mother's well-being and how my initial loss of competence and self-esteem might, through unconscious identification with Amy, be linked to this ethos of parentification (Boszormenyi-Nagy & Krasner, 1986; Byng-Hall, 2002).

Rather than ask Amy whether she worried about her mother (since the only answer from her perspective that would not worry her mother would probably be "No") I told them that I was getting the feeling that Amy worried a lot about her mother and wondered what they made of that. Amy's mother agreed in a manner that conveyed that she might not need so much consideration from her daughter. Amy was then able to speak a little about her concern for her mother, who had been often been depressed over the preceding two years. However, Amy quickly moved on to say that she also felt responsible for her father and this felt a more comfortable topic for mother and daughter. He had lived alone since leaving the family several years previously and she felt she had to visit him regularly or he too would get depressed. He "moaned" if she didn't go but really she would prefer sometimes to be off with her friends.

After a while, sensing that the ethos would now allow some of the parentification to be challenged, I said what a pain it was to have to be so concerned about both her parents and wondered if she needed to take the whole business of being a selfish teenager far more seriously. She laughed and said, with what I took to be a roguish pride, that "unselfish" wouldn't be one of the things she would be known for at school among her teachers. I felt she was much freer and robust in talking about her school self than her home self. I then asked her what she thought she was known for among her teachers. I felt her withdraw a little at that point and realized that, despite the bravado, her "bad reputation" was painful for her. When I acknowledged this, the connection between us was restored and she was able to move on to speak of her reputation in more general terms.

She had been a "quiet girl" all the way through junior school but she had now made quite "a name for herself" for anger and defiance with teachers, which in many ways she was sorry about, because it was hard to get out of. I felt surprisingly sad at this point and thought that Amy might be very lonely. I said that it can be horrible to be at a new school when no one knows your name and that sometimes the need to be recognized can feel more important than the need to be well behaved. She agreed and looked very sad and thoughtful and I felt that she was, for the first time in the session, allowing both me and her mother to be compassionately in contact with her lonely self.

The ethos at this point had become appropriately parental with due consideration (Boszormenyi-Nagy & Krasner, 1986) now available to Amy. I sensed that the mother was, however, stronger than Amy assumed. I felt that Amy might have defended herself against her loneliness and vulnerability by perceiving these aspects of herself—through projective identification—in her parents, thereby increasing her perception of her parents' vulnerability and intensifying the system of parentification.

In this emotional climate it now seemed possible to risk suggesting that Amy might also have felt forgotten at home, given that her grandmother had died, her mother had a new partner, her sister had rejoined the family, there was a new baby in the family, and she felt she had to look after her parents. Amy seemed hesitant but her mother helpfully affirmed that Amy might well have felt left out. This emotional permission made it possible for Amy to begin to explain how bad and alone she had felt at times, especially when she felt her mother take her new stepfather's side against her.

Gradually other aspects of Amy's adaptation within the family ethos became possible to understand. What, I asked, had she done with the hurt feelings and anger that usually go with feeling unimportant? Had she been able to get those known about within the family? Had she been able to feel furious with her mother, for example? Both agreed that Amy had not been able to do that. Amy said she had been aware that her mother wasn't very happy with the new partner and this, together with Mother's grief at the death of her mother, made Amy feel that she must try hard not to add to her mother's upset.

I asked the mother whether she felt she truly needed that much looking after by her daughter or could she, in fact, cope with some good teenage anger? She replied warmly and very robustly that she didn't need looking after at all and that she really wanted her daughter to be happy and to enjoy herself even if that meant she was more difficult at home.

I said that I was very glad to hear it (and it did feel quite believable that the mother could rise to the challenge of surviving ordinary anger). I explained that angry hurt feelings that can't be expressed have to be hidden and that perhaps Amy cutting herself was an attempt to keep the hurt out of their relationship. But, I said, hurt needs recognition and sometimes cutting is the only way to achieve this if it is being dealt with alone. I explained that the reason children are often protective of their parents is because they are trying to protect them from their own furious feelings and I wondered if, instead, Amy had also used the teachers as expendable targets for her rage at feeling unimportant at home. They were both able to accept that this might be the case. Amy added thoughtfully that some of the teachers who still seemed to like her, even after she hated them, were the ones she got on with best now. This seemed to be a message to her mother and I agreed that we as human beings do seem to trust most those who can accept both our loving and hating feelings.

At the end of the session they felt they could go on a waiting list for further work and we parted on friendly terms. Only after they had left did I become fully aware of the significance of forgetting Amy's name and especially the feeling that this was unforgivably uncaring and could not be confessed. Outside of my conscious awareness I had been moved to feel how terrible it was for Amy to be forgotten and this was, perhaps, the only way this knowledge could be communicated. But I felt the system of the heart had registered this "unthought known" (Bollas, 1987) somewhere in my mind, allowing me to feel sadness and then compassion for Amy's lonely, hurt, angry self which, through destructive self-regulatory processes of recognition at school and hurting her body, had been kept out of her relationships at home.

Notes

1. Although I am using the terms "emotions" and "feelings" interchangeably I prefer the latter both for its widespread usage and because it seems more suited to describe a pre-Cartesian unity of bodily sensation, mood, cognition, and interpersonal communication. For example, the statement "I feel gutted" contains all of the above facets.
2. For a full discussion see Frie, 2003.
3. Containment of destructive rage in children requires more than parental empathy but a benign authority that can meet the infantile wish to destroy without parental collapse or retaliation. See, for example, Benjamin (1999) who, from an analytic and feminist perspective sees this robust meeting of destructive rage as essential in order that a child can move from seeing the mother as an extension of his or her own wishes (an object) to experiencing her as an equivalent but separate subject. See also Minuchin & Fishman (1981) and Byng-Hall (1995) on the importance of benign hierarchy and parental coalition.

CHAPTER TEN

Shame and the therapeutic relationship

Ellie Kavner and Sue McNab

Stories about emotion were not privileged in the development of systemic therapy with the interest being focused instead on communication patterns, life cycle issues, transgenerational patterns and belief systems. The move from the metaphor of systems to language has re-activated attention to emotions and the ways they are expressed within relationships. For ourselves, we have reflected upon our interest in working with communication at an emotional level. We have connected to the idea of Greenberg and Paivio (1997) that meaning is emotion based and that emotions both move and inform us. The expression of emotions may provide a signal to the therapist about what may be significant to the client and a "directional compass" (Greenberg & Johnson, 1994) about where and how to intervene.

Helmeke and Sprenkle (2000) have researched those moments in therapy that both clients and therapists feel were particularly significant and change related. They concluded that focusing and refocusing on subject material that is emotionally important to a client seems to be a key factor related to the occurrence of such pivotal moments. In a similar way, Maher (1988) produced a "good moment" list of therapeutic moments, of which six out of the twelve categories were emotion based, including expressing a high level of emotion towards the therapist.

In this chapter we are focusing on one particular but powerful emotion: shame. We initially became interested in the power of shame through our work with mothers and daughters where there have been traumatic experiences that have fostered shameful feelings (McNab & Kavner, 2001). We are working to understand more about shame—its definition, its relationship to ideas of self, family, community, and the way in which thinking about the influence of shame can enhance the therapeutic relationship. We will be thinking about the shameful stories that clients bring and elaborate our ways of working with these. We also explore our ideas about therapists' own shame and the way our stories and clients' stories interact within the therapeutic relationship.

Shame as an emotion

Theories of emotion have trodden a long and diverse path and their elements have been much debated. Are emotions simply Darwinian primitive states of physiological arousal, or are they more complex entities, inseparable from thought and thus from social and cultural contexts, as originally proposed by Aristotle?

While rarely mentioned in the family therapy literature, shame has been more fully explored within the psychoanalytic therapies. For example, in her very recent study of shame in context, Susan B. Miller (1996), a psychoanalytic psychologist, defines shame as a family of related emotions (Miller, 1996, p. 7). She highlights these groups of experience: feeling inadequate, in disarray, not comfortably exposable to others; the urge to hide, silence or reform the disturbed self; embarrassment, humiliation, disgrace, and the idea of the diminished self. Miller also identifies shame as the experience of feeling ashamed of oneself, or viewing oneself as flawed.

Guilt and shame are often linked as experiences and so it is important to differentiate them. Shame differs from guilt in that guilt supposes an understanding that one's behaviour can harm another or cause damage through the "violation of a valued standard" (Miller, 1996, p. 15). Guilt allows the possibility to make amends—"I made a mistake"—whereas shame arises from the consideration of how our behaviours reflect on ourselves—"I am a mistake" (Karan, 1992, p. 48). Shame stops the behaviours of confident social interaction. Anything can evoke shame if it is thought to imply something about our character or the way we are divided from others. Shame can link to anxiety, through internalizing the contempt of others, or depression—the feeling of failure, inadequacy, not being loved enough or successful enough.

For other psychoanalytic thinkers, the origins of shame can be found in the facial mirroring between mother and infant. A face that is not responsive is disturbing to the baby, who may withdraw in a way that gives an impression of being a precursor of shame (Broucek, 1982; Mollon, 2002). Repeated experiences of psychological needs going unmet may lead to those needs being concealed and the development of a "false self" in the belief that the more authentic feelings (the true self) will not be recognized or accepted. So shame acts to inhibit honest communication between people—it involves "a hole where our connection to others should be" (Mollon, 2002, p. 23). Kohut (1972) draws on the work of Sartre (1956) who, within philosophy, described the powerful experience of becoming the "object of the other's look" that can leave us feeling vulnerable and exposed. If such looks, particularly in childhood, are actively shaming, Kohut argues that they influence the development of positive self-esteem and may result in chronic rage or depression.

Shame and the therapeutic relationship came to the attention of another group of psychodynamic therapists through the work of practitioners in the 1970s. Helen Block Lewis (1971) recognized through her research on the differing cognitive experiences of shame and guilt that shame was omni-present and powerful in the therapeutic relationship. Therapy may aggravate shame due to its power imbalances. Mollon (2002) emphasizes that some aspects of the psychoanalytic encounter can evoke shame and impede the therapeutic process. Block Lewis began to think that the therapeutic task was to enable the articulation of attitudes and feelings about oneself that are hidden, thereby challenging self-contempt and feelings of defect while remaining in connection with the client through empathic affirmation. Her work was influential in the relational ideas of the Stone Centre and here the developing themes were mutuality, empathy, the development of authenticity, and helping therapists understand the way that shame can result in disconnection between client and therapist.

All these ideas drawn from the psychoanalytic arena are useful in broadening our understandings of shame and the experience of shame within the therapeutic process. However, in the past few decades, theories of emotion have also been placed in the socio-cultural domain rather than remaining solely "within the province of physiology, psychology or philosophy" (Coulter, 1996, p. 120). Coulter proposes that such socio-cultural dimensions are primary and that "we cannot even begin to identify the emotion we are dealing with unless we take account of how a person is appraising an object or situation" (Coulter, 1996, p. 121)—that is, the context in which the emotion arises. Shame may also, therefore, be understood as functioning through the societal and cultural transmission of beliefs and values and influenced by dominant discourses and power imbalances. Lutz posits that emotion is "about social life rather than internal states" and talks of its "close involvement with issues of sociability and power" (Lutz & Abu-Loghod, 1990, p. 2). She challenges us to consider how emotions, as physiological forces, came to be located within individuals and whether this "psychobiological" frame has been used as a locus of social control.

The attributes of emotions, such as desires, beliefs, and judgements are therefore not necessarily "natural", nor are they solely internal to the individual's experience—they are determined and shaped by the cultural beliefs and values of the particular communities in which they are embedded. So, to comprehend shame, you need to understand the cultural stories recounted about personal success, pride, and admiration as well as those told about humiliation, disgrace, and inadequacy. While we may all, to some extent, internalize the powerful societal beliefs that serve to control us through shaming practices, minority or powerless cultures can be further diminished in the process of comparison, idealization and inequality. Indeed, from within the family therapy field, Parry (1998) encourages us to access the intensity of emotions to help people reflect on the emotional impact that their actions, cognitions, and feelings are having on others in the system. He quotes the idea of philosopher Martha Nussbaum (1998) that stories teach us how to feel, and refers to Gergen (1994) in arguing that emotions "are the activity of relationships" (Parry, 1998, p. 69) and "when emotions are allowed entrance into a story shared by two or more people, they become the means for each person to reach across to the other" (Parry, 1998, p. 77).

The idea that emotions can be understood within the context in which they are expressed is a comfortable fit with systemic thinking and may be added to insights from other fields. Hence, for us, shame as an emotion is interrelational and operates at a number of different levels from the socio-political, the familial and relational to the internal states of mind and bodily physiological responses. This frame allows for exploration of the mutual influence and impact of shame within a relationship—whether it be within family relationships or therapeutic relationships—and how in turn these relational interactions are shaped by wider cultural shaming discourses. We will now be assuming and drawing on this frame in the following explorations of clients" shame and shame in the therapeutic relationship.

Clients' shame

Clients' stories of shame

Clients come to therapy with personal histories where shame may be a constitutive part of their emotional experience affecting their identity and self regard. This might include experiences of abuse and other victimization. We can think about this using a cultural lens, acknowledging that we live in a society where there are power imbalances and privacy is privileged over exposure of violence. Within the dominant culture, there is an emphasis on individual blame, responsibility, and achievement in place of communal and cultural responsibility. Also, we believe that individuals internalize wider societal/cultural shame stories relating, for example, to gender, race, and religion and these serve as a method of social control. In approaching the therapist, a client may feel the ambivalence of seeking to be understood but fearing exposure of hidden, shaming aspects of themselves and their story.

Maria and Antony Scarpino, from Venezuela and Italy respectively, came to our clinic with their fourteen-year-old daughter, Carina, who

> was very sad and isolated following months of bullying at school, resulting in her refusal to return. She also refused to consider alternative schools. The family were feeling desperate; they were conscious of being immigrants and valued education highly for future success but also to aid in presenting a "respectable" face to the majority culture. The early focus was on Carina—helping her return to a different school with more courage, safety plans in place, increasing her sense of agency. Despite their love and interest in Carina, it proved difficult to use the resources of both mother and father in helping her. Maria was the chief spokesperson for the parents, with better English and more confidence; mostly she came alone with her daughter. We talked about how Maria experienced shame and anger as an immigrant mother in a previous school. She felt her concerns were not given sufficient attention and her children suffered from discrimination. She battled to stand strongly for her children but she felt very sad inside. We learned that coming to the clinic took courage for fear of intensifying the shamefulness.

Sometimes there are different layers of shaming stories that unfold:

> Jo and Richard Adams brought their two young children, Freddie and Sarah, for help following the stillbirth of their third child, Helen. Jo was experiencing an extreme grief reaction to this loss and appeared lost in herself. It was very difficult for the therapist to connect with her and form any sort of therapeutic relationship. Very slowly, however, Jo began to speak of the shame she felt about her baby's death—a feeling shared by other family members. Freddie, aged six, had spoken of not wanting another brother or sister as he felt "there would not be enough love to go around". He was feeling very responsible, believing that his bad thoughts had caused Helen's death. Freddie spoke of wanting to join Helen. The picture was further complicated for Jo as the sudden bereavement had put her back in touch with the abuse she had suffered as a child. This story added another layer of shame that could not be spoken.

The complexity increases further when family members sit down together possibly unaware of each other's hidden shaming constructs and where the therapist is prevailed upon to form a number of therapeutic relationships and to be sensitive to the potential for different shaming narratives.

Working with clients' shame

In thinking about the power of shame we do not anticipate its presence, but consider whether difficulties in talking and understanding the meaning of experience might reflect the influence of shame. We are aware that it may impact upon the conversations we have and perhaps the relationships we make with families. There are experiences and beliefs in all cultures that are shaming, but we remind ourselves to make no assumptions about their meaning. As in any therapeutic work we are conscious of pacing and timing. In particular we listen for cues, both verbal and emotional, to weigh up how much to intensify by helping the client to elaborate at that point, or to mark the importance of the cue or partial disclosure but return to it at a later date.

> In the Scarpino family we were curious about Maria's fear of marital separation when she denied that there had been violence in the relationship history. One of us met with Maria on her own and the story unfolded further. I asked if she thought it would help for me to understand how it might be that if Antony had not hurt her she feared violence. Maria looked at me then looked away. "Do you want to tell me what Antony might have done?" I asked. Maria smiled, looked away, then looked at me. I returned the gaze and then she said that "Antony was a very bad boy in Italy". In his adolescence and young adulthood, he was a violent delinquent involved with drug dealing and violent crime, in prison many times, which was traumatic for him. Antony's migration pathway was directed by his mother—she sent him to England to "reform" and there he met Maria and never committed future crimes. However, the couple were always in fear that his shameful past would infect the present and Antony feared that if anyone found out, including his children "they would never think of me the same again".
>
> This past and its connected shame impacted on their life in many ways. Maria was always alert to the need to protect the family and worried when she witnessed Antony's outbursts of anger that his violence would be released, but felt shamed by her doubts. It transpired that Antony had become very aggressive towards his daughter when she went to secondary school because he kept fearing that his shameful past would be recreated in his daughter's life. This anger inadvertently further incapacitated his daughter's sense of self-worth and agency in her own life. Maria was then clear that it would be good to bring

Antony back to the therapy, where we could speak together in an open way about how shame had affected his own personhood and his ability to be the kind of father he wanted to be for his teenage daughter.

It is important to attend to issues of therapeutic engagement in order to enable the exploration of shaming experiences. The relational therapy practised at the Stone Centre talks of the importance of "listening into voice" stressing that "critical listening dries you up" (Judith Jordan, Workshop, Oxford Family Institute, 1998). They pay close attention to skills of listening and responding, such as nodding, maintaining eye contact, tone of voice, and active encouragement to put shame into words. We pay attention to the moments when affect is not congruent to the discourse as a trigger to our curiosity. With the Scarpino family, a more open relationship between couple and therapist was helpful in allowing different conversations to unfold and a positive model of developing relationships free from the influence of shame. We were able to think about the infiltration of shame on different contextual levels—relationship, family, work, community, society—that encouraged Antony to work towards greater openness about his past, and his strengths and weaknesses, with his children.

We introduce the idea of social and cultural influences in the shaming process and the way in which individuals construct their sense of self. These might be ideas about dominant narratives in relation to gender (for example, men's shame in being "weak" when believing they should be "strong') or ethnicity (for example, dominant white culture shaming minority cultures in relation to attributes of success and achievement), or it might be socially reinforced secrecy in relation to violence (for example, victims' feelings of responsibility for being complicit in their attack). The role of the therapist would be to introduce new meanings and to join with the individual or family in recognizing the injustices perpetuated against them. Tomm (2002) and other narrative therapists seek to honour the story of survival, uniqueness, and confidence of the individual through the use of externalization and outsider witnesses, while introducing the influence of familial or societal narratives that have increased the need to hide, to feel inadequate or diminished.

With Jo and her family, the therapist attempted to help Jo identify and acknowledge the injustices she had suffered as a child and to discover her own acts of resistance. This was painful work and shame acted forcibly to maintain its stranglehold that kept Jo silenced and isolated from her family. While the shame around the bereavement could be shared together, the shame around the abuse could not be spoken because Jo was adamant that her husband should not know. The children were very watchful of their mother. Freddie appeared particularly close to her as they shared their grief and shame together. Richard could only understand his wife's distress as a consequence of the loss and strove to keep a semblance of normality for the family. In this family, shame was so deeply rooted that it seemed impossible to shift its influence and the subsequent discourse of self-condemnation.

The dilemma for us is how to hear the shame, respect its seriousness, but not to continue the shaming process in the therapeutic relationship. When working with an Asian family where the daughter was suffering from a diagnosed major mental illness, the therapist encouraged them to be more open in their community and seek support, until she realized her ignorance about the shame brought upon families in these circumstances and that she had been underestimating the perceived potential damage to their futures.

When working with more than one person, there is the need to explore the meaning of these shameful constructions on their relationship with one other. We need to know how much is known by other family members and, if so, how they came to know this story. In considering whether to say the "unsaid", there is often a fear for the person experiencing the shame that she or he will never be viewed as the same person again by the therapist, family, and outside world.

For example, Mark and Sally Peters are a young couple seeking help with managing their eldest daughter's behaviour following the birth of the second child. Quite quickly, cracks in the marital relationship are revealed, but it is not until the sixth session that the couple feel trusting enough to respond to the therapist's innocent enquiry about how they met—with the answer that Sally was Mark's teacher and their relationship began at a time when Mark was underage. The therapist was alerted to the risk being taken in this disclosure by the rise in emotional temperature in the room and by the pause and glances between the couple before answering. These were all cues for her to be mindful that her reactions to whatever information was forthcoming might be closely monitored for censure and judgement. The impact on their relationship of its shameful origins was an imbalance in roles in which Mark could never be seen as a "man" or equal partner, and Sally had to continue to take responsibility while resenting it.

As systemic practitioners we believe in the importance of communication patterns and understand how helping our clients to alter these can lead to important changes in relationships. Emotions are another vital part of this communication and we think that when partners or other family members can see each other experiencing and expressing a new emotion this leads to them seeing and experiencing each other in new ways. For example, angry feelings can often be a mask for sadness, hurt, or shame and unveiling these can result in changes in interpersonal perceptions and hence relationships. Mark Peters' shame at failing to keep employment and care for his family led to angry outbursts and violence between the couple. When he was able to talk about these shameful feelings in a tearful manner, Sally was more willing to empathize with his situation.

Shame and the therapeutic relationship

Therapists' stories of shame

Therapists have their own version of potentially shaming experiences, both personal and professional, that they bring to the therapeutic encounter. We have been exploring how these shameful feelings and experiences of flawed identity also affect the therapist and have discovered that it can take considerable time and a shift in understanding and thinking to enable voice to be given to our own shameful thoughts and feelings. The therapist's role engenders an expectation of expertise and the ability to promote change in a wide variety of situations. We have to believe we have something to offer our clients and our only tool is ourselves. However, the work is difficult and not always successful so there is much room for self doubt and shame to creep in and a belief that someone else would make a better job of it. After all, books and articles emphasize the successful moments, not usually the moments of therapeutic failure or impasse.

> Feeling that you are failing your client by not being able to help them shift a fixed narrative is not a pleasant experience. Such impasses invite therapists to blame themselves for the lack of progress, to question their skills and to feel ashamed by their failure. Working with Jo and her family gave rise to much self doubt and to memories of other failed therapeutic encounters. Why were the questions the therapist was asking making no difference? Why was the therapist unable to reach Jo? If she failed to do this, how could the children's development be safeguarded in such difficult circumstances? At times, feelings of anger and resentment arose in the therapist, "empathy fatigue" set in and disconnection ensued. She felt at the edge of her learning and at the end of her reserves.

At times, therapists are asked to justify their authority and knowledge and this may result in them feeling deskilled and defensive, which can be further intensified when working from a position of difference. The therapist might feel advantaged or disadvantaged by virtue of class, gender, race, or cultural difference. In the family of one of the authors, there was a strong generational transmission of shaming narratives about culture and Judaism that continues to impact on her confidence. For the other author, her history of a privileged, colonial upbringing and her shame at being seen as having been "born with a silver spoon in her mouth" has meant many silent shaming moments over the years.

In working across classes and cultures, the fear of getting it wrong, of being experienced as patronizing or racist freezes creativity and risk-taking, making real connection and the possibility of rich conversations less attainable. Psychotherapy calls upon "the presence of the whole being of the therapist" (Jordan, 1997, p. 153) so when a professional mask is employed to hide our shame, the authenticity of the therapeutic relationship is again called into question. We have been greatly helped by Maxwell Mudarikiri's injunction (Workshop, Institute of Family Therapy, London, 2001) that being clumsy about matters of difference is preferable to avoiding them, together with the realization that our responsibility for uncovering oppressive, shaming stories is more critical than our own sense of shame.

Working with teams and screens further amplifies the public performance aspect of our work. All these things place high expectations on our ability to make a difference and, like our clients, expose us to the gaze of others. The potential for embarrassment and shame is high. These stories may never have been shared in training, and kept secret from the supervisor or colleagues. They may affect the stories we tell about ourselves as family therapists and may serve to keep us in the professional shadows or working harder to impress.

Sometimes, our feelings of shame lead to disconnection from the client and what is happening in the room. Disconnection can occur on a number of different levels. At a physical level, we might experience a flooding sensation, blushing, or an increase in heartbeat. This may lead us to avert our eyes or change our body posture for fear of exposure or humiliation. In turn this may send the wrong signal to our clients about our ability to understand their shaming stories. At a cognitive level, shame may affect our ability to think, and/or we might become more preoccupied with our own inner dialogues: for example, "if you only knew", "don't rumble me", "this makes me feel bad—what do I do now". Here our inner talk is used, not in the service of the client, but to protect ourselves. Disconnection may also show at the behavioural level, where shame may stop us listening, asking questions, being curious, taking risks, losing empathy. We may also become defensive and angry and even find ourselves instructing clients to change or blaming them for their resistance.

These disconnections are cues for asking ourselves questions: does this signal a connection to shame stories related to our professional identity or to our personal identity?; dare we take the risk of exposure?; which aspects of our own experiences are helpful to bring directly into the work? As therapists, we recognize that some experiences or situations are known triggers to our own personal vulnerabilities or shaming histories. In relation to other therapeutic encounters, the shame may arise from our response to the family's experience and the subsequent interweaving of client and therapist shamefulness.

The interaction of shame in the therapeutic relationship

When we consider our response to families, we as therapists may need to take a position that feels shaming.

In the work with Jo and Richard, the situation was further compounded when the need to move into a protective stance arose. Jo remained shrouded in her grief, shame, and guilt that distanced her from the needs of her growing children. The professional network became increasingly alarmed about the safety of Freddie and Sarah and discussions took place about how to intervene in the most helpful way. Jo would not consider psychiatric inpatient treatment and finally the therapist had to initiate child protection proceedings. It goes without saying that this decision reactivated shameful feelings for both therapist and clients and, unremarkably, this move into the production domain (Lang, Little, & Cronen, 1990) dealt the therapeutic relationship a mortal blow. At the subsequent session, the therapist had to weather Jo's fury, but instead of her usual practice of reaching out to the client, she experienced a closing down of empathic connection and retreated into cold silence. Although shocked by her response, any attempt to connect with her inner talk proved useless and the session and the work ended badly.

The therapist felt shamed both by the previous treatment failure and her behaviour towards the family, who were themselves paralysed by the shame of the public nature of the child protection conference. Consultation helped the therapist to consider the role that transference played in the therapeutic relationship and the placing of the therapist in the position of a mother who had failed to protect her daughter. However, it did not sufficiently explain the intensity of the feelings and the deadly power of shame to put a stop to conversations.

The move towards more transparent systemic practice has encouraged new dialogues between families and therapists that have strengthened the therapeutic relationship. It is, however, our belief that the shame that therapists feel, either by something being triggered in their own personal story, or when shaming stories on both sides of the therapeutic encounter interact together, is rarely given voice. Working in a shaming context or within shaming institutional practices can also affect the quality of the therapeutic relationship. It is not easy to open up conversations about the ways in which we hurt, humiliate, or marginalize one another as co-workers or team members. Speaking out against such customs takes courage. So, in the work with Jo and her family, the therapist and client were both suffering from the shame of oppressive practices and silenced by their own shameful emotions of failure—

perhaps a conversation that explored the mutuality of these feelings might have gone some way to repairing the therapeutic relationship.

Sometimes the sharing of the therapist's personal shaming histories in support of a family's dilemmas is possible and can be helpful:

> In the work with the Scarpino family, the therapist was reminded of the way shame was integrated into her grandparents' stories of migration and adjustment in the New World. Histories were lost and mysteries pervasive. The therapist talked about these resonances with Antony and Maria in thinking about how history can distort relationships and paradoxically harm rather than protect.

At other times, such conversations might best be conducted in the supervisory process.

The moment when client and therapist stories of shame are simultaneously activated in a session may only be momentary but the disruption in the therapeutic relationship may be serious and can be further intensified when shaming stories of diversity or traumatic experiences are echoed. Jordan (1997) addresses one of the central paradoxes in the therapeutic relationship in which the sense of unworthiness in being in connection with another, alongside the awareness of how much one wants to be connected, may lead the client to keep "shameful" parts of themselves out of the relationship in order to make and maintain the relationship.

Thus, shame is not simply one-sided, confined only to clients' stories, but may also be relational between therapist and client. Unmediated shame may result in losing the authenticity of the therapeutic relationship. The disjunction in therapeutic connection will remain until shameful feelings can be named, acknowledged, and accepted—in other words, until persons can be truly known. This, then, is the importance of an authentic therapeutic relationship.

Conclusion

We favour adopting a wide view of understanding emotions, seeing them as operating on many different levels from individual bodily sensations to discourses "created in rather than shaped by speech" (Lutz & Abu-Loghod, 1990, p. 12). We find it helpful to think about the ways in which we work on an emotional level and how that connects with other systemic ideas. In this chapter we have explored our understanding and familiarity with shame and the way that it operates on different levels from the individual construction of identity in professional and personal domains, to the institutional and societal. When working with the shame that might be significant in the dilemmas brought by clients and ourselves into the therapeutic relationship, we are alert to non-verbal communication, and to the reminder by Bertrando (2000) of the need to observe as well as listen to gain entry to people's emotional lives in a way that words cannot convey.

When working with families we are conscious of the importance of family members witnessing the intensity of each other's accounts that may give new meaning to their experience. As self-reflexivity has become an important component of systemic theory, we have come to appreciate the relevance of accessing our own inner dialogues, both at a cognitive and emotional level, and considering how these may be put to good use in the therapeutic work. Shame can create a disconnection in the therapeutic relationship that prevents meaningful and authentic engagement if not brought forth and understood.

CHAPTER ELEVEN

Relational risk-taking and the therapeutic relationship

Barry Mason

Introduction

This chapter comprises three interlinked, mutually influencing elements.

1. I am writing from a view that there are problems in the field about risk-taking and the therapeutic relationship that come out of some of the more recent developments around the construction of collaborative practices. In particular, I wish to raise some of the associated issues related to the systemic therapist's ownership of expertise and some of the disingenuousness that I think is still around in relation to this matter.
2. In particular, I wish to explore some of the thinking around the not-knowing position (Anderson & Goolishian, 1992b) and the preferred meanings that have been attached to this concept. While there has been an encouraging trend more recently (Anderson, 1997) to clarify the original thinking around the not-knowing position, I still believe that the concept can be misunderstood, not least in the very nature of the terminology

itself. In this respect I suggest in this chapter another, additional way of looking at the nature of the therapeutic relationship (and this complements the work of Silver, 1991; Larner, 2000, and Flaskas, 2002). The not-knowing position will remain with us and I am not seeking here to expunge it from the literature. I wish to offer an alternative way of looking at how the therapist owns their own position and how this influences the nature of the therapeutic relationship. For some people this may not seem a risk at all, but for many I do think it involves the risk of thinking and practising in some different ways.

3. After looking at how I think recent developments have influenced the nature of the therapeutic relationship and the place of risk within that relationship, I will offer a number of ideas for practice, both from within the therapy domain itself and from a supervisory perspective. Further, I will offer some suggestions as to how my thinking about risk and the therapeutic relationship may need to be addressed in the training of supervisors, family therapists, and systemic practitioners.

Definitions of risk-taking

If you look up in any dictionary the word "risk" you will come across the following: *to dare, to venture, to speculate, danger, threat, exposure, hazard, jeopardy, peril, ordeal, uncertainty, anxiety*. Of course, whether any of these terms describes the taking of risk depends on the person and their history, culture, life experience, and training. In addition, our ideas about what is risky may change over time. What was a risk at one point in our lives may no longer be a risk at another time, personally and/or professionally. In defining risk it is also important to note that this chapter is not about risk-taking in terms of sky-diving or driving cars fast. It is a paper about risk-taking in the context of relationships, specifically the therapeutic relationship. Our relationship with risk informs our practice and its effectiveness, and our practice and effectiveness is informed, in part, by how the nature of the therapeutic relationship is perceived by our clients (Hubble, Duncan & Miller, 1999; Lambert, 1992).

The development of the importance of the therapeutic relationship

The pioneers of family therapy were generally analytically trained. In the 1950s, however, dissatisfaction grew with how therapy and change were perceived. There developed an increasing shift to an emphasis on the interactional; that the problems and difficulties that people experience exist not only because of an intrapsychic disposition, but also because of wider contextual influences. These influences (initially concentrating on family relationships, later expanding to discourses concerning culture and society) introduced the seeds of the idea that mind—as Bateson (1979) argued—is also social, not just skull bound.

However, in wishing to establish its difference, these early pioneers, especially in the USA, rejected many of the ideas to which they had previously been attached. While family therapy was against pathologizing clients (or at least thought it was taking this view) it had no problems at all in pathologizing psychoanalysis. The emphasis for many years in family therapy was to explore the relationship between theory and technique. The nature of the self of the therapist and the nature of the therapeutic relationship was very much in the background.

This was despite the fact that in the early 1980s there was a paradigm shift from a first order to a second order perspective (Hoffman, 1985). In working from a first order perspective therapists would tend to concentrate on the nature of the problem presented to them (rather than the nature of the therapeutic relationship, the families' relationship to help, or the self of the therapist) and, one hopes, use their skills (including their preferred theoretical attachments) to contribute to useful change. Any struggles they might have would tend to be viewed in this context. And much good work was done. I do not want to get into a position here of taking the easy swipe (as is all too often heard in the field) of suggesting that first order is, somehow, intrinsically bad and second order good. While this author would describe his work as coming from a second order perspective, it is plainly disrespectful (and not very second order!) to dismiss first order ideas and practice as such. The shift to a second order perspective was a development in the field, not a shift from bad to good.

In moving to a second order perspective there emerged an emphasis that was less on finding certainty and more one of finding fit, one that included the contribution of the therapist in constructing reality. Thus, a second order perspective became defined in terms of a mutually influencing relationship; that the act of observation influenced that which is observed (Heisenberg, 1962; Von Foerster, 1990). One of the things that was seen to be important was that we should not get into what Stewart, Valentine, and Amundsen (1991) have termed premature certainty, and which Anderson and Goolishian (1988) have talked of in terms of not understanding too quickly. Cecchin's (1987) notion of curiosity also informed the developing view that the balance between what the therapist thought and what the client thought perhaps had to be revisited.

The shift from a first to a second order position, with its view that we could no longer play the role of detached observers, that we are involved in the world we observe, implied that we needed to start asking questions of ourselves and, thus, the process of therapy of which we were considered to be a part. But while a second order perspective implied such a belief, it was not until the late 1980s/early 1990s that the practice implications of the theory caught up with the theory itself.

The not-knowing position

This background became the context, then, for Anderson and Goolishian's (1992b) concept of the "not-knowing" position. In that paper they described such a position as

> a general attitude or stance in which the therapists' actions communicate an abundant genuine curiosity. That is, the therapists' actions and attitudes express a need to know more about what has been said, rather than convey preconceived opinions and expectations about the client, the problem or what must be changed. The therapist, therefore, positions himself or herself in such a way as always to be in the state of being informed by the client. [Anderson & Goolishian, 1992b, p. 29]

Elsewhere in the same article they write that "not-knowing requires that our understandings, explanations and interpretations in therapy must not be limited by prior experience or theoretically informed truths and knowledge" (*ibid.*, p. 28). I think one of the problems since this was written is that prior professional experience, prejudices, and beliefs have at times been judged as being akin to a "knowing" position, one that has been defined, more recently, by Anderson (1997) as "the delusion of understanding or the security of methodology", a somewhat one-dimensional definition as it seems to give the idea that knowing is only absolutist.

Interestingly, Anderson, in the same book, has realized that the "not-knowing" position has been taken a little too literally and that, of course, prior knowledge, experience, cultural background, amongst other factors, are important in terms of how a therapist creates a relationship with clients. She quotes Derrida (1978) who has suggested that not-knowing "does not mean that we know nothing" (Anderson, 1997, p. 137) but rather that we may not have absolute knowledge.

I would suggest that the concept of "not-knowing" has *both* contributed usefully to the development of the therapeutic relationship in systemic work *and* constrained this development. It has contributed, in the sense of helping therapists open themselves up to being influenced more by the clients' perspectives; and constrained therapists, through encouraging them (perhaps inadvertently) to refrain from expressing ideas and knowledge that might be beneficial to clients, *in addition* to taking a stance of curiosity. In writing this, there is a danger that I may come across as making this point as a polarization between curiosity and (the risk for some) of taking a position and I do not wish to place these two stances as if they are in opposition. Rather, I see them as complementary. However, from my position of being a trainer in the field, I have found myself at times coming up against therapists pulling back from offering expertise in the form of ideas, as if to do so might be seen as marginalizing the client and thus oppressive. Such concerns, in respect of race and culture led some of us to put together a book on taking risks in working cross-culturally (Mason & Sawyerr, 2002).

One of the ideas that this author treasures from systems theory is that the theory is one of mutual influence (not, it should be noted, equal influence) and that it follows that the therapeutic relationship is thus a relationship of mutual influence. Indeed, Anderson & Goolishian (1992, p. 31) themselves acknowledge that the therapeutic relationship is one of mutual influence. And while I would agree with them that we should prioritize the clients' world views, our useful influence on clients may sometimes be through saying to them, "This is what I am thinking based on some of the things you are saying here and/or my experience/research", not from a position of authoritative certainty but from a position of authoritative doubt. That is, to take the risk of stating a position. It is important that the therapeutic work be informed both by the clients' expertise and also the expertise of the therapist, including their prior knowledge and experience. It is important that we do not marginalize aspects of our own expertise, for it offers the potential of doing a disservice to clients (see also Byng-Hall, 2004).

I remember some years ago watching someone who was training as a supervisor having a mid-session discussion with the therapist and with the team behind the screen. The supervisor asked, sensitively and clearly, how the therapist was thinking about the session at this point and what ideas they had for the remainder of the time left. She (the supervisor) then asked what ideas the other members of the team had. At the end of the discussion the interview with the family continued. A similar process with the team took place after the family had left. In my feedback to this trainee supervisor the following day I said how much I appreciated her sensitivity towards the therapist and the team but that there was just one thing missing—she hadn't expressed any of her own ideas that might have been useful, particularly to the therapist—only asked questions. She replied that she had not wanted to marginalize their ideas. The supervisor was, and is, very talented and had plenty of ideas that could have been potentially useful by sharing them, without such sharing being necessarily seen as somehow dismissing supervisee expertise.

On another occasion I saw a session with a male/female couple struggling to obtain from the therapist what the latter was thinking. The more the ("not-knowing') therapist was curious the more the couple asked what the therapist thought about their situation. The couple, particularly the man, started to become frustrated. This frustration was eventually discussed. The man came from a family where he had always experienced a frustration with both his parents about not getting clear feedback as to what they were thinking. He experienced his parents as withholding help. He experienced the therapist similarly. In effect, the client had invested the therapist with a constructive ownership of power (knowledge) (Young *et al.*, 1997). The therapist, in an attempt to remove power from the relationship, only "concealed its visibility" (Guilfoyle, 2003, pp. 334).

It is this self-marginalization of aspects of the ownership and use of therapists' expertise that has led me to further develop a concept I first raised in a previously published paper (Mason, 1993)—a concept called authoritative doubt.

A position of authoritative doubt is the ownership of expertise in the context of uncertainty. It is an attempt to shift the therapist's position to acknowledging that clients pay us, indirectly or directly, to have some ideas about what may contribute to positive change. The ownership of such a position can be a constructive use of therapists' power. Clients have some rights to feel informed by the ideas of the therapist so that they may have a wider range of options and knowledge that might enable them to address the difficulties and concerns that they have brought to therapy. I stress, however, that the therapist does not get into authoritative certainty.

Lambert (1992) and Hubble, Duncan, and Miller (1999) have suggested that the quality of the therapeutic relationship as perceived by clients is considerably more important than technique in contributing to positive therapeutic outcome. I would suggest, though, that this quality of relationship is unlikely to be enhanced if we cannot widen our definition and practice about what is the meaning of expertise. It involves us owning a position of authoritative doubt and exploring the nature of risk-taking in the therapeutic relationship. I suggest in the next section that this has implications for the way therapists are trained.

Some ideas that may contribute to the development of risk-taking in the therapeutic relationship

Trust and risk

There is a general idea that you need to establish trust in the therapeutic relationship before you can take risks. While this is undoubtedly a perfectly legitimate position to take, there is a danger in this idea being limiting. In the last couple of years in my teaching and practice I have begun to see the relationship between trust and risk-taking in a different way, that of a relationship of mutual influence.

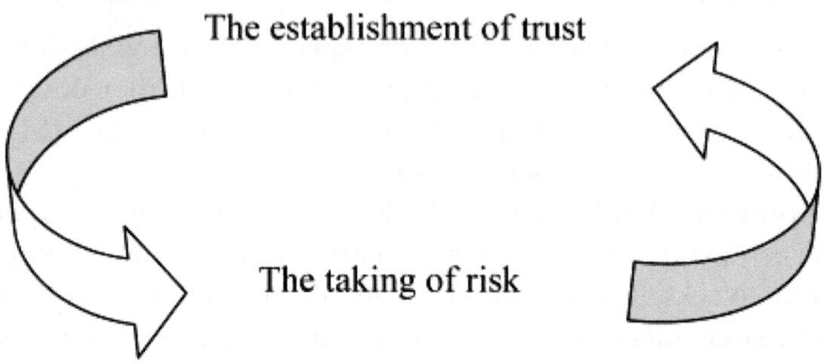

As a therapist, one needs to contribute both to the establishment of a therapeutic context where clients and therapist can feel safe enough to explore uncertainties (Mason, 1993), and to a therapeutic context where appropriate risk can be taken such that greater trust in the therapeutic relationship can develop.

Questions around the negotiation of risk-taking in the therapeutic relationship

In the last few years I have been asking questions fairly early on in the therapeutic relationship around the meaning and negotiating of risk-taking and playing safe. Some of the questions I tend to ask are as follows:

1. Suppose I were to take more risks in working with you. What advice would you give me regarding talking about an issue that you think might be uncomfortable but potentially useful/helpful?
2. If I were to really challenge you on what you've just said, what would be the most useful thing that I could say, even if it felt uncomfortable for you?
3. If you were to really challenge me on the way I was working with you, what would you say to me that might be uncomfortable for me, but potentially very useful to the way we work together in therapy?

4. Suppose I were to play safe in my work with you in that you felt comfortable but it wasn't very effective—what would that look like? What would I be doing?
5. When you are playing safe in your relationship(s) but in a way that is not satisfying, what happens? What do you do?
6. When you are taking risks in your relationship(s) and it's difficult but ultimately beneficial what happens? What do you do?

It is important to note that these questions vary in the language used; it is important to find a fit with the use of language the clients bring.

The "not the miracle question"

Although on occasion I have used it to good effect, I have, at times, been put off by the way I have heard some clinicians talk about the miracle question (Berg, 1991), as if a miracle in the therapeutic work will happen as a result of asking it. That aside, the question, if used carefully, can be very helpful. The question can be put as follows:

> Suppose that tonight while you were sleeping a miracle happened and you woke up in the morning and things were much better in your life, what would have happened? What would you notice and what would other people notice that was different about you?

In working with people with chronic illness and chronic pain (which is a specialism of the author) asking the miracle question might seem a little insensitive. Further, people are sometimes reluctant to engage in therapy. They may be there because somebody else wants them to come more than they may do. This may be linked to experiences with professionals in the past that have, from their perspective, been unsatisfactory. One of the tasks of the therapist is to explore and engage with the logic of reluctance. This has led the author to develop a new question—the not the miracle question.

The question is usually posed as follows:

> Suppose we were to work together for a number of sessions and I was to work with you in such a way as to be of little or no use to you, what would *I* have to do to get it so wrong?

Some examples of the use of the question are as follows:

(i) I see a family where the mother has been depressed for some time. She has a fifteen-year-old daughter and a ten-year-old son. I ask them the question. The mother says I would get it wrong if I thought she was "putting it on" (exaggerating or making up the depression). I ask her where that idea has come from and she says that her father has expressed the view that she is putting on the depression to get attention. When I ask the boy the question he says I would get it wrong if I insist he has to come. The girl starts to cry when I ask the question. She says that I would get it wrong if I blame her for not being able to help her mother get out of her depression. She has never said before that she feels so responsible for her mother. Her mother turns to her, takes her hand, raises it to her cheek and then gently caresses it.

(ii) I see an individual woman of forty-two and ask her the question. She says I would get it wrong if I tell her about my personal experiences as a way of trying to help her with her concerns. She tells me she has come to tell me about her, not to hear about me. (That is, don't be like my previous therapist.)

(iii) I see a family (mother, father, sixteen-year-old daughter, and thirteen-year-old son). The mother has had a chronic pain condition for many years and the hospital consultant feels there is little more that can be done beyond medication. The consultant says she is concerned about the impact on the family. In the first meeting I get the clear impression from all the family members that they do not really want to be at this meeting. Mrs A, in particular, is unhappy about some of the treatment she has had in the past. When I ask the question, Mr A replies that I would get it wrong if I wasn't able to offer some practical advice to them about how the family could help Mrs A. Mrs A says I would be of no use if I suggested that her pain was all in the mind, if I didn't believe her—"isn't that what the hospital think by referring me to you?" The daughter says that I would be of no use if I didn't realize how bad a state her mother was in, and the son said he didn't know. Apart from the son's response, the question gave information to me that was useful in ultimately gaining a mandate to work with this family. With all clients, no matter what they say in response to the question, I say to them that it is helpful for me to hear what I could do that would be potentially unhelpful. It is crucial that I explore their relationship to "help".

(iv) I see an American couple working in London. I ask them the question. The man pauses, looks at me somewhat despondently and says "Not a very can do question, is it?" Initially, I put this response down to a clash of cultures. I eventually realize, however (the question works well with other American clients), that it is very much more to do with a poor piece of therapy on my part. I had fallen in love with technique (Cecchin, workshop presentations, 1983, 1995) at the expense of staying connected with therapeutic content and process.

There is also a variation on the question which I tend to use once I perceive a trusting relationship between myself and the client(s) has been established. I often use it when we spend some time reviewing the work we have done thus far. Like the initial "Not the miracle question" used above, it is an example of authoritative doubt in action. I usually preface the question by referring to the original (not the miracle) question I will have asked earlier on in the therapy, and that I would now like to ask something similar but different.

The variation of the question is usually posed as follows:

> Suppose in the continuation of our work together *you* were to be of little or no use to yourself in the way you contributed to these meetings, what would *you* have to do to get it so wrong?

The creation of this question has been influenced, in part, by a strong belief I have about the issue of personal responsibility as part of a systemic frame of seeing, not separate from it; that the self of the person is embedded and embodied (Hardham, 1996).

An example:

> I see a man who initially only came to see me because he said that if he didn't his girlfriend said she would leave him. After a few sessions he starts to talk positively about the sessions. At a review of the work after six sessions I ask the variation. He chuckles in an engaged way and replies that he would get it wrong if he continued to blame his girlfriend for all the problems in the relationship rather than to take "a good portion of responsibility" himself—something he had not previously said.

With both the not the miracle question and its variation, I sometimes also widen it to include significant others. So, for example, I might say: "Suppose (name of significant other(s)) was here at the moment and I was to ask him/her the same question about what I/you would have to do to get it so wrong, what response(s) might s/he give?"

It is also important to note that these questions, as examples of authoritative doubt in action, can feel risky to ask. They need to be delivered with some authoritativeness rather than delivered with such tentativeness that the asking of the questions is more likely to contribute to a position, or exacerbation, of unsafe uncertainty (Mason, 1993).

Risk-taking, the supervisory process and issues of personal development

As indicated earlier in this chapter, the shift to a second order perspective has opened up issues of self-reflexivity and the self of the therapist. In family therapy development in the UK, while there has not been a move to personal therapy for trainees and those who are qualified, there has been a shift towards personal development issues needing to be addressed (for example, see Hildebrand, 1998). There is a widely held view (for example, see Walsh & McGoldrick, 2004) that systemic therapists need to address, and be aware of, personal history (including attention to gender, culture, sexual orientation, for example) that may both aid and/or constrain our work with clients. Supervision and consultation thus become very important aspects of this professional responsibility.

As part of a contribution to this responsibility, I have been asking the following questions in the last few years, both of myself and of those whom I supervise.

> What themes/issues/feelings do you feel you might be pulling back from addressing in your work with clients? and
>
> How do you explain to yourself, or how might others who know you and your work, explain why this process of pulling back is occurring? [Mason, 2002]

In the last three years of the advanced training programme in supervision at the Institute of Family Therapy in London, the addressing of trainees' relationship to risk-taking has now become a core part of the training. This development has been introduced as part of a second order, collaborative approach to training. In particular, helping people take the risk of owning their expertise through the taking of a position as well as showing the ownership of expertise through the utilization of therapeutic curiosity (Cecchin, 1987) has been encouraged. (It is important to add here that risk-taking for some people might be more through utilizing a position of curiosity rather than the utilization of taking a position.)

As part of the attention to risk-taking a number of questions/areas are explored. For example:

- What are your personal and professional relationships over time to the taking of risks?
- How do your preferred theoretical ways of seeing both aid and/or constrain your ability to take risks in your work? It is important that we do not get into what John Burnham has elegantly termed, theoretical ageism (Burnham & Harris, 2002).
- What risks are you taking on the course and in your work in terms of how you address sex, sexual orientation, race and culture, gender, religion, and disability? In terms of working cross-culturally, for example, I do not think we develop therapeutic intimacy if we play safe and, writing from the perspective of being a white male, just say "the right thing". If we can take the risk of learning to challenge cross-culturally from respectful positions, rather than just play safe, we are more likely to develop collaborative, trusting relationships (Mason & Sawyerr, 2002).

Conclusion

In this chapter I have attempted to put across the view that some of the developments in family therapy, particularly those that have been seen as taking a non-expert position, can be seen to have a constraining influence on the development of risk-taking in the therapeutic relationship, as well as an enabling influence. The bias of my practice is towards curiosity, and it will continue to remain so. My concern is that there is a danger that in the desire to be collaborative and respectful to clients we play so safe that we ultimately do a disservice to those clients (and our colleagues) by withholding potentially useful aspects of our therapeutic (and supervisory) expertise. It is my belief that the vast majority of clients come to therapy with a view that they will need to take some risks. Indeed, we know that coming is in itself a risk for many. These clients deserve therapists who will do likewise.

CHAPTER TWELVE

Adopting a research lens in family therapy: a means to therapeutic collaboration

Amaryll Perlesz and Rhonda Brown

Introduction

Collaborative approaches have become widely popular, in theory and practice, within the family systemic and narrative therapies. In this paper we revisit the ideal of collaboration and explore how it fits best with different research and therapy conceptual frameworks. We propose that the participatory, cooperative research inquiry paradigm may be more synchronous with the idea of collaboration than other frameworks, such as the social constructionist therapies that are founded on a basic assumption that the co-creation of meanings in therapy is an automatically collaborative process. We explore the process of collaboration, or lack thereof, in different knowledge generation and therapeutic interview contexts: a grounded theory, research family interview; an anthropological, ethnographic research project; and a family therapy interview.

In examining the implications of adopting a "cooperative/participatory researcher lens" in family therapy, we discuss the concept of "co-research" created by David Epston and explore the relationship of "co-research" to the collaborative, participatory paradigm. Knowledge generation is examined at the different levels of local and archival knowledge and experience, with implications for the therapeutic/research relationship.

A grounded theory, research family interview

> I arrive at the family's home for dinner and am offered a glass of wine soon after arriving. Neither the lesbian couple nor their adult children—all of whom I am about to interview—are known to me. They are friendly and communicative and interested in my work and the research project in which they will be participants. The dinner is much fun—the food and wine of high quality—and we cover a range of social topics that include sharing information about work, study, and leisure interests.
>
> The table is cleared as we begin to focus on the task at hand—the research interview. We are here to explore this lesbian-parented family's experiences of family formation, the "coming out" process and their interactions with mainstream organizations. The interview is interspersed with more laughter, focused questions by me to each of them, as well as occasional questions by each of them to others in the family, thoughtful silences, careful listening to each other's responses, and respectful words of agreement or correction as they *collaborate* in this research process.
>
> As I prepare to leave, the lesbian couple is thanking me for the evening. They've enjoyed the interview and they think it's been good for their family. They observe that it has been valuable hearing each other's opinions and perspectives as they have explored their family formation and their wide ranging experiences of total acceptance, social homophobia, and fear of coming out. They've enjoyed meeting me, we've established that we have things in common, and they make it clear that they would be happy to reconnect socially. I am pleased by the suggestion, and have no hesitation in saying yes.
>
> It seems inconceivable that a clinical interview would have taken a similar course. I've accepted a dinner invitation from "strangers", I've stayed for four hours, I've not disclosed much personally, but shared enough of my lesbian parenting experience to make it "useful" for the family, and now I'm agreeing to meet with my research participants socially.

It appears that the participants in this research interview collaborated willingly in the research process. What, if any, are the implications of this research experience for the process of therapy and the therapeutic relationship? What does working together collaboratively really mean? We know that the therapeutic relationship is an important factor in determining successful counselling outcomes. Does the same hold for research interviews? Is there something we can learn from our research interviews that will affect how we conduct clinical interviews?

An anthropological, ethnographic research interview

> Margaret Mead was 23 when she went to Samoa to conduct field research for her supervisor, Franz Boas. Boas was interested in collecting evidence for his hypothesis that all human behaviour—and in this case adolescent sexuality—was socially and culturally, rather than genetically, determined. Mead concluded that this was indeed the case, and wrote up her findings about adolescent sexual promiscuity in her famous book *Coming of Age in Samoa*. More than 60 years later, one of her principal informants, Fa'apua'a Fa'amu, in a sworn deposition to the American Anthropological Association, admitted that she and her girlfriends in their interviews with Mead had played a prank by telling stories about their "promiscuity" rather than revealing that they were ceremonial virgins who in fact upheld a strict sexual morality. Mead was totally convinced of the "genuineness" of her respondents' accounts, and subsequently, inadvertently misled and misinformed the entire anthropological establishment and other intellectuals for almost fifty years. The research informants revealed that they had no idea that Margaret Mead was an author who would publish their wild and playful untruths in what was to become a highly influential anthropological study of the twentieth century. [Freeman, 1992: 4–6]

It appears that the informants in this study, unlike the previous example, chose not to be *collaborative* participants in the generation of knowledge. We can create many possible explanations for how this hoax came about. Margaret Mead at the time of conducting the research was inexperienced in field-work and interviewing. She had a fixed preconception about Polynesian sexual promiscuity that she had acquired from a fellow anthropologist on her way to Samoa and she had a famous supervisor whom she wanted to please and whose theory she was attempting to confirm. Mead's respondents had no idea of the potential implications of their prank, and it is unlikely that without fully understanding the context of their interviews that they would choose to fully collaborate. Not all research is a collaborative endeavour. But then therapy is not necessarily collaborative either.

A family therapy interview

The young lesbian couple with their four-year-old daughter, Elise, have sought counselling to improve their relationship around parenting. Elise is not present at the session, because her parents think she may be too disruptive. Jane is the biological mother, and Elise has been conceived via donor sperm from a young gay man, Trevor, who is erratic in his fathering responsibilities, and only helps out "when he feels like it". Both Deb and Jane, the lesbian co-parents are frustrated by Trevor's attitude, because it seems to contravene their parenting agreement at the time he donated sperm. They think of him as Elise's father, rather than simply as a non-involved sperm donor, although Deb has reached the point where she would like Jane to simply give up on him so that they can get on with their lives. Jane says she is unwilling to turn her back on Trevor for Elise's sake, and this has led to much frustration between Deb and Jane, as well as between the women and Trevor.

Deb is not at all keen on therapy and she has come only for Jane's sake. Deb actually doesn't believe in therapy, because she says talking through things doesn't help. Jane believes that Deb needs to be more accepting of Trevor's role. Deb believes that it's Jane's job to sort out things with Trevor.

The discussion in the first session centres around how the women define their family, not just from their point of view, but also from Elise's. Although there are many adults—grandparents, aunts, uncles, friends—involved to varying degrees in Elise's life, Jane and Deb agree that they share a culturally influenced and broadly accepted view that fathers—sometimes even despite their behaviour—have a particular importance for children as designated, primary carers.

The therapist is curious about, and interested, in this belief. Deb and Jane are curious about the choices made by other lesbian parents, including the therapist's own experience of lesbian parenting. They are

> curious about what the research and clinical literature says about outcomes for children raised in lesbian-led families. This conversation seems like new territory to Deb and Jane. This conversation is new territory for the therapist, too, because although she is familiar with the general discourse around lesbian parenting there are many specific and unique aspects to Deb and Jane's life experience that she begins to explore with them. Even Deb begins to engage more collaboratively in these general discussions of lesbian family formation, parenting issues, and balancing the roles of multiple parents.

The shift to an increasing collaborative partnership occurs for Deb at the point at which she begins to scrutinize and investigate external information about lesbian parenting. Therapists and researchers are likely to hold ideals about collaboratively working together with clients and research participants, but there are endless variants in the degree to which this can be achieved. *The number of therapists it takes to change a light bulb depends on whether or not the light bulb wants to change!* These brief scenarios indicate that collaboration is likely to involve an interactive partnership, and this paper is about exploring ways to facilitate such collaboration in both family research and therapy.

Defining the landscape of collaboration

Before we can begin to talk about collaborative research approaches, we have to remind ourselves of the positioning of collaboration within the systemic and narrative therapies. The "collaborative" metaphor slipped into the language of family therapy in the mid 1980s, initially as a stance of second order therapies where "collaboration" in the systemic therapies gained its footing more generally in opposition to an objective, observing therapist and to the hierarchical structure of therapy (Hoffman, 1985); soon after in reflective team work (Andersen, 1987); then under the banner of Harry Goolishian and Harlene Anderson (Anderson, 1997; Anderson & Goolishian, 1988, 1992b), as an actual therapeutic "collaborative language systems approach"; and finally quite specifically and simultaneously within other social constructionist and narrative approaches (Jenkins, 1990; McNamee & Gergen, 1992; White &

Epston, 1990). Although "collaborative" is sometimes linked more closely with the social constructionist and narrative positions, *most* therapists would lay claim to a collaborative ethic.

But *what* is "collaborative", and *how* collaborative is "collaborative"? To *collaborate* in non-therapeutic parlance means to "... work in combination with; share in production; work or act jointly; cooperate voluntarily; willingly comply with; cooperate with ..." (*Webster's Dictionary*). Such a description implies a conscious working partnership shared equally between the members of the partnership. "Collaboration" as a concept in therapy, although used pervasively and in many different senses by family and narrative therapists, will always run into difficulties because of the problematic of therapists' power, influence, and expertise, and the question marks riding over how collaborative partnerships can develop in unequal relationships. This dilemma has been discussed at length elsewhere (e.g., Churven, 2000; Golann, 1988; Strong, 2000).

Collaborative therapists will say that they address issues of influence through attending to clients' preferences and choices and negotiating a "shared intentionality" or co-creating multi-authored and co-constructed meanings and understandings between therapist and client (Anderson, 1997). The introduction of reflecting teams was deemed to be a way of making therapy more transparent and allowing clients more power and control over the process as they collaborated with team members around the co-construction of meaning and experience in therapy (Andersen, 1987). Other techniques designed to be more collaborative included extending invitations to take responsibility for violence and engage in the process of change (Jenkins, 1990), and collaborating with clients in re-authoring their lives (White, 1995).

These examples of collaborative therapies—and of course there are many more—require particular therapeutic "stances" to achieve this "collaborative ideal" or collaborative ethic. The kind of language that dominates collaborative approaches includes: respect and empathic listening; radical listening (Weingarten, 1995); knowing not to know (Larner, 2000); curiosity (Cecchin, 1987); not-knowing (Anderson & Goolishian, 1988); authoritative doubt and safe uncertainty (Mason, 1993); co-constructing responsibility (Tomm, 1998); poetic activism (Penn & Frankfurt, 1994); a sensitivity to *différance* (Pocock, 1997) and so on.

Each of these examples and the way they are described gives emphasis to the therapist's stance. They are saying something about the therapist, a little about the client, and sometimes indirectly about the relationship. But collaboration, as we have seen above, is a willing, working partnership—it is a relational, interactional term requiring more than one key player. It is not about inherent characteristics of either the therapist or the client, but about a shared activity (Harlene Anderson, in Holmes, 1994). There is no language in these descriptions of the therapist's "collaborative stance" for the role of the client. We understand how the therapist's stance contributes to freeing the client, making them feel heard, understood, respected and that conditions are created in which new meanings can be generated. Missing here, though, is a language to describe the client's "collaborative stance" *as a more active participant in the collaborative process*. What shape might this collaborative partnership take if we attend to the role of the client as well as that of the therapist?

Some research paradigms and therapeutic styles are clearly more collaborative than others, and although social constructionist frameworks have been favoured by family therapists, particularly those with narrative leanings, a cooperative, participatory research frame is a particular research paradigm or inquiry stance that could also be useful for family therapists wishing to engage in more collaborative processes. Let us take a closer look, then, at the implications of adopting a *research* lens in the exploration of collaborative partnerships between clients and therapists.

The case for a research lens

The therapist's *raison d'être* could be labelled in many ways because there are a vast array of therapeutic frameworks engaging in different processes and leading to different outcomes. A therapist could define her role as to help, transform, understand, reflect on, change, bear witness to, be curious about, co-construct meaning, and so on.

"Therapy" is actually defined as the "... treatment of disease", where the *therapist* is one skilled in the "application of remedies for diseases". A *patient* is "... a person under treatment or care, as by a physician or surgeon ... the object or recipient of an action ..."

Many therapists prefer words like *client* to refer to the person/family who seeks out their services, yet "client" has also been defined as "... one of a class of dependents attached to patrician families ... one under the protection of another ... one who buys the services of another ..." To *help* refers to aiding and assisting "... to furnish with relief—as from pain, disease or distress; to succour; to change for the better; to improve ..." (*Webster's Dictionary*)

Not many therapists reading this paper will define themselves or their clients thus! However, the popular or common discourse around therapy carries with it strong connotations of disproportionate power, influence, and control. Patients and clients are dependent on the help they receive from expert therapists, who are frequently of a higher social class than their clients—particularly in public settings.

Research, on the other hand, is a process that requires "... careful searching ... a close searching ... studious enquiry ... critical and exhaustive investigation ... having for its aim the revision of accepted conclusions, in the light of newly discovered facts ..." (*Webster's Dictionary*) Ironically, this definition of research captures an essence of therapy more incisively than the actual definition of therapy and helping cited here.

A process of collaboration could sit comfortably within a research paradigm—particularly if *all* research participants partake in a "careful, close searching and studious enquiry". Of course, this position will hold better for some types of research than others. Researchers, just like therapists, can hold very different views about their research roles, seeking variously to know, discover, prove, test, understand, transform through participatory action, thickly describe, be curious about, and so on. Methods of inquiry and research goals will obviously differ depending on one's ontological position or construction of "reality", or epistemological stance—the nature of the relationship between the knower and what can be known. A positivist researcher will be more interested in testing hypotheses and discovering truths via rigorous, objective, often quantitative methods. There is unlikely to be much that is collaborative in such research.

A researcher working from a constructivist[1] framework, on the other hand, holds a relativist ontology and a subjectivist epistemology. There is no independent reality but local and specific constructed realities are "created" through an interpretivist research method. The interesting point to make here about constructivist research approaches is that they *need not necessarily* be collaborative. This is a brave assertion, but a point worth making, because all too often there is an assumption made by both therapists and researchers that the social constructionist stance is necessarily collaborative. It *is* the case that narratives and meaning are socially constructed through interactional dialogue and language. However, not all conversations all of the time are deliberate, active partnerships around meaning-making. One cannot "not communicate", but we believe that one must be able to "not collaborate" or otherwise the concept of willing participation loses its meaning.

This leads us to a distinct method of inquiry that has been called the participatory/cooperative[2] paradigm (Heron, 1996; Heron & Reason, 1997; Lincoln & Guba, 2000). Most frequently characterized by participatory action research, the goal here is transformation of social and personal experience through action, analysis, and reflection, learning and more action. Some research paradigms, such as feminist standpoint research and participatory action research, are more closely identified with cooperative, participatory approaches because they specifically include research participants in their meaning-making. It is this research stance that most comfortably gives us a language of collaboration and sits well, too, with the process of therapy. The territory of collaboration can include vastly different kinds of "action", such as conversations in the therapy room, homework tasks, reflecting teams/outsider witness groups, large scale interventions in school communities, and so on.

A participatory/cooperative research paradigm involves the therapist/researcher and client/research participant working together to discover and transform an as yet unarticulated and unknown territory into a different space that is new for both parties. Within the family therapy literature there already exists useful discussions of different aspects of this territory in descriptions of the intersubjectivity between the therapist and the client (Flaskas, 2002), and the idea of *différance*—those parts of the story or narrative that remain untold and are waiting to be discovered or articulated in the process of therapy (Pocock, 1997). Our focus here is on the client's own collaborative stance in this discovery process, because thus far, the story of collaboration has been better told from the therapist's perspective.

The second part of our argument about preferring the development of a research lens to make sense of the collaborative process in therapy is that the synchronicity between post-positivist research and the collaborative therapies is already extant with key concepts like curiosity, not-knowing, and co-constructed meanings—concepts that require further development from the client's perspective and the all-important collaborative partnership. Moreover, key influential exponents of the collaborative therapies have already argued that there is no difference between their research and their therapy—they are one and the same thing (Epston, 1999; Harlene Anderson in Holmes, 1994). "I think research should always be part of clinical practice and not separate from it. I use the same process in my research as I do in therapy" (Harlene Anderson, in Holmes, 1994, p. 161).

We agree with Anderson's sentiment as expressed here, though it is David Epston who has most explicitly promoted a collaborative, clinical inquiry paradigm—co-research—that privileges the client as the practitioner researcher.

Generating local and archival knowledges in co-research

Epston's idea about "co-research" as a description of a type of therapeutic collaborative partnership is a classic example of a therapist adopting a research lens. Within the narrative therapies, the term "co-research" was initially used in very specific ways with particular client groups (e.g., anorexia and bulimia), and only recently has been applied more widely. The idea has little currency within the field of systemic family therapy, and even in its brief heyday there was virtually no discussion within the family therapy literature about "co-research" beyond Epston's own personal exploration—more often presented at conferences and workshops than written about.[3] What does "co-research" mean and why are we revisiting the idea here?

Epston defines co-research as "two persons seeking knowledge and understanding in a common conversational endeavour, one as *participant researcher*, and the other as *practitioner researcher*" (from

"Notes on a co-researching practice": David Epston, 2nd September 2000). "Participant researcher" is defined as the therapist or professional whose role is to interview the practitioner researcher with openness and curiosity for her or his "inside" knowledge of the problem, and to collate and archive this knowledge. The "practitioner researcher" is the client who has inside knowledge of the problem and how they have overcome it.

Already we find a twist in the language here that privileges the position of the client. It is she or he who is the practitioner, and it is the therapist who participates in the client's journey of discovery. The co-production of knowledge requires the generation of inside knowledge or *local knowledge*[4] by the practitioner researcher. Local knowledge is that knowledge which is often hidden from view or lacking sufficient credibility to be either voiced or heard—and this knowledge might not only serve the interests of its membership but it can provide an effective critique of dominant knowledges (Epston & White, 1992; White & Epston, 1990). Giving voice to this local knowledge, or bearing witness to local and situated wisdoms is that unsettling part of the research and therapy process that requires both participant and practitioner researchers to revise previously accepted conclusions in the light of newly discovered understandings. The "collating and warehousing" of these local knowledges in an archival system by the participant researcher (the therapist) leads to the creation of *archival knowledges*.

> The local knowledge that began to emerge in the conversation with Jane and Deb was the deconstruction around the choices they had made to have a known and involved donor/father for their child, a decision they believed to be in the best interests of their child. It emerged that many of their friends, also with seemingly well-adjusted children, had made quite different choices such as anonymous donors, or non-involved but known donors. Again these were choices made in what was believed to be in the best interests of the child.
>
> It was Deb and Jane's own curiosity and rigorous investigation around their own social and kinship networks that allowed an alternative knowledge to emerge that perhaps there were *many* legitimate ways of raising children. They identified many interested and available adults in their wider kinship and friendship groups who could, and in some cases already did, play a significant mentoring and caring role in their child's life. The dominant knowledge of the importance of the role of

> the biological father began to recede into the background. Deb and Jane began to privilege their own parenting relationship and make commitments to working on it together. They were now valuing their relationship as parents as a valuable asset for their child.
>
> Curiosity and respect fuelled a shared exploration of the participant and practitioner researchers' different experiences of lesbian-led parenting arrangements. Together they compiled their local knowledges, and created an extended archival knowledge of the territory of lesbian parenting.

This collated, archival knowledge is available for potential inspiration for other co-researchers rather than as a repository of right answers or prescriptions and proscriptions, because it is always knowledge-in-the-making rather than "completed knowledge" (Epston, 1999). The generation of local and archival knowledge is not a static process, but an ongoing recursive loop that leads both the participant and practitioner researchers to unarticulated, unknown territory.

Epston has traditionally collected his archival knowledge in the form of letters written by himself as a participant researcher and personal accounts and replies written by practitioner researchers. The correspondence is in the form of local knowledge accounts from *all* participants in the co-research process (practitioner and participant researchers). The collating, sharing, and disseminating of these accounts generates the archival knowledge for use by others.

An alternative archival resource of local knowledges or wisdoms has been collated at the Bouverie Centre[5] following the recording of clients" accounts of their experiences of survival after a wide range of traumatic experiences (Ingram, 2002; Ingram & Perlesz, 2004). The Wisdoms collection is housed in a large bound folder in the waiting room at the Centre, and clients read it as they wait for interviews. Sometimes they choose to add their own story to the collection, or discuss another client's story with their own therapist.

Of course, archival and local knowledges need not be bound in folders or available in a stack of letters or on a web site. They are ever-present in the ongoing conversations in our therapy rooms as we co-research our lived experiences and share our wisdoms—from both sides of the therapeutic fence. Inviting clients on board as practitioner researchers is not just a pragmatic tool or manipulation to ensure their collaboration in the therapy, but if it is to work therapeutically it requires a genuine sharing of the unknown—a territory where curiosity and not-knowing co-exist with the inside and local knowledges for all participants.

When research is therapeutic

Witnessing is an essential feature of our role as therapists. Witnessing other people's suffering, or their joy, their hope and despair, their complaints, or their understandings and explanations of events. This is the nature of our job. The process of "bearing witness" requires both a listener and a speaker (Perlesz, 1999; Weingarten, 2000), it is just as much the job of the researcher to bear witness to his or her research participants" stories, or very real accounts of their life experiences. This act of "being witness to" is an important part of the research process—not just a collateral by-product. Because the *outcomes* of research are more generally focused on the generating of knowledge and information, (or the testing of these), the centrality of a research *process* that allows the witnessing of significant life events—and the therapeutic impact of this— can be overlooked.

Remember the responsive family in our earlier research interview?

> During the research interview, Tess (one of the adult children in the family) shares her experiences of having been uncomfortable with her own mother's lesbianism while at school. Her brother Jim, on the other hand, had embraced the idea and was delighted that his mother had found a new partner. Tess told none of her friends at school, and spoke to no one outside the family about her mother's sexual orientation between years nine and twelve at school, because she was worried about her friends being judgemental. As she reflects on this past experience in the research interview, she is also curious about the difference between her and her brother's reactions to their mother's lesbianism and wonders if she ought not to have been more accepting.
>
> All family members listen intently when I confirm that other teenage and adult children, particularly girls, in our research family interviews

have reported similar experiences. I add that within my own family our son, too, had not been concerned, whereas our daughter had experienced similar fears of discrimination and had been very reluctant to talk to school friends about my lesbianism.

This disclosure of my own inside experience or local knowledge and the broader archival information gathered from other families leads to an excited discussion amongst family members about gender issues and identification with the parent who is gay or lesbian. It is they who begin to ask each other questions about how different it might have been for the children if it were their father who had been gay. Family members ask "what if" questions of each other and explore their experiences of sexual identity and of child–parent relationships. The knowledge generation moves to and fro between local and archival as they begin to theorize about their personal experiences.

As the interview finishes and I am packing up my recording equipment, Tess again asks me about my daughter. She is curious about their shared experiences at school. It is as though Tess wishes to confirm that she is not the only one who has had this experience. It seems as though a weight has lifted from her shoulders—as though her experience has been acknowledged. Tess has borne witness to her suffering or discomfort as a daughter of a lesbian mother, and the researcher has listened or witnessed from a position that is both aware (a shared local knowledge) and empowering (Weingarten, 2000).

Conclusion

These examples taken from family therapy and research family interviews show that a participatory, cooperative inquiry paradigm is a useful lens for family therapists to adopt in their clinical work and research, because it can paint clients back into the collaborative process in a more particular way around clients" own experiences as practising researchers. Such a framework invites us as therapists and researchers to be more attuned to the *shared* exploration of local knowledges, and the careful searching and scrutiny of insider experiences that contribute to archival knowledge generation and dissemination.

A commitment to collaboration by the therapist, or researcher, does not of course automatically ensure that it takes place. For instance, not only does the example of Margaret Mead's research show us that research participants may not always choose to collaborate with researchers, but that professionals—therapists and researchers alike—can cling to their dominant knowledges in a way that suppresses and subjugates local knowledges and stifles a collaborative ethic in knowledge generation.

When Derek Freeman's refutation of Margaret Mead's research findings in Samoa were first considered by the American Anthropological Association (AAA) in 1983, his own research conclusions were soundly denounced by the AAA and declared to be "unscientific" by a vote of more than 1000 members, even though there was no strong "scientific" evidence to the contrary, in support of Mead's findings, put to the AAA. Moves were eventually made to rescind this motion more than ten years later when it was finally accepted to be the case that Mead's conclusions had been erroneous and subject to a hoax (Freeman, 1992).

We use this example here because it so clearly shows that curiosity and openness to new ideas does not come easily. The fact that we talk so much in our literature about curiosity and collaboration does not mean that such a stance can be easily held in the rough and tumble of everyday therapy, in the painful witnessing of life-long trauma, or in tending to the ordinariness and extraordinariness of each person's unique life. A research lens is just one of many useful lenses or metaphors for change in family therapy—particularly when applied to all players—because it is the very process of research that has the capacity to privilege curiosity and rigorous scrutiny of lived experience in a collaborative manner.

Notes

1. Rather than always writing the more cumbersome "constructionist/constructivist approach", we use "constructivist" as a research paradigm (as used by Lincoln & Guba, 2000) without making a distinction between biological constructivism and social constructionism (see (Hoffman, 1990)
2. Heron & Reason (1997) articulated a research framework they called the "cooperative paradigm" that actually referred not just to cooperative participation, but also to collaborative participatory research endeavour. So, although the words "cooperative" and "collaborative" actually

have a different emphasis—the former refers more to the act of being helpful, supportive, obliging, accommodating, whereas the latter refers more to teamwork, group effort and partnership—'participating cooperatively" as in the case of "working together" can also be used interchangeably with "participating collaboratively," and it is in this sense that we use cooperatively. Not in the sense of the patient cooperating with the doctor, or the student cooperating with the teacher. Harlene Anderson (in Holmes, 1994) also makes this distinction between cooperation and collaboration.

3. Dulwich Centre Publications (2004) have recently compiled a short history of how the term "co-research" was initially brought into the therapy realm by David Epston, and how narrative therapists have practiced as co-researchers since the mid 1980s.
4. White & Epston, (1990) cite Foucault's use of "local knowledge" as the hidden, subjugated voice. Clifford Geertz (1983) the anthropologist, uses "local knowledge" in the sense of situated and localized cultural knowledges: ". . . the small imaginings of local knowledge and the large ones of cosmopolitan intent" (Geertz, 1983, p. 15).
5. A publicly funded family therapy service in Melbourne, Australia. The Wisdoms collection is available on The Bouverie Centre website at www.lalvobt.edu.au/Bouverie.

CHAPTER THIRTEEN

Research on the therapeutic alliance in family therapy

Alan Carr

Introduction

The chapter opens with a brief description of therapeutic alliance assessment scales that may routinely be used in clinical practice and then discusses research that highlights the strong relationship between the therapeutic alliance and outcome in marital and family therapy. The remainder of the chapter is a selective review of process research which points to specific practices that therapists may incorporate into their own styles to improve the quality of therapeutic relationships.

In the integrative approach to practice that informs my clinical work (Carr, 2000) I assume that the formulations which emerge from talking with families about their problems and exceptions to these are social constructions. The primary frame of reference for this aspect of the work is observing systems. Since it is possible to co-construct multiple formulations to explain any problem or exception to it, it is important to have a criterion by which to judge the merit of any particular one. In my approach it is the *usefulness* of formulations in suggesting a variety of feasible solutions that are acceptable to families which is the sole criterion for judging the merit of one formulation over another. In deciding about the usefulness of formulations and interventions, I take account of the results of empirical research, such as those reviewed in this chapter, on the process and outcome of couples and family therapy. The primary frame of reference for such research is observed systems. Thus, the integrative approach I have developed attempts to bridge the frames of reference, often referred to within the field of family therapy, as observed and observing systems. A fine harvest may be reaped from both of these fields. This chapter is largely concerned with fruits from the field of observed systems. I have tried within the space constraints of the chapter to draw together empirical findings that may be useful to practitioners and which may have important implications for practice.

Recent reviews of the literature on marital and family therapy process have concluded that the relationship between the therapist and family members is important for effective therapy (Friedlander, 1998; Liddle, Santisteban, Levant, & Bray, 2002; Reimers, 2001; Sprenkle, Blow, & Dickey, 1999).

Assessing therapeutic alliance

The self-report Family Therapy Alliance Scale (Pinsof & Catherall, 1986) and the Family Therapeutic Alliance Observer Rating Scale (Martin & Allison, 1993) are good examples of the best available methods for assessing client–therapist relationships in marital and family therapy. Pinsof and Catherall's (1986) self-report Family Therapy Alliance Scale is designed to measure family members' perceptions of the quality of therapeutic alliances involving (1) themselves and the therapist; (2) other family members and the therapist; and (3) the family as a whole and the therapist. In each of these three domains it yields a total score and scores on content subscales concerned with therapy tasks, goals and bonds. The following are some sample items from this instrument: "I trust the therapist"; "The therapist understands my goals in therapy"; and "The therapist is helping my family". For each item, responses are given on seven-point Likert-type scales that range from "completely agree" (7) to "completely disagree" (1), with a "neutral" (4) midpoint. Higher scores indicate stronger alliances.

MFT therapeutic alliance and outcome

Studies of couples therapy consistently show that the quality of the therapeutic alliance or the client–therapist relationship reported by clients during therapy is associated with therapeutic outcome (Bourgeois, Sabourin, & Wright, 1990; Johnson & Talitman, 1997; Quinn, Dotson & Jordan, 1997; Reif, 1998). For example, Johnson & Talitman (1997), in a study of emotionally focused couples therapy, found that the couple's alliance with therapist accounted for 22% of variance in post-treatment satisfaction and 29% of variance in follow-up satisfaction. Studies of family therapy, like those of couples therapy, also show that the quality of the therapeutic alliance reported by clients during therapy is consistently associated with the outcome of therapy (Beck & Jones, 1973; Johnson, 1998; Joseph, 1997; Lyness, 1999; Van Orman, 1996). For example, Beck and Jones (1973), in a study of over 3,000 family therapy cases, found that the therapeutic alliance was the most powerful service-based predictor of therapeutic outcome and a better predictor of outcome than all client characteristic variables combined.

Convening whole family sessions is a pre-requisite for the development of a good alliance with all family members. Where all family members are motivated to attend therapy, convening a whole family session is rarely problematic. But in those cases where only some members of the family wish to attend therapy, then working towards convening whole family sessions becomes the first step in establishing a therapeutic alliance with the family.

Convening whole family sessions

Convening whole family sessions where adolescents have drug problems or adults have alcohol problems can be very challenging. Systemic interventions are particularly effective in helping families whose members have substance use problems engage in therapy and maintain an ongoing therapeutic relationship (Liddle & Dakof, 1995; Stanton & Shadish, 1997).

For adult alcohol abuse, family-based engagement techniques such as family intervention (Liepman, Silvia, & Nirenberg, 1989) and community reinforcement training (Sisson & Azrin, 1986) can help 57–86% of cases engage in treatment (either individual or family based) compared with the typical engagement rate of about 0–31% (Edwards & Steinglass, 1995). Family-based engagement techniques help family members create a context within which the chances of the family member with a drink problem entering treatment are maximized. This involves coaching family members in skills required to motivate the person with the alcohol problem to enter therapy and pinpointing the right time to use these so as to maximize the chances of success. The skills include relationship building, confrontation, requesting treatment entry, and supporting sobriety.

In two studies it has been shown that a systemic approach to engaging adolescent drug abusers and their families in therapy can be about twice as effective as routine methods for convening family therapy sessions (Santisteban *et al.*, 1996; Szapocznik *et al.*, 1988). With systemic engagement, the concerned family member was coached in ways to involve other less motivated family members in therapy. The invitations for treatment-resistant family members to participate in therapy were reframed so as to highlight the benefits of attending therapy in terms of the resistant family members' expressed concerns and wishes. Where appropriate, invitations to attend therapy were offered to treatment-resistant family members during home visits.

These techniques for convening family therapy sessions in substance abuse cases may probably be adapted for use in other types of cases where convening whole family sessions is problematic (Carr, 2000). However, once family therapy sessions have been convened, aspects of the therapeutic context such as the use of teams and screens may compromise the formation of a good therapeutic relationship with clients.

Engagement and the use of teams and screens

There is evidence that certain practices can pre-empt clients' negative reactions to teams and one-way screens. Knott & Espie (1997), in a survey of families attending family therapy service, found that clients who felt at ease working with a family therapy team and screen had been informed about the team and screen before the first session; had read a leaflet explaining the team and screen; and felt able to discuss concerns about the team and screen with the therapist. Only about half of the participants in this study had read the leaflet they were sent, and these tended to be the more motivated clients.

Höger, Teme, Reiter, & Steiner (1994) found that families valued the many positive ideas offered from multiple perspectives by reflecting teams. Smith and colleagues, in a qualitative study of clients' perceptions of reflecting team processes, found that clients valued the impartial reflections offered by reflecting teams, appreciated mixed-gender reflecting teams, and found teams were less threatening when the team was not behind the one-way screen (Smith, Sells, & Clevenger, 1994). Stith, in a study of children's views of therapy, found that certain practices helped children to be more comfortable with teams and screens. These were showing children how the screen worked; including the team, therapist and family in therapeutic conversations; involving children actively in therapy through the use of charts, board games and homework tasks; and not leaving children in the waiting room while the therapist talked to their parents (Stith, Rosen, McCollum, Coleman, & Herman, 1996).

Questioning styles that enhance alliances

Much of family therapy, but particularly much of the early sessions, involves the therapist asking questions and clients responding to these. Certain styles of questioning, especially those that are based on circular or systemic assumptions, are more supportive of alliance formation than other questioning styles. Scheel & Conoley (1998) investigated the relationship between questioning style and loss of neutrality in three families. After four sessions of family therapy, individual family members viewed videotape replays of moments when questions were posed and rated their perceptions of therapist side-taking and feelings of discomfort for each questioning event. Ratings of non-neutrality were associated with interventive questions.

In two analogue studies, non-clinical families viewed brief videotaped vignettes illustrating each of Karl Tomm's (1988) four questioning styles and subsequently rated the quality of the alliance between the therapist and the family for each vignette (Dozier, Hicks, Cornille, & Peterson, 1998; Ryan & Carr, 2001). For both studies, compared with strategic and lineal questioning styles, circular and reflexive questions led to higher ratings of therapeutic alliance. These results support Karl Tomm's (1988) hypothesis that questioning styles based on circular assumptions lead to a better therapeutic alliance than do questions based on lineal assumptions.

Reframing and alliance formation

Building an alliance with families in the early sessions of therapy is challenging because of the potential for punitive blaming to occur when families are explaining their understanding of their difficulties and how these arose. There is a risk that the therapeutic conversation will revolve around family members' explanations of problems being due to their perceptions of the identified as intrinsically "bad", "sad", "sick", or "mad". Such negative framings of problem behaviour may further reinforce scapegoating and other problem-maintaining family processes. In a study of functional family therapy for delinquent adolescents and their families, Alexander and his team found that reframing was more effective than reflection, questioning, or structuring interventions in promoting engagement and reducing defensive family communication, and that adolescents responded even more favourably to reframes than mothers and fathers (Robbins, Alexander, Newell, & Turner, 1996).

In a qualitative study of the reframing process, Coulehan, Friedlander, and Heatherington (1998) compared families in which early relational reframing of the problem occurred successfully with families in which it did not. A clear sequence characterized successful relational reframing. In the first stage, family members' individual constructions of the problem and exceptions to it were explored. In the second stage, positive aspects of the child with the problem, family strengths, and individual and family factors that contributed to problem formation were acknowledged. During this stage there was an emotional shift from blaming the child to a softer, more supportive position. In the third stage, family members expressed hope and recognized that change may be possible.

These studies support the value of using reframing, particularly during the early stages of therapy to strengthen the relationship between the therapist and family members.

Engaging adolescents

For adolescents to benefit from family therapy, it is important for them to form good working relationships with their therapists. Often this is challenging, and particular attention needs to be paid to the process of building an alliance with the adolescent. There is evidence that certain techniques are particularly effective in facilitating this process. Diamond, Liddle, Hogue, and Dakof (1999) rated videotapes for the presence or absence of a range of alliance-building interventions from five improved and five unimproved cases. In all of these cases families with adolescent drug abusers were participating in multi-dimensional family therapy. Diamond and his colleagues found that orientating adolescents to the collaborative nature of therapy; helping adolescents to form personally meaningful goals; and generating hope that these tangible goals could be achieved were particularly effective techniques for improving initially poor therapist–adolescent alliances.

The importance of support and collaboration

There is good evidence for a link between therapists' supportive or collaborative behaviour on the one hand and client cooperation on the other. Frankel and Piercy (1990) showed that client cooperation within therapy was associated with supportive behaviour on the part of the therapist and that this relationship between support and cooperation was strengthened if supervisors in turn were supportive of therapists. Moorehouse and Carr (2001) also found that client cooperation was associated with therapists' collaborative behaviour. Verwaaijen and VanAcker's study of thirteen families of conduct-disordered female adolescents at risk for institutionalization found that, in successful cases, therapists put more emphasis on collaborating with parents by elucidating problems, evaluating possibilities, and enhancing commitment, and less on stating conclusions and attempting to directly change clients' experiences (Verwaaijen & VanAcker, 1993).

Balancing support and structure

A principle of systemic practice is that for couples and families to change, alternatives to their problem-maintaining routines and beliefs require exploration. There is evidence that a balance of collaborative support on the one hand, and providing structure and direction on the other, may help clients explore new ways of resolving their difficulties. In a study of functional family therapy with the families of delinquent adolescents, Alexander, Barton, Schiavo, and Parsons (1976) found that, supportive relationship-building skills such as warmth and humour and directive structuring skills together accounted for 60% of the variance in treatment outcome. Relationship skills accounted for 45% of the outcome variance and structuring skills for 15%. Sells, Smith, and Moon (1996), in a qualitative study, found that clients valued therapy in which the therapist showed competence by being goal-focused rather than directionless and also maintained a warm, trusting, informal, down-to-earth relationship.

Different strokes for different folks

In a study of couples therapy, Cline, Mejia, Coles, Klein, and Cline (1984), found that middle-class couples benefited most when therapists became less directive over the course of therapy. In contrast, working-class couples benefited most when therapists became increasingly directive as therapy progressed. Cline and colleagues argued that middle-class couples used the increasingly non-directive therapeutic climate to spontaneously increase their emotional expressiveness, acceptance, agreement, and approval, while the working-class couples used the increasingly directive therapeutic climate to develop a clearer understanding of the dynamics of their marriage.

Hampson and Beavers (1996), in a study of 434 families who participated in Beavers' Family Systems therapy with trainee therapists, found that families who benefited most had the following profile. They formed a good therapeutic partnership with the therapist, attended at least six sessions, were rated as more competent and more enmeshed on the Beavers Interactional Scales (Beavers & Hampson, 1990). More competent families who were characterized by a more enmeshed style fared best when their therapists were more open about their therapeutic strategy, more egalitarian in the power differential they established with their clients, and more joined in partnership with families within the therapeutic alliance. Families rated as less competent and more disengaged in their style on the Beavers Interactional Scales made greater therapeutic progress when their therapists were less open about their therapeutic strategy, and established a more hierarchical therapeutic relationship characterized by interpersonal distance and directiveness. These results suggest that partnership, openness, and low power differential are the hallmarks of an effective therapeutic alliance with families rated as more competent on the Beavers' scales. It is only with less competent families, as rated by Beavers' scales, that therapeutic effectiveness is increased by maintaining an overt power differential and by not disclosing therapeutic strategy.

An important concern in interpreting these results is the meaning of "family competence". Ratings on the Beavers' Interactional Scales, which have good reliability and validity (Beavers & Hampson, 1990), are made from observations of ten-minute family discussions of what family members would like to see changed in their families. Competence within this context refers to a family's overall status on a range of factors such as goal directed negotiation, clarity of expression, conflict resolution, and empathy.

Managing resistance

Research on behavioural family therapy for families of aggressive boys conducted by Patterson's group at the Oregon Social Learning Centre has provided some of the most important empirical findings on the process of resistance (Patterson & Chamberlain, 1994). Resistance is elicited by therapists directly instructing clients in parenting skills or confronting them when they do not follow through on the use of such skills. The highest levels of resistance (as assessed by behavioural ratings of non-cooperation) occur in the middle phase of therapy and are associated with dropping out of therapy before completion. In successful therapy, mid-therapy resistance is gradually resolved and diminishes over the second half of therapy. Stoolmiller, Duncan, Bank, and Patterson (1993) found that this pattern of high resistance in mid-therapy with resolution by termination was associated with reduced arrest rates for aggressive boys two years after the end of therapy. This finding supports a model of therapy in which the first phase is devoted to building an alliance using largely supportive interventions. Once this supportive therapeutic relationship has been formed, the therapist uses the alliance as a context within which to confront and challenge ineffective parenting practices and to teach new ones based on behavioural principles. During this mid-phase of therapy, resistance is at a maximum. Once clients develop competence in using new parenting skills, their resistance begins to abate and they receive increasing support from therapists for their effective use of behavioural parenting skills.

While parent–therapist conflict about implementing parenting practices is the main type of resistance encountered in working with families containing pre-adolescent children, parent–adolescent difficulties in engaging in cooperative problem-solving is one of the most common forms of resistance found in working with families of adolescents. Friedlander and Heatherington identified a series of steps that facilitated therapeutic progress during episodes where families containing adolescents showed resistance to engaging in constructive problem-solving (Friedlander, Heatherington, Johnson, & Skowron, 1994). They compared four successful and four unsuccessful cases and found that members of successful families first acknowledged their own contribution to the resistance process. Then they communicated their thoughts and feelings about the impasse to other family members, who validated these sentiments. This led to a change in the emotional climate within the family from cold and conflictual to warm and accepting. This new climate created a context within which family members found new ways of understanding each others' behaviour and recognized the value of engaging in constructive problem-solving.

In a study of families of adolescent drug abusers in multidimensional family therapy, Diamond and Liddle (1996) identified a similar set of processes for dealing with therapeutic impasses where parents expressed frustration and hopelessness and adolescents expressed anger and resentment. First, the therapist supported and contained the adolescents within the therapy session and allowed them to feel understood as being both sad and angry. Next, the parents were supported to help them move from a position of accusation and blame to one of disappointment and loss. This was accompanied by a softening of the emotional tone of the interaction. Then adolescents were helped to articulate their sense of loss (of attachment to parents) underlying the anger and resentment. This "parent–adolescent re-attachment" process created a context within which constructive problem-solving could be resumed.

These two studies suggest that helping families with adolescents disclose beliefs and emotions associated with unresolved attachment issues within a supportive and accepting emotional climate may facilitate a move towards joint dialogue and constructive problem-solving when therapy reaches an impasse.

Implications for practice

This review suggests that a strong therapeutic alliance is important for achieving a good therapeutic outcome, because it provides the relational context essential for achieving therapeutic goals (Friedlander, 1998; Liddle, Santisteban, Levant, & Bray, 2002; Reimers, 2001; Sprenkle, Blow, & Dickey, 1999). The overriding implication is that all other aspects of marital (Bourgeois, Sabourin, & Wright, 1990; Johnson & Talitman, 1997; Quinn, Dotson, & Jordan, 1997; Reif, 1998) and family (Beck & Jones, 1973; Johnson, 1998; Joseph, 1997; Lyness, 1999; Van Orman, 1996) therapy should be subordinate to the therapeutic relationship. Probably, the only exception to this rule is where the safety of a family member is at risk and in such cases protection takes priority over alliance building.

Therapists should use a supportive and invitational approach in which family members are invited (not directed) to participate in therapy (Frankel & Piercy, 1990; Moorehouse & Carr, 2001; Verwaaijen & VanAcker, 1993) and in which a style of questioning, based on circular or systemic assumptions is predominantly used (Dozier, Hicks, Cornille, & Peterson, 1998; Ryan & Carr, 2001).

Therapists should form a collaborative partnership with families (Moorehouse & Carr, 2001). In this partnership, family members are experts on the specific features of their own family and its difficulties and therapists are experts on general scientific and clinical information relevant to family development and the broad class of problems of which the presenting problem is a specific instance (Carr, 2000). (This is a "knowing and not-knowing" position.)

There should be an attempt to match the way therapy is conducted to the clients' readiness to change, since to do otherwise may jeopardize the therapeutic alliance (Stoolmiller *et al.*, 1993). Early in therapy the emphasis should be on offering support (rather than direction) and reducing blame thorough reframing problems in relational terms, and in terms of family members strengths and good intentions (Robbins, Alexander, Newell, & Turner, 1996). Later in therapy the emphasis may shift to collaborative problem-solving. There should also be an attempt to match the therapy style to suit the structure and culture of the family (Cline, Mejia, Coles, Klein, & Cline, 1984; Hampson & Beavers, 1996).

There should be a balanced focus on individual and family strengths and resilience on the one hand, and on problems and constraints on the other (Carr, 2000). A focus on strengths promotes hope and mobilizes clients to use their own resources to solve their problems. However, a focus on understanding why the problem persists and the factors that maintain it is also important, since this information informs more efficient problem-solving.

Explanations of the way teams and screens work and add value to the service families receive may offset any potentially negative impact they might have on the therapeutic alliance (Knott & Espie, 1997) in. For family members who find it difficult to engage in therapy, specific techniques may be valuable. With substance abusers, other family members may be coached in how to help them engage in therapy (Santisteban *et al.*, 1996; Szapocznik *et al.*, 1988). For adolescents, helping them to view therapy as a collaborative process in which they can pursue personally meaningful goals is particularly effective (Diamond, Liddle, Hogue, & Dakof, 1999).

There should be an acknowledgement that both therapists and clients inadvertently bring to the therapeutic relationship attitudes, expectations, emotional responses, and interactional routines from other areas of their lives, notably early significant care-giving and care-receiving relationships (Carr, 2000). These relationship habits, if unrecognized, may compromise therapeutic progress and so should be addressed when resistance to therapeutic change occurs.

The degree to which the research findings summarized in this chapter can be generalized to settings outside those in which the studies were conducted is limited. While participants in some studies were from a range of social classes (e.g., Cline, Mejia, Coles, Klein, & Cline, 1984) and ethnic minority groups (e.g., Santisteban *et al.*, 1996; Szapocznik *et al.*, 1988), we do not have evidence from controlled empirical studies or narrative qualitative investigations on the impact of broader cultural, contextual, and socio-political factors on the therapeutic relationship. Clearly, these huge gaps in our knowledge need to be addressed in future research.

REFERENCES

Alexander, J., Barton, C., Schiavo, R, & Parsons, B. (1976). Therapist characteristics, family behaviour and outcome. *Journal of Consulting and Clinical Psychology*, *44*: 656–664.

Anderson, H. (1997). *Conversation, Language and Possibilities: A Post-modern Approach to Therapy*. New York: Basic Books.

Anderson, H., & Goolishian, H. (1988). Human systems as linguistic systems: Preliminary and evolving ideas about the implications for clinical theory. *Family Process*, *27*(4): 371–393.

Anderson, H., & Goolishian, H. (1992a). Therapeutic process as social construction. In: S. McNamee & K. J. Gergen (Eds.), *Therapy as Social Construction* (pp. 40–53). London: Sage.

Anderson, H., & Goolishian, H. (1992b). The client is the expert: a not-knowing approach to therapy. In: S. McNamee & K. J. Gergen (Eds.), *Therapy as Social Construction* (pp. 25–39). London: Sage.

Anderson, T. (1992). Reflections on reflecting with families. In: S. McNamee & K. Gergen (Eds.), *Therapy as Social Construction* (pp. 54–68). London: Sage.

Augusta-Scott, T. (2001). Dichotomies in the power and control story: Exploring multiple stories about men who choose abuse in intimate relationships. *Gecko*, *2*: 31–54.

Baldwin, M. (Ed.) (2000). *The Use of Self in Therapy* (2nd edn). Binghamton, NY: Haworth Press.

Balint, M. (1957). *The Doctor, his Patient and the Illness.* London: Pitman.

Bateson, G. (1972). *Steps to an Ecology of Mind.* London: Paladin.

Bateson, G. (1973)[1969]. Double bind. In: G. Bateson (Ed.), *Steps to an Ecology of Mind* (pp. 242–249). London: Paladin.

Bateson, G. (1979). *Mind and Nature.* London: Wildwood.

Beavers, W. R., & Hampson, R. B. (1990). *Successful Families: Assessment and Intervention.* New York: W. W. Norton.

Beck, D., & Jones, M. (1973). *Progress on Family Problems: A Nation-wide Study of Clients' and Counsellors' Views of Family Agency Services.* New York: Family Service Association of America.

Beebe, B., & Lachmann, F. (2002). *Infant Research and Adult Treatment: Co-constructing interactions.* Hillsdale, NJ: Analytic Press.

Benjamin, J. (1999). Recognition and destruction: an outline of intersubjectivity. In: S. Mitchell & L. Aron (Eds.), *Relational Psychoanalysis: The Emergence of a Tradition* (pp. 181–210). Hillsdale, NJ: Analytic Press.

Berg, I. M. (1991). *Family Preservation: A Brief Therapy Workbook.* London: BT Press.

Bertrando, P. (2000). Text and context: narrative, postmodernism and cybernetics. *Journal of Family Therapy, 22*: 83–103.

Bion, W. (1963). *Elements of Psycho-Analysis.* London: Heineman [reprinted London: Karnac, 1984].

Bion, W. R. (1967). *Second Thoughts: Selected Papers on Psycho-Analysis.* London: Maresfield Library [reprinted London: Karnac].

Bion, W. R. (1970). *Attention and Interpretation.* London: Tavistock.

Block Lewis, H. (1971). *Shame and Guilt in Neurosis.* New York: International Universities Press.

Bollas, C. (1987). *Shadow of the Object: Psychoanalysis of the Unthought Known.* London: Free Association Books.

Bor, R., Mallandain, I., & Vetere, A. (1998). What we say we do: results of the 1997 UK Association of Family Therapy Members Survey. *Journal of Family Therapy, 20*: 333–351.

Boscolo, L., & Bertando, P. (1992). The reflexive loop of past, present and future in systemic therapy and consultation. *Family Process, 31*: 119–130.

Boscolo, L., & Bertrando, P. (1993) *The Times of Time: A New Perspective in Systemic Therapy and Consultation.* New York: Norton Press.

Boscolo, L., Cecchin, G., Hoffman, L., & Penn, P. (1987). *Milan Systemic Family Therapy: Conversations in Theory and Practice.* New York: Basic Books.

Boszormenyi-Nagy, I., & Krasner, B. R. (1986). *Between Give and Take: A Clinical Guide to Contextual Therapy*. New York: Brunner/Mazel.

Bourdieu, P. (1977)[1972]. *Outline of a Theory of Practice*. Cambridge: Cambridge University Press.

Bourgeois, L., Sabourin, S., & Wright, J. (1990). Predictive validity of therapeutic alliance in group couples therapy. *Journal of Consulting and Clinical Psychology, 58*: 608–613.

Bowlby, J. (1951). *Maternal Care and Mental Health*. Geneva:.World Health Organisation.

Bowlby, J. (1958). The nature of the child's tie to his mother. *International Journal of Psycho-Analysis, 39*: 350–373.

Bowlby, J. (1969). *Attachment and Loss, Vol. 1 Attachment*. London: Hogarth Press and The Institute of Psycho-Analysis.

Bowlby, J. (1988). *A Secure Base: Clinical Applications of Attachment Theory*. London: Routledge.

Box, S., & Thomas, J. (1979). Working with families: a psychoanalytic approach, thoughts on the conference workshop. *Journal of Family Therapy, 1*(2): 177–182.

Box, S., Copley, B., Magagna, J., & Moustaki, E. (Eds.) (1994). *Crisis at Adolescence: Object Relations Therapy with the Family*. New York: Aronson.

Boyd-Franklin, N. (1989). *Black Families in Therapy: A Multisystems Approach*. New York: Guilford Press.

Boyd-Franklin, N., & Hafer Bry, B. (2000) *Reaching Out in Family Therapy, Home Based, School, and Community Interventions*. New York: Guilford Press.

Broucek, F. (1982). Shame and its relation to early narcissistic developments. *International Journal of Psychoanalysis, 63*: 369–378.

Burnham, J. (1993). Systemic supervision: the evolution of reflexivity in the context of the supervisory relationship. *Human Systems. The Journal of Systemic Consultation and Management*, 4(3–4): 349–381.

Burnham, J., & Harris, Q. (2002). Cultural issues in supervision. In: D. Campbell & B. Mason (Eds.), *Perspectives on Supervision*. London: Karnac.

Byng-Hall, J. (1985). The family script as a useful bridge between theory and practice. *Journal of Family Therapy, 3*: 301–306.

Byng-Hall, J. (1995). *Rewriting Family Scripts: Improvisation and Systems Change*. New York: Guilford.

Byng-Hall, J. (1999). Family therapy and couple therapy: toward greater security. In: J. Cassidy & P. R. Shaver (Eds), *Handbook of Attachment:*

Theory, Research, and Clinical Applications (pp. 625–645). New York: Guildford.

Byng-Hall, J. (2002). Relieving parentified children's burdens in families with insecure attachment patterns. *Family Process, 41*: 375–388.

Byng-Hall, J. (2004). Towards effective and versatile expertise. *Context, 74*: 18–20.

Campbell, D. & Mason, B. (Eds.) (2002). *Perspectives on Supervision.* London: Karnac.

Carr, A. (1989). Counter-transference reactions to families where child abuse has occurred. *Journal of Family Therapy, 11*(1): 87–98.

Carr, A. (2000). *Family Therapy: Concepts, Process and Practice.* Chichester: Wiley.

Cecchin, G. (1983). Workshop presentation, London.

Cecchin, G. (1987). Hypothesizing, circularity and neutrality revisited: an invitation to curiosity. *Family Process, 26*(4): 405–413.

Cecchin, G. (1995). Workshop presentation, Cardiff.

Cecchin, G., Lane, G., & Ray, W. (1991). *From Strategizing to Non-Intervention: Towards Irreverence in Systemic Practice.* London: Karnac.

Churven, P. (2000). A critique of "collaborative influence"—Is there a role for expertise? *Australian and New Zealand Journal of Family Therapy, 21*(3): 149.

Clarkson, P. (1995). *The Therapeutic Relationship.* London: Whurr.

Cline, V., Mejia, J., Coles, J., Klein, N., & Cline, R. (1984). The relationship between therapist behaviours and outcome for middle- and lower-class couples in couples therapy. *Journal of Clinical Psychology, 40*: 691–704.

Cooklin, A. (1999). *Changing Organisations: Clinicians as Agents of Change.* London: Karnac.

Coulehan, R., Friedlander, M., & Heatherington, L. (1998). Transforming narratives: A change event in constructivist family therapy. *Family Process, 37*: 17–33.

Coulter, J. (1986). Affect and social context: emotion function as a social task. In: R. Harre (Ed.), *The Social Construction of Emotion* (pp. 120–133). Oxford: Blackwell.

Crittenden, P. (2000). A dynamic–maturational approach to continuity and change in patterns of attachment. In: P. Crittenden & A. Clausson (Eds.), *The Organisation of Attachment Relationships: Maturation, Culture and Context* (pp. 343–357). New York: Cambridge University Press.

Cronen, V., & Lang, P. (1994). Language and action: Wittgenstein and Dewey in the practice of therapy and consultation. *Human Systems The Journal of Systemic Consultation and Management*, *5*(1–2): 5–43.

Csordas, T. J (1994). *Embodiment and Experience. The Existential Ground of Culture and Self.* Cambridge: Cambridge University Press.

Csordas, T. J (2002). *Body/Meaning/Healing*. Basingstoke: Palgrave Macmillan.

Dalal, F. (2002). *Race, Colour and Processes of Racialization*. Hove: Brunner-Routledge.

Damasio, A. (2003). *Looking for Spinoza. Joy, Sorrow and the Feeling Brain.* London: William Heinemann.

Davies, D., & Neal, C. (Eds.) (1996). *Pink Therapy: A Guide for Counsellors and Therapists Working with Lesbians, Gay and Bisexual Clients.* Buckingham: Oxford University Press.

Derrida, J. (1978). Quoted in Anderson, H. (1997, *op. cit.*).

de Shazer S. (1994). *Words were Originally Magic*. New York: Norton Press.

Diamond, G., & Liddle, H. (1996). Resolving a therapeutic impasse between parents and adolescents in multidimensional family therapy. *Journal of Consulting and Clinical Psychology*, *64*: 481–488.

Diamond, G., Liddle, H., Hogue, A., & Dakof, G. (1999). Alliance-building interventions with adolescents in family therapy: A process study. *Psychotherapy Theory, Research, Practice & Training*, *36*: 355–368.

Douglas, M. (1966). *Purity and Danger. An Analysis of the Concepts of Pollution and Taboo.* London: Ark Paperbacks.

Douglas, M. (1970). *Natural Symbols*. [Reprinted Harmondsworth: Penguin, 1978].

Dozier, R., Hicks, M., Cornille, T., & Peterson, G. (1998). The effect of Tomm's therapeutic questioning styles on therapeutic alliance: A clinical analogue study. *Family Process*, *37*: 189–200

Dulwich Centre Newsletter (1993). Other wisdoms other worlds. *Colonisation and Family Therapy*, *1*: 15–19.

Dulwich Centre Publications (2004). Narrative therapy and research *The International Journal of Narrative Therapy and Community Work*, *2*: 29–36.

Dupont-Joshua, A. (1998). Towards healing the splits between black and white people in counselling. *Counselling*, 271–284.

Edwards, M., & Steinglass, P. (1995). Family therapy treatment outcomes for alcoholism. *Journal of Marital and Family Therapy*, *21*: 475–509.

Epston, D. (1999). Co-research: The making of an alternative knowledge. *Narrative Therapy and Community Work: A Conference Collection*. Adelaide: Dulwich Centre Publications.

Epston, D., & White, M. (1992). Consulting your consultants: The documentation of alternative knowledges. In: *Experience, Contradiction, Narrative and Imagination. Selected Papers of David Epston and Michael White 1989–1991*. South Australia: Dulwich Centre Publications.

Evans-Holmes, D. (1992). Race and the transference in psychoanalysis and psychotherapy. *International Journal of Psycho-analysis, 73*: 1.

Ferard, M. L., & Hunnybun, N. K. (1962). *The Caseworkers Use of Relationships*. London: Tavistock.

Flaskas, C. (1992). A reframe by any other name: On the process of reframing in strategic, Milan, and analytic therapy. *Journal of Family Therapy, 14*(2).

Flaskas, C. (1994). Exploring the therapeutic relationship: a case study. *Australian and New Zealand Journal of Family Therapy, 15*: 185–190.

Flaskas, C. (1996). Understanding the therapeutic relationship: using psychoanalytic ideas in the systemic context. In: C. Flaskas & A. Perlesz (Eds.), *The Therapeutic Relationship in Systemic Therapy*. (pp. 34–52).London: Karnac.

Flaskas, C. (1997). Engagement and the therapeutic relationship in systemic therapy. *Journal of Family Therapy, 19*(3): 263–282.

Flaskas, C. (2002). *Family Therapy Beyond Postmodernism: Practice, Challenges, Theory*. Hove: Brunner-Routledge.

Flaskas, C. (2004). Thinking about the therapeutic relationship: emerging themes in family therapy. *Australian and New Zealand Journal of Family Therapy*, 25(1): 13–20.

Flaskas, C., & Perlesz, A. (Eds.) (1996a). *The Therapeutic Relationship in Systemic Therapy*. London: Karnac.

Flaskas, C., & Perlesz, A. (1996b). The return of the therapeutic relationship in systemic therapy. In: C. Flaskas & A. Perlesz (Eds.), *The Therapeutic Relationship in Systemic Therapy*. London: Karnac.

Fletchman-Smith, B. (2000). *Mental Slavery, Psychoanalytic Studies of Caribbean People*. London: Rebus Press.

Frances, R. (1996). Ethical, methodological and gender issues in assessing intervention programs for violent men. *Psychiatry, Psychology and Law*, 3(2): 143–151.

Frankel, B., & Piercy, F. (1990). The relationship among selected supervisor, therapist and client behaviour. *Journal of Marital and Family Therapy, 16*: 407–421.

Freedman, J., & Combs, G. (1996). *Narrative Therapy: The Social Construction of Preferred Realities*. New York: Norton Press

Freeman, D. (1992). *Paradigms in Collision*. Canberra: Research School of Pacific Studies, The Australian National University.

Freud, S. (1922e). Two encyclopaedia articles, (a) Psycho-analysis. *S.E., XVIII*: 239. London: Hogarth.

Frie, R. (Ed.) (2003). *Understanding Experience: Psychotherapy and Postmodernism*. London: Routledge.

Friedlander, M. (1998). Family therapy research: Science into practice, practice into science. In: M. Nichols (Ed.), *Family Therapy: Concepts and Methods* (Fourth edn) (pp. 503–526). Boston: Allyn and Bacon.

Friedlander, M., Heatherington, L., Johnson, B., & Skowron, E. (1994). Sustaining engagement: A change event in family therapy. *Journal of Counselling Psychology, 41*: 438–448.

Friedlander, M. L., Wildman, J., Heatherington, L., & Skowron, E. A. (1994). What we do and don't know about the process of family therapy. *Journal of Family Psychology, 8*: 390–416.

Frosh, S. (1997). Postmodern narratives: or muddles in the mind. In: R. K. Papadopoulos & J. Byng-Hall (Eds.), *Multiple Voices: Narrative in Systemic Family Psychotherapy* (pp. 86–99). London: Duckworth.

Frosh, S. (2002). *Afterwords: The Personal in Gender, Culture and Psychotherapy*. Basingstoke: Palgrave.

Frugerri, L. (1992). Therapeutic process as social construction. In: S. McNamee & K. J. Gergen (Eds.), *Therapy as Social Construction*. London: Sage.

Geertz, C. (1983). *Local Knowledge*. New York: Basic Books.

Gergen, K. (1991). *The Saturated Self: Dilemmas of Identity in Contemporary Life*. New York: Basic Books.

Gergen, K. (1994). *Realities and Relationships: Soundings in Social Constructionism*. Cambrige, MA: Harvard University Press.

Gibney, P. (1996). To embrace paradox (once more with feeling): a commentary on narrative/conversational therapies and the therapeutic relationship. In C. Flaskas & A. Perlesz (Eds.), *The Therapeutic Relationship in Systemic Therapy* (pp. 90–107). London: Karnac.

Golann, S. (1988). On second-order family therapy. *Family Process, 27*: 51–65.

Goldenberg, I., & Goldenberg, H. (1996). *Family Therapy: An Overview*. Pacific Grove: Brooks/Cole.

Goldner, V., Penn, P., Sheinberg, M., & Walker, G. (1990). Love and violence: gender paradoxes in volatile attachments. *Family Process, 29*: 343–364.

Gondolf, E. W. (1993). Reconceptualising batterer program evaluation. Paper presented to the Third National Conference for Professionals Working with Men Who Batter, Minneapolis, MN, 14–17 April.

Gorell Barnes, G., & Henessy, S. (1994). Reclaiming a female mind from the experience of sexual abuse. In: C. Burck & B. Speed (Eds.), *Gender, Power and Relationships* (pp. 69–85). London: Routledge.

Gorell Barnes, G., & Campbell, D. (1982). The impact of structural and strategic approaches on the supervisory process: a supervisor is supervised. In: R. Whiffen & J. Byng-Hall (Eds.), *Family Therapy Supervision: Recent Developments in Practice* (pp. 137–152). London: Academic Press.

Green, J., & Goldwyn, R. (2002). Annotation: Attachment disorganisation and psychopathology: new findings in attachment research and their potential implications for developmental psychopathology in childhood. *Journal of Child Psychology and Psychiatry, 43*: 835–846.

Greenberg, L., & Johnson, S. (1994). *The Heart of the Matter: Perspectives on Emotion in Marital Therapy*. New York: Bruner/Mazel.

Greenberg, L., & Marques, C. (1998). Emotions in couples systems. *Journal of Systemic Therapies, 17*(2): 93–107.

Guilfoyle, M. (2003). Dialogue and power; a critical analysis of power in dialogical therapy. *Family Process, 42*: 331–343.

Haber, R. (1994). Response-ability: therapist's "I" and role. *Journal of Family Therapy, 16*: 269–284.

Hacking, I. (1999). *The Social Construction of What?* Cambridge, MA: Harvard University Press.

Hampson, R., & Beavers, W. (1996). Family therapy and outcome: Relationships between therapist and family styles. *Contemporary Family Therapy, 18*: 345–370.

Hardham, V. (1996). Embedded and embodied in the therapeutic relationship: understanding the therapist's use of self systemically. In: C. Flaskas & A. Perlesz (Eds.), *The Therapeutic Relationship in Systemic Therapy* (pp. 71–89). London: Karnac.

Heisenberg, W. (1962). *Physics and Philosophy*. New York: Harper and Row.

Helmeke, K. B., & Sprenkle, D. (2000). Clients' perceptions of pivotal moments in couples therapy. *Journal of Marital and Family Therapy*, 26(4): 469–483.

Heron, J. (1996). *Cooperative Inquiry: Research into the Human Condition*. London: Sage.

Heron, J., & Reason, P. (1997). A participatory inquiry paradigm. *Qualitative Inquiry, 3*: 274–294.

Hildebrand, J. (1998). *Bridging the Gap: A Training Model in Personal and Professional Development*. London: Karnac.

Hilderbrand, J., & Speed, B. (1995). The influence of the therapist's personal experience on their work with couples. In: J. Van Lawick & M. Sanders (Eds.), *Family, Gender and Beyond*. Heemstede, The Netherlands: LS Books.

Hoffman, L. (1985). Beyond power and control: towards a "second order" family systems therapy. *Family Systems Medicine, 3*(4): 381–396.

Hoffman, L. (1988). A constructivist position for family therapy. *The Irish Journal of Psychology, 9*: 110–129.

Hoffman, L. (1990). Constructing realities: An art of lenses. *Family Process, 29*(1): 1–12.

Hoffman, L. (1992). A reflexive stance for family therapy. In: S. McNamee & K. J. Gergen (Eds.), *Therapy as Social Construction*. London: Sage.

Hoffman, L. (2002). *Family Therapy: An Intimate History*. New York: Norton.

Höger, C., Teme, M., Reiter, L., & Steiner, E. (1994). The reflecting team approach: Convergent results of two exploratory studies. *Journal of family Therapy, 16*: 427–437.

Holmes, J. (2001). *The Search for the Secure Base: Attachment Theory and Psychotherapy*. London: Brunner-Routledge.

Holmes, S. (1994). A philosophical stance, ethics and therapy: An interview with Harlene Anderson. *Australian and New Zealand Journal of Family Therapy, 15*(3): 155–161.

Hubble, M. A., Duncan, B. L., & Miller, S. D. (1999). Introduction. In: M. A. Hubble, B. L. Duncan, & S. D. Miller (Eds.), *The Heart and Soul of Change: What Works in Therapy* (pp. 1–19). Washington: American Psychological Association.

Hubble, M. A., Duncan, B. L., & Miller, S. D. (Eds.) (1999a). *The Heart and Soul of Change: What Works in Therapy*. Washington: American Psychological Association.

Hughes, C. (1997). Women challenging men: The role of female facilitators in men's behaviour change programs, V-Net Training Session Notes, Melbourne, 17th September

Hughes, C., & Weiss, K. (1997). Women challenging men: Men's responsibility groups, V-Net Training Session Notes, Melbourne, 17th September.

Ingram, C. (2002). The getting and giving of wisdoms. Unpublished Master of Family Therapy (Minor Thesis), La Trobe University, Melbourne.

Ingram, C., & Perlesz, A. (2004). The getting of wisdoms. *The International Journal of Narrative Therapy and Community Work, 2*: 49–56.

Irvine, E. E. (1956a). Some implications of Freudian theory for casework. *The Almoner, 9*(2): 39–44.

Irvine, E. E. (1956b). Transference and reality in the casework relationship. *The British Journal of Psychiatric Social Work, 3*(4): 1–10.

Jenkins, A. (1990). *Invitations to Responsibility: The Therapeutic Engagement of Men who are Violent and Abusive.* Adelaide, Dulwich Center Publications.

Johnson, S. (1998). Listening to the music: emotion as a natural part of systems theory. *Journal of Systemic Therapies, 17*(2): 1–9.

Johnson, S., & Talitman, E. (1997). Predictors of success in emotionally focused couples therapy. *Journal of Marital and Family Therapy, 23*: 135–152.

Jones, M. A., & Gabriel, M. A. (1999). Utilization of psychotherapy by lesbians, gay men, and bisexuals: findings from a nationwide survey. *American Journal of Orthopsychiatry, 69(2):*209–219.

Jordan, J. (1997). *Women's Growth in Diversity.* New York: Guilford Press.

Joseph, S. (1997). Exploration of the therapeutic relationship with families. *Dissertation Abstracts International Section A: Humanities and Social Sciences, 57*(12-A): 5048.

Kaffman, M. (1987). Failures in family therapy: and then what? *Journal of Family Therapy, 9*(4): 307–328.

Kapferer, B. (1983). *A Celebration of Demons. Exorcism and the Aesthetics of Healing in Sri Lanka.* Indiana: Indiana University Press [reprinted Oxford: Berg Smithsonian Institution Press, 1991].

Karan, R. (1992). Shame. *Atlantic Monthly, February*: 40–70.

Kareem, J. (1988). Outside in . . . inside out . . . Some considerations in intercultural psycho-therapy. *Journal of Social Work Practice, 39*(3): 57–71.

Kareem, J., & Littlewood, R. (Eds.) (1992). *Intercultural Therapy, Themes Interpretation and Practice.* Oxford: Blackwell.

Karl, Cynthia, Andrew, & Vanessa (1992). Therapeutic distinctions in an ongoing therapy. In: S. McNamee & K. J. Gergen (Eds.), *Therapy as Social Construction.* London: Sage.

Kassis, J. P., & Matthews, W. J. (1987). When families and helpers do not want the mirror: a brief report of one team's experience. *Journal of Strategic and Systemic Therapies, 6(*4): 33–43.

Kaufert, J. M. (1990). Sociological and anthropological perspectives on the impact of interpreters on clinician/client communication. *Sante Culture Health, VII*(2–3): 209–235.

Kazan, Z., Anderson, L., Law, I., & Swan, V. (1993). Training in narrative therapy. *Human Systems. The Journal of Systemic Consultation and Management*, 4(3–)4: 349–381.

Kingston, W., & Bentovim, A. (1981). Constructing a focal formulation and hypothesis in family therapy. *Australian & New Zealand Journal of Family Therapy*, 4: 37–50.

Klein, M. (1957). *Envy and Gratitude*. London: Tavistock.

Klein, M. (with Joan Riviere) (1937). *Love Guilt and Reparation. Hate and Reparation*. London: Hogarth.

Knott, F., & Espie, C. (1997). Families' perceptions of the one-way screen in the first meeting. *Journal of Family Therapy*, *19*: 431–439.

Knudson, M. C. (1997). The politics of gender in family therapy. *Journal of Marital and Family Therapy*, *23*(4): 421—437.

Kohut, H. (1972). Thoughts on narcissism and narcissistic rage. *The Psychoanalytic Study of the Child*, *27*: 360–400.

Kozlowska, K., & Hanney, L. (2002). The network perspective: an integration of attachment and family systems theories. *Family Process*, *41*: 285–312.

Kraemer, S. (1991).The origins of fatherhood. *Family Process*, *30*: 377–392.

Krause, I. (1993). Family therapy and anthropology: a case for emotions. *Journal of Family Therapy*, *15*: 35–56.

Krause, I.-B. (1998). *Therapy Across Culture*. London: Sage.

Krause, I.-B. (2002). *Culture and System in Family Therapy*. London: Karnac.

Laderman, C., & Roseman, M. (1996). *The Performance of Healing*. New York: Routledge.

Laing, L. (2001). Working with women: exploring individual and group work approaches. *Australian Domestic and Family Violence Clearinghouse, Issues Paper 4*.

Laing, R. D., & Esterson, A. (1964). *Sanity, Madness and the Family*. London: Tavistock.

Lambert, M. J. (1992). Implications of outcome research for psychotherapy integration. In: J. C. Norcross & M. R. Goldfried (Eds.), *Handbook for Psychotherapy Integration* (pp. 157–212). New York: Basic Books.

Lambert, M. J., Shapiro, D. A., & Bergin, A .E. (1986). The effectiveness of psychotherapy. In: S. L. Garfield & A. E. Bergin (Eds.), *Handbook of Psychotherapy and Behavior Change* (3rd edn) (pp. 157–212). New York: Wiley.

Lang, P., Little, M., & Cronen, V. (1990). The systemic professional domains of action and the question of neutrality .*Human Systems: The Journal of Systemic Consultation and Management*, *1*: 40–55.

Lannaman, J. W. (1998). Social construction and materiality: the limits of interdeterminancy in therapeutic settings. *Family Process*, *37*: 393–413.

Larner, G. (2000). Toward a common ground in psychoanalysis and family therapy: on knowing not to know. *Journal of Family Therapy*, *22*(1): 61–82.

Lau, A. (1984). Transcultural issues in family therapy. *Journal of Family Therapy*, *6*: 91–112.

Layton, M. (1995). Mastering mindfulness. *Networker*, *Nov/Dec*: 28–31.

Leslie, L. A. (1995). The evolving treatment of gender, ethnicity, and sexual orientation in marital and family therapy. *Family Relations*, *44*: 359–367.

LeVine, R. A., Dixon, S., LeVine, S., Richman, A., Leiderman, P. H., Keefer, C. H., & Brazelton, T. B. (1996). *Childcare and Culture. Lessons from Africa*. Cambridge: Cambridge University Press.

Levi-Strauss, C. (1963). *Structural Anthropology*. Harmondsworth: Penguin.

Levi-Strauss, C. (1970). *The Raw and the Cooked. Introduction to a Science of Mythology 1*. London: Jonathan Cape.

Liddle, H., & Dakof, G. (1995). Efficacy of family therapy for drug abuse: promising but not definitive. *Journal of Marital and Family Therapy*, *21*: 511–543.

Liddle, H., Santisteban, D., Levant, R., & Bray, J. (2002). *Family Psychology. Science-Based Interventions*. Washington, DC: American Psychological Association.

Lieberman, S. (1980). *Transgenerational Family Therapy*. London: Groom Helm.

Liepman, M., Silvia, L., & Nirenberg, T. (1989). The use of family behaviour loop mapping for substance abuse. *Family Relations*, *38*: 282–287.

Lincoln, Y. S., & Guba, E. G. (2000). Paradigmatic controversies, contradictions, and emerging confluences. In: N. K. Denzin & Y. S. Lincoln (Eds.), *Handbook of Qualitative Reseaerch* (pp. 163–188). Thousand Oaks, CA: Sage.

Lutz, C., & Abu-Loghod, L. (1990). *Emotion, Discourse and the Politics of Everyday Life*. Cambridge: Cambridge University Press.

Lyness, K. (1999). The role of the therapeutic relationship in successful family therapy outcome. *Dissertation Abstracts International: Section B: The Sciences and Engineering*, *60*(3-B): 1307.

Madigan, S. P. (1993). Questions about questions: Situating the therapist's curiosity in front of the family. In: S. Gilligan & R. Price (Eds.), *Therapeutic Conversations*. New York. W. W. Norton.

Maher, A. (1988). Research and clinical applications of "good moments" in psychotherapy *Journal of Integrative and Eclective Psychotherapy*, *7*(1): 81–93.

Malik, R. (2000). The cultural construction of emotions: depression amongst Pakistanis. In: C. Squire (Ed.), *Culture in Psychology* (pp. 147–162). London: Routledge.

Malley, M. (2002). Straight talking? Lesbians, gay men and psychotherapists. Thesis submitted for D. Psychotherapy, London, IFT/ Birkbeck.

Malley, M., & Tasker, F. (1999). Lesbians, gay men and family therapy: a contradiction in terms? *Journal of Family Therapy*, 21(1): 3–30.

Marcos, L. (1979). Effects of interpreters on the psychopathology in non-English-speaking patients. *American Journal of Psychiatry*, *136*: 171–174.

Marris, P. (1996). *The Politics of Uncertainty: Attachment in Private and Public Life*. London: Routledge.

Martin, G., & Allison, S. (1993). Therapeutic alliance: a view constructed by a family therapy team. *Australian and New Zealand Journal of Family Therapy*, *14*: 205–214.

Mason, B. (1993). Towards positions of safe uncertainty. *Human Systems: The Journal of Systemic Consultation and Management* (Special Issue) *4*(3–4): 189–200.

Mason, B. (2002). A reflective recording format for supervisors and trainees. In: D. Campbell & B. Mason (Eds.), *Perspectives on Supervision*. London: Karnac.

Mason, B., & Sawyerr, A. (2002). Introduction. *Exploring the Unsaid: Creativity, Risks and Dilemmas in Working Cross-Culturally*. London: Karnac.

Mason, B., & Sawyerr, A. (Eds.) (2002). *Exploring The Unsaid; Creativity, Risks, and Dilemas in Working Cross-Culturally*. London: Karnac.

Mauss, M. (1954). *The Gift*. London: Cohen & West [reprinted London: Routledge, 1990].

McDougall, J. (1989). *Theatres of the Body: a Psychoanalytical Approach to Psychosomatic Illness*. London: Free Association Books.

McGoldrick, M (Ed.) (1998). *Revisioning Family Therapy: Race, Culture and Gender in Clinical Practice*. New York: Guilford Press.

McGoldrick, M., Pearce, J., & Giordano, J. (Eds.) (1982). *Ethnicity and Family Therapy*. New York: Guilford Press.

McNab, S., & Kavner, E. (2001).When it all goes wrong—challenge of motherhood: forging connections between mothers and daughters. *Journal of Family Therapy, 23*: 189–207.

McNamee, S. (2004). Promiscuity in the practice of family therapy. *Journal of Family Therapy,* 26: 224–245.

McNamee, S., & Gergen, K. (Eds.) (1992). *Therapy as Social Construction*. Newbury Park, CA: Sage.

McNamee, S., Gergen, K. (Eds.) (1999). *Relational Responsibility: Resources for Sustainable Dialogue.* London: Sage.

Menzies, I. (1988). *Containing Anxiety in Institutions, Vol. 1*. London: Free Association Books.

Merleau-Ponty, M. (1962). *Phenomenology of Perception*. London: Routledge and Kegan Paul.

Merleau-Ponty, M. (1964). *The Primacy of Perception*. Evanston, IL: Northwestern University Press.

Miller, A. C., & Thomas, L. K. (1994). Introducing ideas about racism and culture into family therapy training. *Context, 20* (Autumn): 25–29.

Miller, S. B. (1996). *Shame in Context*. Hillsdale, NJ: Analytical Press.

Milton, M., & Coyle, A. (1999). Lesbian and gay affirmative psychotherapy: Issues in theory and practice. *Sexual and Marital Therapy, 14*(1): 43–59

Minuchin, S. (1974). *Families and Family Therapy*. London: Tavistock.

Minuchin, S., & Fishman, H. C. (1981). *Family Therapy Techniques*. Cambridge, MA: Harvard University Press.

Minuchin, S., Wai-Yung, L., & Simon, G. M. (1996). *Mastering Family Therapy, Journeys of Growth and Transformation*. New York: Wiley.

Mitchell, J. (1974). *Psychoanalysis and Feminism*. Harmondsworth: Penguin.

Mollon, P. (2002). *Shame and Jealousy: the Hidden Turmoils*. London: Karnac.

Moloney, B., & Moloney, L. (1996). Personal relationships in systemic supervision. In: C. Flaskas & A. Perlesz (Eds.), *The Therapeutic Relationship in Systemic Therapy* (pp. 195–214). London: Karnac.

Montagu, A. (1978). *Touching*. New York: Harper and Row.

Moorehouse, A., & Carr, A. (2001). A study of live supervisory phone-ins in family therapy: Correlates of client co-operation. *Journal of Marital and Family Therapy, 27*: 241–250.

Mudarikiri, M (2001). Race and culture workshop held at the Institute of Family Therapy, London.

Nussbaum, P. (1988/1989). Narrative emotion: Beckett's genealogy of love. In: S. Hauerwas & L. G. Jones (Eds.), *Why Narrative? Readings in Narrative Theology*. Grand Rapids, MI: William B. Eerdmans.

Nyland, D., & Corsiglia, V. (1998). Internalised other questioning with men who are violent. *Dulwich Centre Newsletter, 199*(2): 29–34.

O'Brian, C. (1990). Family therapy with black families. *Journal of Family Therapy, 12:* 3–16.

Ogden, T. (1994). The analytic third: working with intersubjective clinical facts. *International Journal of Psycho-Analysis, 76*: 3–19.

O'Hanlon, W. H., & Weiner-Davis, M., (1989). *In Search Of Solutions: A New Direction In Psychotherapy*, New York. Norton.

Orange, D. (1995). *Emotional Understanding: Studies in Psychoanalytic Epistemology*. New York: Guilford.

Parry, A., & Doan, R. E. (1994). *Story Re-Visions: Narrative Therapy in the Postmodern World*. New York: Guilford Press.

Parry, T. A. (1998). Reasons of the heart—narrative construction of emotions. *Journal of Systemic Therapies, 17*(2): 65–79.

Paterson, T. (1996). Leaving well alone: a systemic perspective on the therapeutic relationship. In: C. Flaskas & A. Perlesz (Eds.), *The Therapeutic Relationship in Systemic Therapy* (pp. 15–33). London: Karnac.

Patterson, C., & Chamberlain, P. (1994). A functional analysis of resistance during parent training therapy. *Clinical Psychology: Science and Practice, 1*: 53–70.

Pearce, W. B. (1989). *Communication and the Human Condition*. Chicago, IL: Chicago University Press.

Pease, B. (2001). Political issues in working with men in the human services, women against violence. *Relatewell, Journal of Family Relationships, 5*(1): 12–15.

Penn, P. (1985). Feedforward: Future questions, future maps. *Family Process, 24*(3): 299–310.

Penn, P., & Frankfurt, M. (1994). Creating a participant text: Writing, multiple voices, narrative multiplicity. *Family Process, 33*: 217–232.

Perelberg, R. J., & Miller, A. C. (1990). *Gender and Power in Families*, London: Routledge.

Perlesz, A. (1999). Complex responses to trauma: Challenges in bearing witness. *Australian and New Zealand Journal of Family Therapy, 20*(1): 11–19.

Perry, R. (1993). Empathy—still at the heart of therapy: the interplay of context and empathy. *Australian and New Zealand Journal of Family Therapy, 14*: 63–74.

Pinsof, W., & Catherall, D. (1986). The integrative psychotherapy alliance: Family, couple and individual scales. *Journal of Marital and Family Therapy, 12*: 137–151.

Pocock, D. (1995). Searching for a better story: Harnessing modern and postmodern positions in family therapy. *Journal of Family Therapy, 17*(2): 149–174.

Pocock, D. (1997). Feeling understood in family therapy. *Journal of Family Therapy, 19*(3): 283–302.

Pocock, D. (1997). Feeling understood in family therapy. *Family Process, 19*(3): 283–302.

Ptacek, J. (1988). Why do men batter their wives? In: K. Yllo & M. Bograd (Eds.), *Feminist Perspectives on Wife Abuse* (pp. 133–157). Newbury Park, CA: Sage.

Quinn, W., Dotson, D., & Jordan, K. (1997). Dimensions of therapeutic alliance and their associations with outcome in family therapy. *Psychotherapy Research, 7*: 429–438.

Raval, H. (1996). A systemic perspective on working with interpreters. *Clinical Child Psychology and Psychiatry, 1*: 29–43.

Raval, H. (2002) Interpreters as co-workers: why is this relationship hard to achieve? *Context, 59*: 13–15.

Raval, H. (2003). An overview of the issues in the work of interpreters In: R. Tribe & H. Raval, (Eds.), *Working with Interpreters in Mental Health* (pp. 8–29). London: Routledge.

Raval, H. (2005). Being heard and understood in the context of seeking asylum and refuge: communicating with the help of bi-lingual co-workers. *Clinical Child Psychology and Psychiatry, 10*(2): 197–216.

Raval, H. & Smith, J. A. (2003). Therapists' experiences of working with language interpreters. *International Journal of Mental Health, 32*: 6–32.

Real, T. (1990). The therapeutic use of self in constructionist/systemic therapy. *Family Process, 29*(3): 255–272.

Reif, C. (1998). Therapeutic alliance in couples therapy. *Dissertation Abstracts International: Section B: The Sciences and Engineering, 58*(10-B): 5653.

Reimers, S. (2001). Understanding alliances. How can research inform user-friendly practice? *Journal of Family Therapy, 23*(1): 46–62.

Reimers, S., & Treacher, A. (1995). *Introducing User-friendly Family Therapy*. London and New York: Routledge.

Robbins, M. Alexander, J., Newell, R., & Turner, C. (1996). The immediate effect of reframing on client attitude in family therapy. *Journal of Family Psychology, 10*: 28–34.

Rober, P. (1999). The therapist's inner conversation in family therapy practice: some ideas about the self of the therapist, therapeutic impasse and the process of reflection. *Family Process*, *38*(2): 209–228.

Rodnight, V., & Wright, M. (2002). Gender: issues and dilemmas in a casework/counselling team. Unpublished paper presented at Australian Psychotherapy Conference, Melbourne.

Rogers, C. (1951). *Client Centered Therapy*. Boston: Houghton-Mifflin.

Rose, E. (1997). Daring to work with internalised racism. *Counselling*, May: 92–94.

Rosenbaum, R., & Dyckman, J. (1995). Integrating self and system: an empty intersection? *Family Process*, *34*: 21–44.

Rothbaum, F., Rosen, K., Ujiie, T., & Uchida, N. (2002). Family systems, attachment theory and culture. *Family Process*, *41*: 328–350.

Ryan, D., & Carr, A. (2001) A study of the differential effects of Tomm's questioning styles on therapeutic alliance. *Family Process*, *40*: 67–77

Santisteban, D., Szapocznik, J., Perez-Vidal, A., Kurtines, W., Murray, E., & LaPerriere, A. (1996). Efficacy of intervention for engaging youth and families into treatment and some variables that may contribute to differential effectiveness. *Journal of Family Psychology*, *10*: 35–44.

Sartre, J.-P. (1956). *Being and Nothingness. A Phenomenological Essay on Ontology*. New York: Philosophical Library.

Satir, V. (1972). *Peoplemaking*. Palo Alto, CA: Science & Behaviour Books.

Satir, V. (1987). The therapist's story. In: M. Baldwin (Ed.), *The Use of Self in Therapy* (pp. 17–25). Binghamton, NY: Haworth Press.

Scharff, D. E., & Savege Scharff, J. (1987). *Object Relations Family Therapy*. Northvale, NJ: Jason Aronson.

Scheel, M., & Conoley, C. (1998). Circular questioning and neutrality: An investigation of the process relationship. *Contemporary Family Therapy*, *20*: 221–235.

Schlicht, J. (1991). Logs, windsurfing and the Blitz, or the art of family therapy. *Human Systems: The Journal of Systemic Consultation and Management*, *2*: 57–62.

Sells, S., Smith, T., & Moon, S. (1996). An ethnographic study of client and therapist perceptions of therapy effectiveness in a university-based training clinic. *Journal of Marital and Family Therapy*, *22*: 321–342.

Selvini Palazolli, M, Boscolo, L., Cecchin, G., & Prata, G., (1980). Hypothesizing—circularity—neutrality: Three guidelines for the conductor of the session. *Family Process*, *19*: 3–12.

Selvini Palazzoli, M., Boscolo, L., Cecchin, G., & Prata, G. (1980). Hypothesizing–circularity–neutrality. *Family Process*, *6*(1): 3–9.

Shilling, C. (2003). *The Body and Social Theory*. London: Sage.

Shotter, J. (1993). *Conversational Realities: Constructing Life through Language*. London: Sage.

Silver, E. (1991). Should I give advice? A systemic view. *Journal of Family Therapy*, 13: 295–309.

Sisson, R., & Azrin, N. (1986). Family member involvement to initiate and promote treatment of problem drinkers. *Journal of Behaviour Therapy and Experimental Psychiatry*, *17*: 15–21.

Sloman, L., Atkinson, L., Milligan, K., & Liotti, G. (2002). Attachment, social rank and affect regulation: speculations on an ethological approach to family interaction. *Family Process*, *41*: 313–327.

Smith, J., Osman, C., & Goding, M. (1990). Reclaiming the emotional aspects of the therapist–family system, *Australian New Zealand Journal of Family Therapy*, *11*(3): 140–146.

Smith, T., Sells, S., & Clevenger, T. (1994). Ethnographic content analysis of couple and therapist perceptions of a reflecting team setting. *Journal of Marital and Family Therapy*, *20*: 267–286.

Solomon, M. Z. (1997). From what's neutral to what's meaningful: reflections on a study of medical interpreters. *The Journal of Clinical Ethics*, *8*: 88–93.

Spellman, D., & Harper, D. J. (1996). Failure, mistakes, regret and other subjugated stories in family therapy. *Journal of Family Therapy*, *18*(2): 205–214.

Sprenkle, D., Blow, A., & Dickey, M. (1999). Common factors and other non-technique variables in marriage and family therapy. In: M. Hubble, B. Duncan, & S. Miller (Eds.), *The Heart and Soul of Change* (pp. 329–360). Washington, DC: American Psychological Association.

Stanton, M., & Shadish, W. (1997). Outcome, attrition and family-couples treatment for Drug Abuse: A meta-analysis and review of the controlled comparative studies. *Psychological Bulletin*, *122*: 170–191.

Stewart, K., Valentine, L., & Amundsen, J. (1991). The battle for definition: the problem with (the problem). *Journal of Strategic and Systemic Therapies*, *10*: 21–31.

Stith, S., Rosen, K., McCollum, E., Coleman, J., & Herman, S. (1996). The voices of children. Preadolescent children's experiences of family therapy. *Journal of Marital and Family Therapy*, *22*: 69–86.

Stolorow, R., & Atwood, G. (1999). Three realms of the unconscious. In: S. Mitchell & L. Aron (Eds.), *Relational Psychoanalysis: The Emergence of a Tradition* (pp. 365–378). Hillsdale, NJ: Analytic Press.

Stoolmiller, M., Duncan, T., Bank, L., & Patterson, G. (1993). Some problems and solutions in the study of change: Significant patterns of client resistance. *Journal of Consulting and Clinical Psychology, 61*: 920–928.

Street, E., & Rivett, M. (1996). Stress and coping in the practice of family therapy: a British survey. *Journal of Family Therapy, 18*: 303–319.

Strong, T. (2000). Collaborative influence. *Australian and New Zealand Journal of Family Therapy, 21*(3): 144–148.

Symington, J., & Symington, N. (1996). *The Clinical Thinking of Wilfred Bion*. London: Routledge.

Szapocznik, J., Perez-Vidal, A., Brickman, A., Foote, F. H., Santisteban, D., & Hervis, O. (1988). Engaging adolescent drug abusers and their families in treatment: a strategic structural systems approach. *Journal of Consulting and Clinical Psychology, 56*: 552–557.

Tann, R. (1993). Racism and similarity: paranoid–schizoid structures. *British Journal of Psychotherapy, 10*(1): 33–43.

Taussig, M. (1993). *Mimesis and Alterity. A Particular History of the Senses*. New York: Routledge.

Taylor, C. (1985). *Philosophy and the Human Sciences. Philosophical Papers* 2. Cambridge: Cambridge University Press.

Thomas, L. K. (1992). Racism and psychotherapy: working with race in the consulting room, an analytic view. In: J. Kareem & R. Littlewood (Eds.), *Intercultural Therapy, Themes Interpretation and Practice* (pp. 133–145). Oxford: Blackwell Scientific.

Thomas, L. K. (1995). Psychotherapy in the context of race and culture: an intercultural therapeutic approach. In: S. Fernando (Ed.), *Mental Health in a Multiethnic Society* (pp. 172–190). London: Routledge.

Thomas, L. K. (1999). Communicating with a black child: overcoming obstacles of difference. In: P. Miller & B. Carolin (Eds.), *Time to Listen to Children* (pp. 65–78). London: Routledge.

Thomas, L. K. (2002a). Ethnic sameness and difference in family and systemic therapy. In: B Mason & A. Sawyerr (Eds.), *Exploring The Unsaid: Creativity, Risks, and Dilemmas in Working Cross-Culturally* (pp. 49–68). London: Karnac.

Thomas, L. K. (2002b). Working interculturally with probation and forensic clients. In: A. Dupont-Joshua (Ed.), *Working Interculturally*. (pp. 168–194). London: Routledge.

Tinker, R. H., & Wilson, S. A. (1999). *Through the Eyes of a Child*, New York: Norton.

Tomm, K. (1987a). Interventive interviewing: Part 1: Strategizing as a fourth guideline for the therapist. *Family Process, 26*: 3–13.

Tomm, K. (1987b). Interventive interviewing: Part II: Reflexive questioning as a means to enable self healing. *Family Process, 26*: 167–183.

Tomm, K. (1988). Interventive interviewing Part III. Intending to ask linear, circular, strategic or reflexive questions. *Family Process, 27*: 1–15.

Tomm, K. (1998). Co-constructing responsibility. In: S. McNamee & K. Gergen. (Eds.), *Relational Responsibility* (pp. 129–138). Thousand Oaks, CA: Sage.

Tomm, K. (2002). Deconstructing shame and guilt and opening space for apology, restorative action and forgiveness. Workshop hosted by The Prudence Skinner Family Therapy Clinic, London.

Ussher, J. (1991). Family and couples therapy with gay and lesbian clients: acknowledging the forgotten minority. *Journal of Family Therapy, 13*: 131–148.

Van Orman, W. (1996). The relationship between therapeutic alliance and therapy outcome in home based family therapy. *Dissertation Abstracts International: Section B: The Sciences and Engineering, 57*(3-B): 2169.

Verwaaijen, A., & VanAcker, J. (1993). Family treatment for adolescents at risk of placement: II. Treatment process and outcome. *Family Therapy, 20*: 103–132.

Vessey, J., & Howard, K. (1993). Who seeks psychotherapy? *Psychotherapy, 30*: 546–553.

Von Foerster, H. (1990). Ethics and second order cybernetics. Paper given at the International Conference on Systems and Family Therapy: Ethics, Epistemology, New Methods. Paris.

Vygotsky, L. S. (1978). *Mind in Society: The Development of Higher Psychological Processes*. Cambridge, MA: Harvard University Press.

Walsh, F., & McGoldrick, M. (Eds.) (2004). *Living Beyond Loss: Death in the Family*. New York: W. W. Norton.

Weingarten, K. (1995). Radical listening: Challenging cultural beliefs for and about mothers. *Journal of Feminist Family Therapy*, 7(1–2): 7–22.

Weingarten, K. (2000). Witnessing, wonder and hope. *Family Process, 39*(4): 389–402.

White, M. (1988). *The Process of Questioning: A Therapy of Literary Merit*. Adelaide: Dulwich Centre Publications.

White, M. (1992). Family therapy training and supervision in a world of experience and narrative. In: D. Epston & M. White (Eds.) *Experience, Contradiction, Narrative and Imagination: Selected papers of David Epston and Michael White 1989–1991* (pp. 75–96). Adelaide: Dulwich Centre Publications.

White, M. (1995). *Re-authoring Lives*. Adelaide: Dulwich Centre Publications.

White, M. (2000). *Reflections on Narrative Practice*. Adelaide, South Australia: Dulwich Centre Publications.

White, M., & Epston, D. (1990). *Narrative Means to Therapeutic Ends*. New York: W. W. Norton.

White, M., & Epston, D. (1991). *Narrative Means to Therapeutic Ends*. New York: Norton.

Williams, B. (2002). *Truth and Truthfulness. An Essay in Genealogy*. Princeton: University of Princeton Press.

Winnicott, D. W. (1991). *Playing and Reality*. London: Tavistock

Woodcock, J. (2000). A systemic approach to trauma. *Context, 51* (Autumn): 2–4.

Woodcock, J. (2001). Threads from the labyrinth: therapy with survivors of war and political oppression. *Journal of Family Therapy, 23*(2): 136–154.

Young, J., Saunders, F., Prentice, G., Macri-Riseley, D., Fitch, R., & Pati-Tasca, C. (1997). Three journeys toward the reflecting team. *Australian and New Zealand Journal of Family Therapy, 18*: 27–37.

INDEX

For Product Safety Concerns and Information please contact our EU representative GPSR@taylorandfrancis.com Taylor & Francis Verlag GmbH, Kaufingerstraße 24, 80331 München, Germany

Batch number: 10725893

Printed by Printforce, the Netherlands